IMAGES
of America

MARBLETOWN

On the cover: Please see page 92. (Courtesy Stone Ridge Library.)

IMAGES
of America

MARBLETOWN

Lucy Van Sickle

ARCADIA
PUBLISHING

ISBN 978-0-7385-5683-3

Published by Arcadia Publishing
Charleston, South Carolina

Printed in the United States of America

Library of Congress Catalog Card Number: 2008921590

For all general information contact Arcadia Publishing at:
Telephone 843-853-2070
Fax 843-853-0044
E-mail sales@arcadiapublishing.com
For customer service and orders:
Toll-Free 1-888-313-2665

Visit us on the Internet at www.arcadiapublishing.com

Dedicated to my husband, children, and friends who helped make this book possible, thanks to Dr. Alan V. Tepp for his guidance and advice, and special thanks to my friend Deana Decker for her encouragement

Contents

Acknowledgments

So many people in this area have pictures and knowledge that would be lost without bringing it all together in this book. Thanks to George K. Van Sickle, Ed and Betty Croswell, Jody Ford of the Stone Ridge Library, Paul Wikane, Charles Greene, John Snykus, Donald Newell Jr., Brad Fiore, the Ontario and Western Railway Historical Society, Lawrence Skalla, Barbara Cole, Eric Fedde, Beverly Bennett, Kenneth Cole Sr., and the fire companies in Marbletown that responded to requests for pictures.

INTRODUCTION

In 1668, Col. Francis Lovelace became governor of New Netherland. One of his first projects was to create a new village that would be settled by soldiers living near the Esopus Creek. He ordered Henry Pauling to lay out the new lots in New Dorp at Esopus. He proclaimed that each soldier would receive 10 morgens of lowland and 15 morgens of upland that they could call their own. A morgen was the amount of land that could be plowed in one morning, roughly two acres. Lots were laid out along the roadway, and before long, at least 50 dwellings, mostly log houses, were built. As Esopus Indians still lived in the area, settlers were encouraged to live in clustered groups, but gradually people moved farther apart. The Widow Davis Tavern is thought to be the oldest house in Marbletown. It was built almost directly across the road from the Andrew Oliver house. The Esopus Indians' main council house was farther south in what is now known as Wawarsing, near Ellenville. After the treaty of 1664, they simply moved farther west and joined into other Delaware tribes. Many an archaeologist has found a plentitude of American Indian artifacts at sites along the Rondout and Esopus Creeks in Marbletown.

The name *Marbletown* was derived mainly from the enormous amount of limestone found in the region. Its patent was filed on June 25, 1703, and the town was formally recognized as a township in 1788. The terrain is a combination of hills and lowlands, with streams and valleys dividing it. The Rondout and Esopus Creeks transect the area. The area lays south of Kingston along the Old Mine Road, also known as the Kings Highway. The road connected the Hudson River port of Kingston with the coal and stone mines of Pennsylvania. Marbletown was mostly an agricultural area in those days, as it remains today. Corn was the main crop grown.

On October 16, 1777, the British burned Kingston, which was the capital of New York State. In need of a new place to run the government, Lt. Gov. Pierre Van Courtlandt and 10 other members of the council traveled south to Marbletown and set up headquarters in the home of Andrew Oliver. They ran the government there until November 18 and then moved it to Hurley and finally to Poughkeepsie. The original Oliver house was built sometime around 1740. It was eventually torn down, and a replacement house was built, which still stands today.

The Old Mine Road was probably the longest road built in the early days. It originally was an American Indian trail that joined the Esopus Creek to the Delaware Valley. The Esopus Indians had many items made of copper, which interested the early Dutch settlers. They told of wonderful mines southwest of the area, near the Delaware Water Gap. The Old Mine Road was built to facilitate the transport of minerals from the copper mines to the Hudson River, where they could be shipped back to Europe. Settlers near the water gap used the road to bring salt and other traded items that were not available locally back to their homes from the port cities on the Hudson River.

The seven hamlets that make up Marbletown of today are Marbletown, Stone Ridge, Cottekill, Lomontville, Vly-Atwood, Kripplebush, and High Falls. In this book, you will get a glimpse of life in each of these hamlets, learning what each little area contributed to life as it was known in Marbletown. You will travel from the robust canal life of High Falls to the well-traveled road through Stone Ridge and on "up to the Vly" where the earth meets the sky.

Marbletown is continuing its growth as it did in the 1600s, becoming a mecca for more metro families seeking the same things settlers of old did—the rural beauty and slow pace that drew them to settle in the area. Careful planning is taking place to preserve the historic nature of the area, which will allow generations to come to view the historic stone houses, the old canals, and the wonderful old farms that still continue to thrive in the area. Marbletown is nestled in the foothills of the Catskill Mountains, bordered on the west by the Ashokan Reservoir, on the north by the historic town of Hurley, by the cement mines of Rosendale on the east, and by the town of Rochester on the south. I invite you to look at the pictures and project yourself back in time—back to a simpler time.

—Lucy Van Sickle

One

Marbletown

Many a resident has referred to the area north of Stone Ridge on the Old Mine Road as "North Marbletown." In fact, that is not correct. It is simply known as Marbletown. It is somewhat of a no-man's-land between Hurley and Stone Ridge, not really a part of either hamlet. It did, however, have its own post office and government representation. It is a most integral and history-rich part of the entire town of Marbletown.

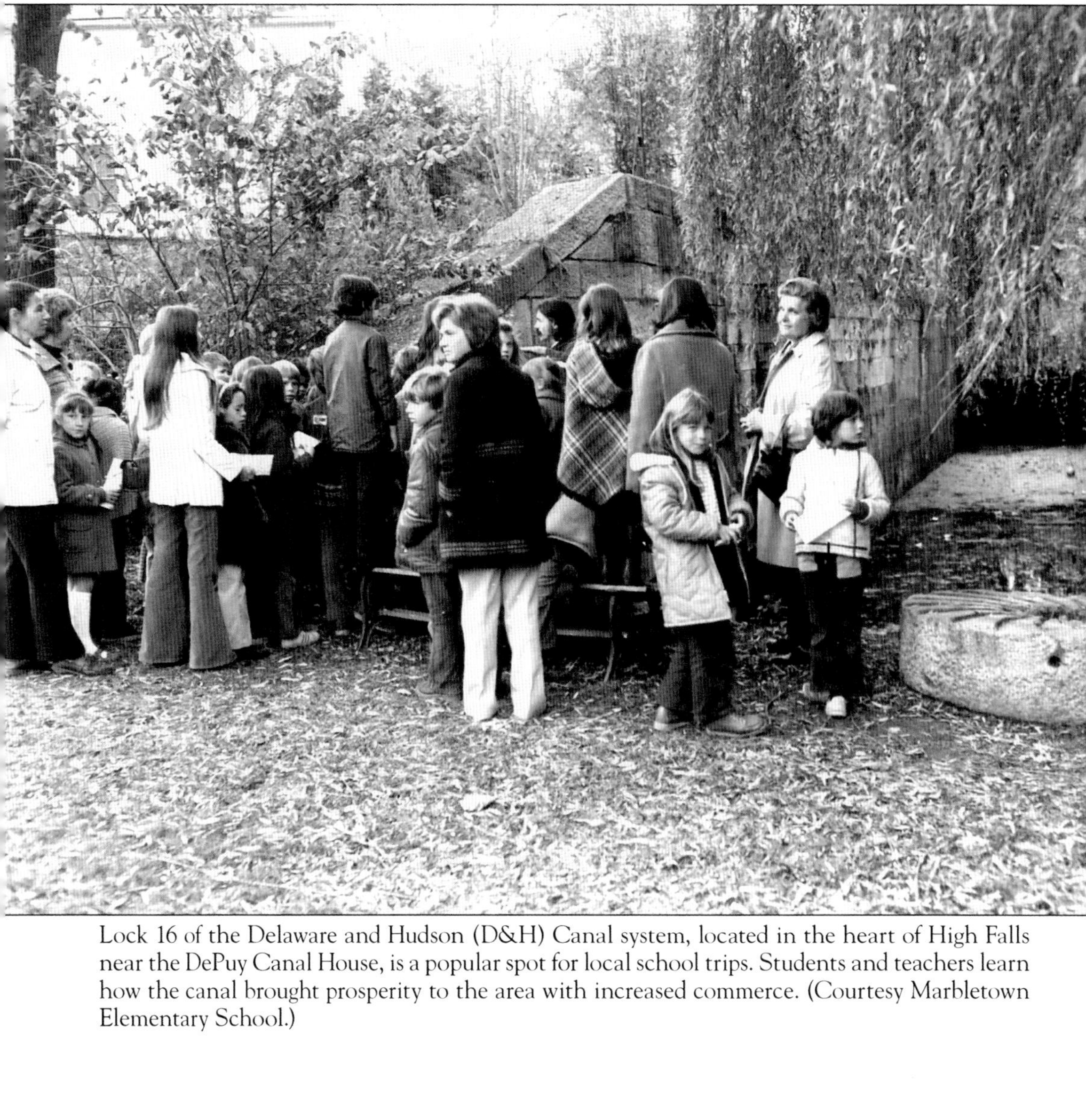

Lock 16 of the Delaware and Hudson (D&H) Canal system, located in the heart of High Falls near the DePuy Canal House, is a popular spot for local school trips. Students and teachers learn how the canal brought prosperity to the area with increased commerce. (Courtesy Marbletown Elementary School.)

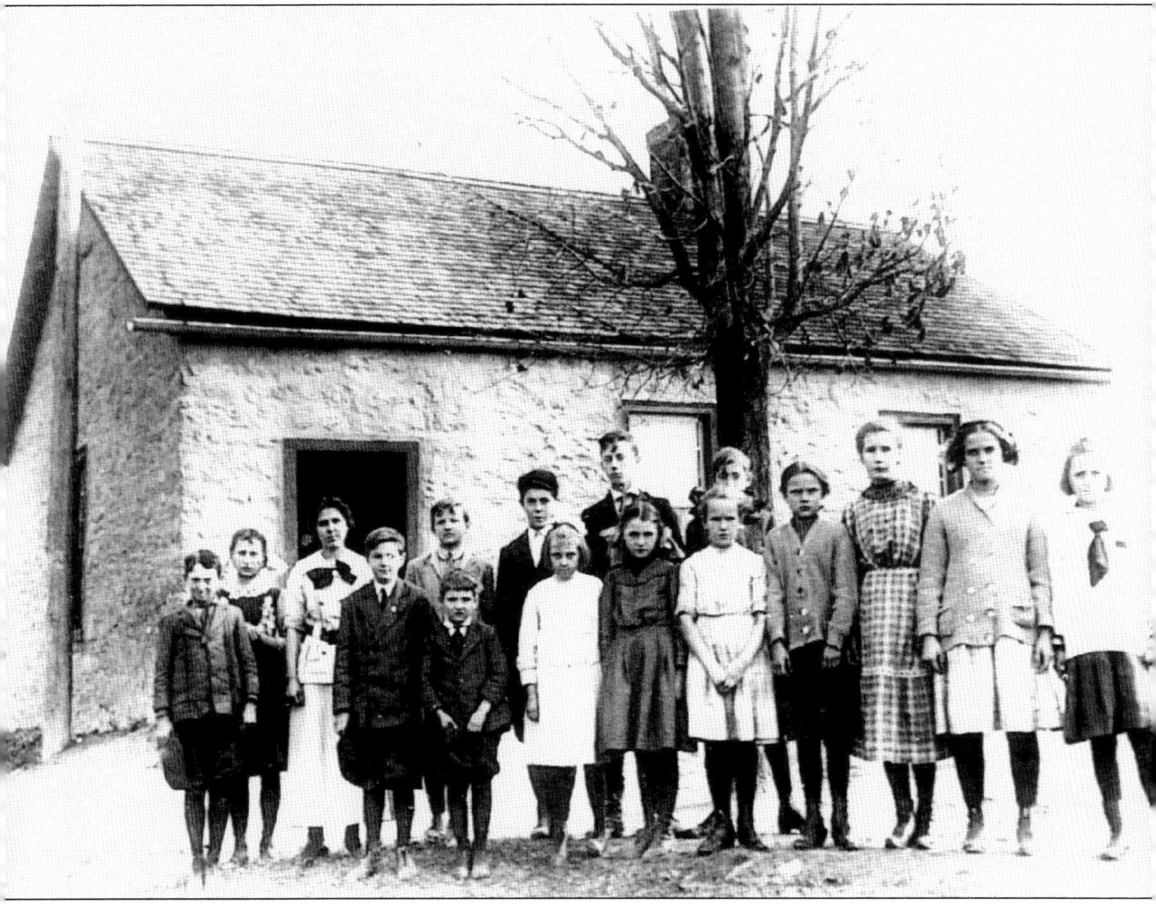

The Marbletown stone school No. 3, built in 1832, served the children of the northern area of Marbletown. There were 14 separate school districts in the town at that time, which were later consolidated into 1 district around 1952. Pictured here is teacher Margaret Foertner Hiller (third from left) with the class of 1912. Hiller (1894–1940) was a 1912 graduate of Kingston Academy. She taught at Marbletown No. 3 from 1912 to 1913. In 1917, she went on to graduate from Vassar Brothers Hospital School of Nursing and served in the U.S. Army Nurse Corps. (Courtesy George K. Van Sickle.)

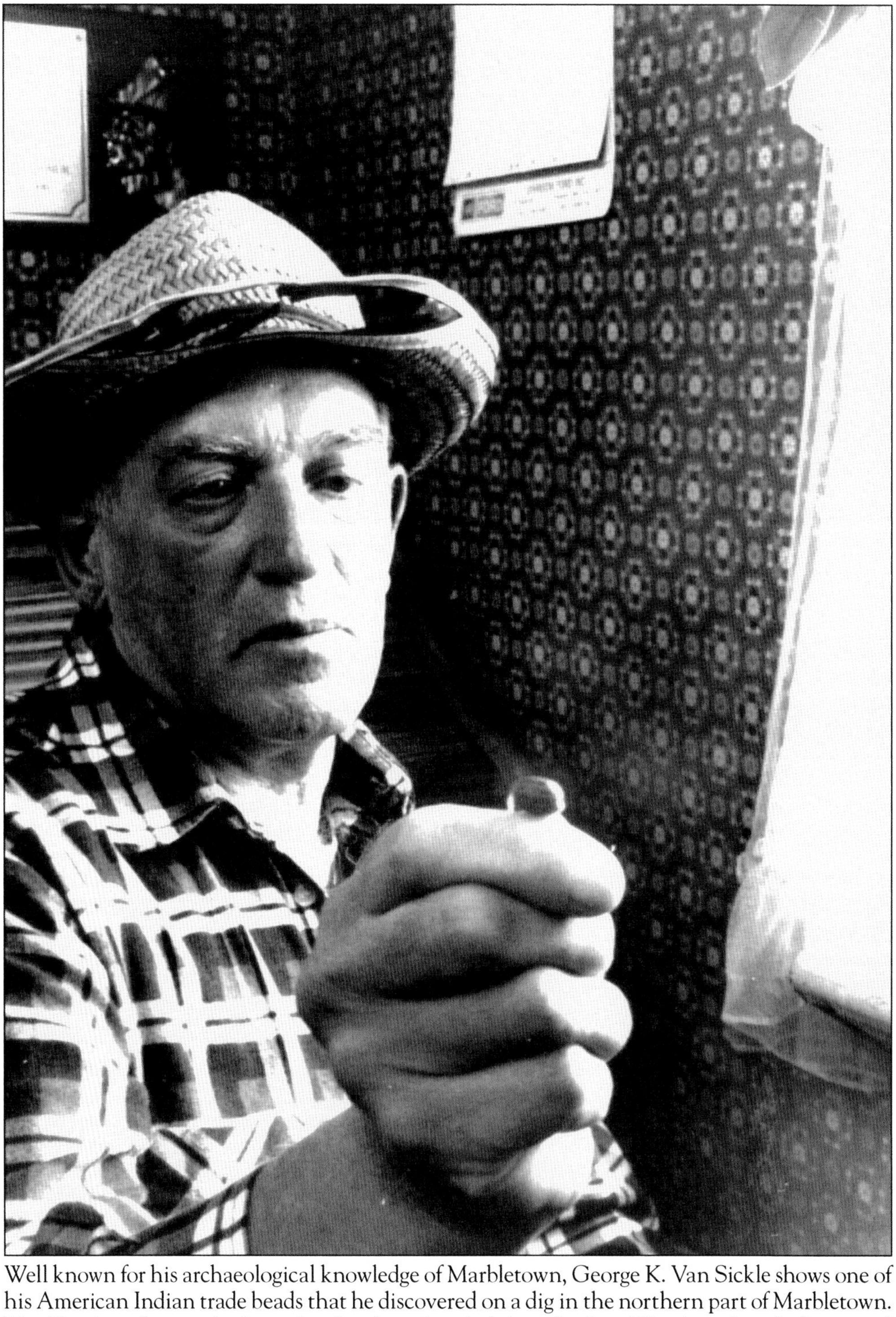

Well known for his archaeological knowledge of Marbletown, George K. Van Sickle shows one of his American Indian trade beads that he discovered on a dig in the northern part of Marbletown. The Dutch traders made these glass beads and traded them for furs. The American Indians used the beads as decorations, wearing them around their necks. (Courtesy Russ Van Sickle.)

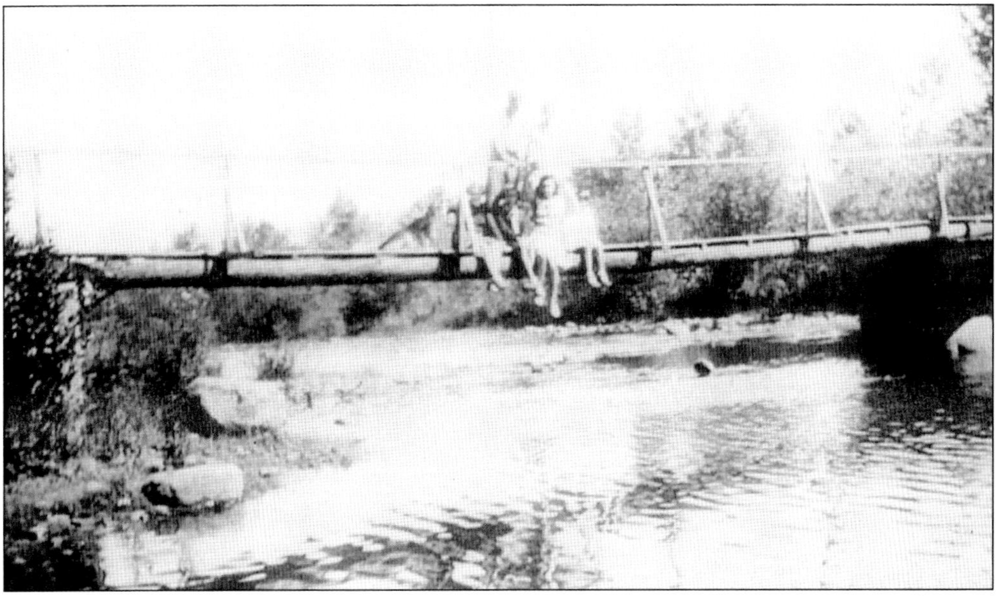

Local children enjoyed sitting on the "fording place" bridge during warm summers. The ford is still passable today during low water. Cars can carefully traverse the cobblestone creek bed. Occasionally someone will try it in high water, requiring rescue from local fire companies and the Ulster County sheriff's dive team. (Courtesy Ed Croswell.)

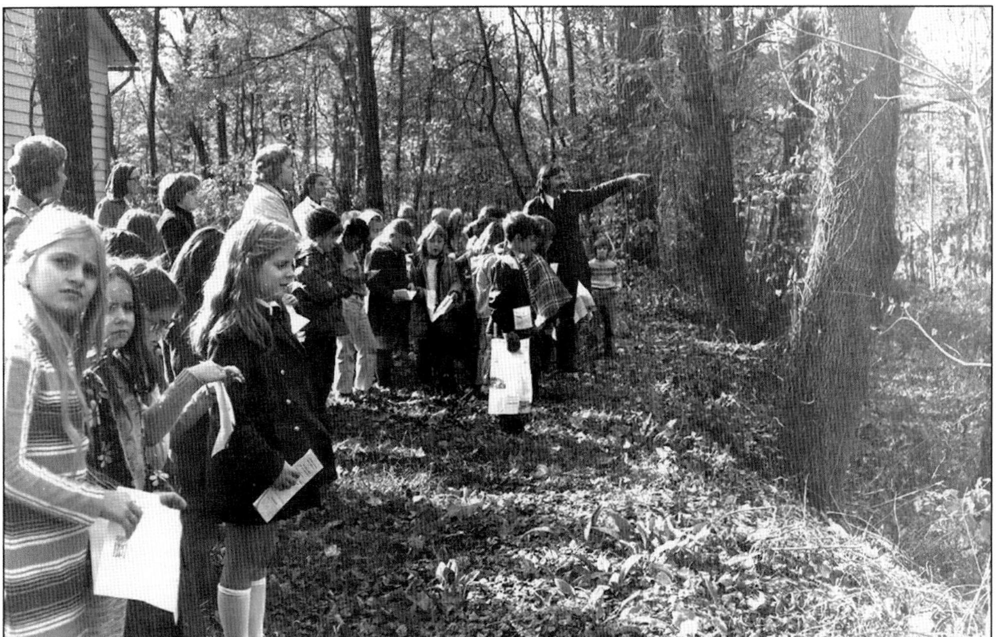

Here John Novi, owner of the DePuy Canal House, educates students from Marbletown Elementary School on the D&H Canal system. The overgrown canal channel can be seen on the right side of the picture. (Courtesy Marbletown Elementary School.)

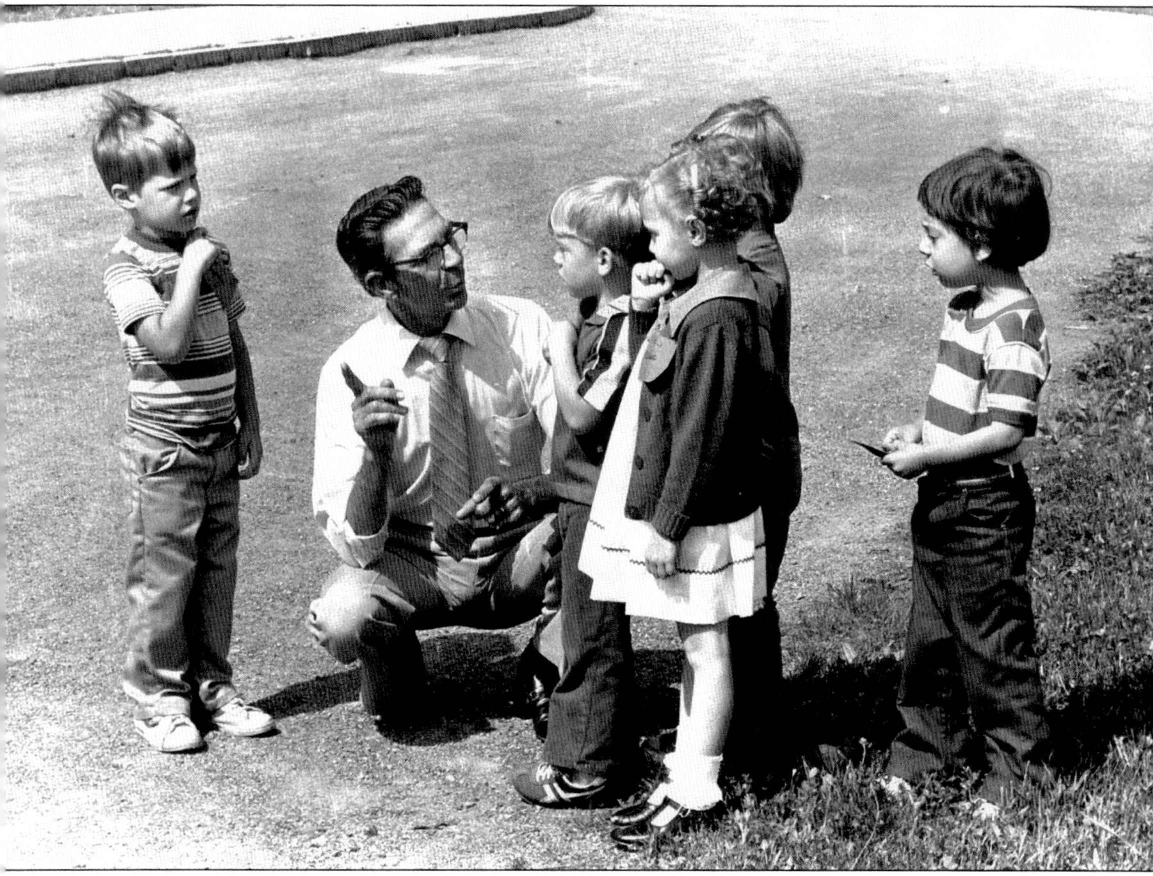

Marbletown Elementary School principal Robert Thornton reassures young students on their first day of school in this c. 1960 photograph. (Courtesy Marbletown Elementary School.)

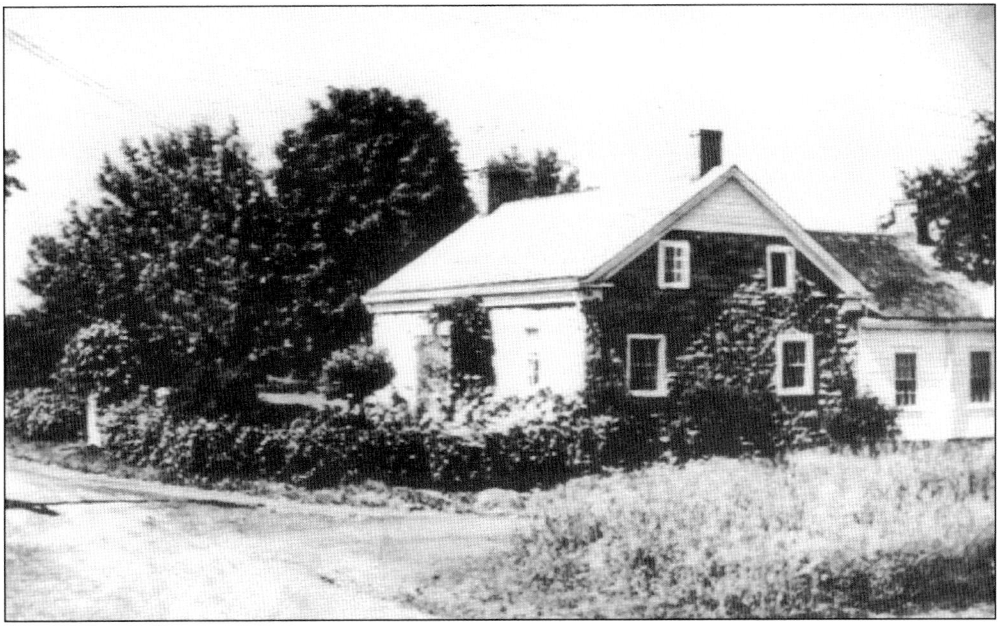

The Rowlands lived in this stone house at the upper end of Fording Place Road. Known as the William Nottingham house, this stone house possesses extremely unique architecture. It was the tenant house to the John A. DeWitt home, also located on North Marbletown Road. John was the son of Andries DeWitt and James Oliver. It was built between 1745 and 1750. The symmetrical exterior and centrally placed staircase inside reflect a "vernacular interpretation of fashionable Renaissance architecture." (Courtesy Ed Croswell.)

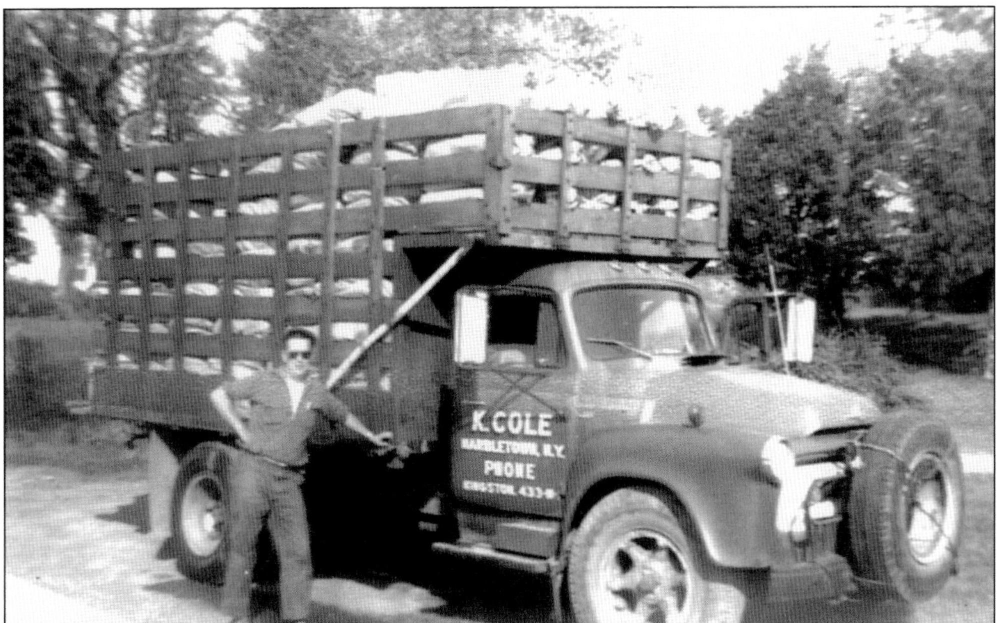

Kenneth Cole Sr. stands by his 1950s vintage International truck. It is loaded with sweet corn, headed for sale in New York City. Much of the Hudson Valley corn comes from Marbletown farmers. (Courtesy Ed Croswell.)

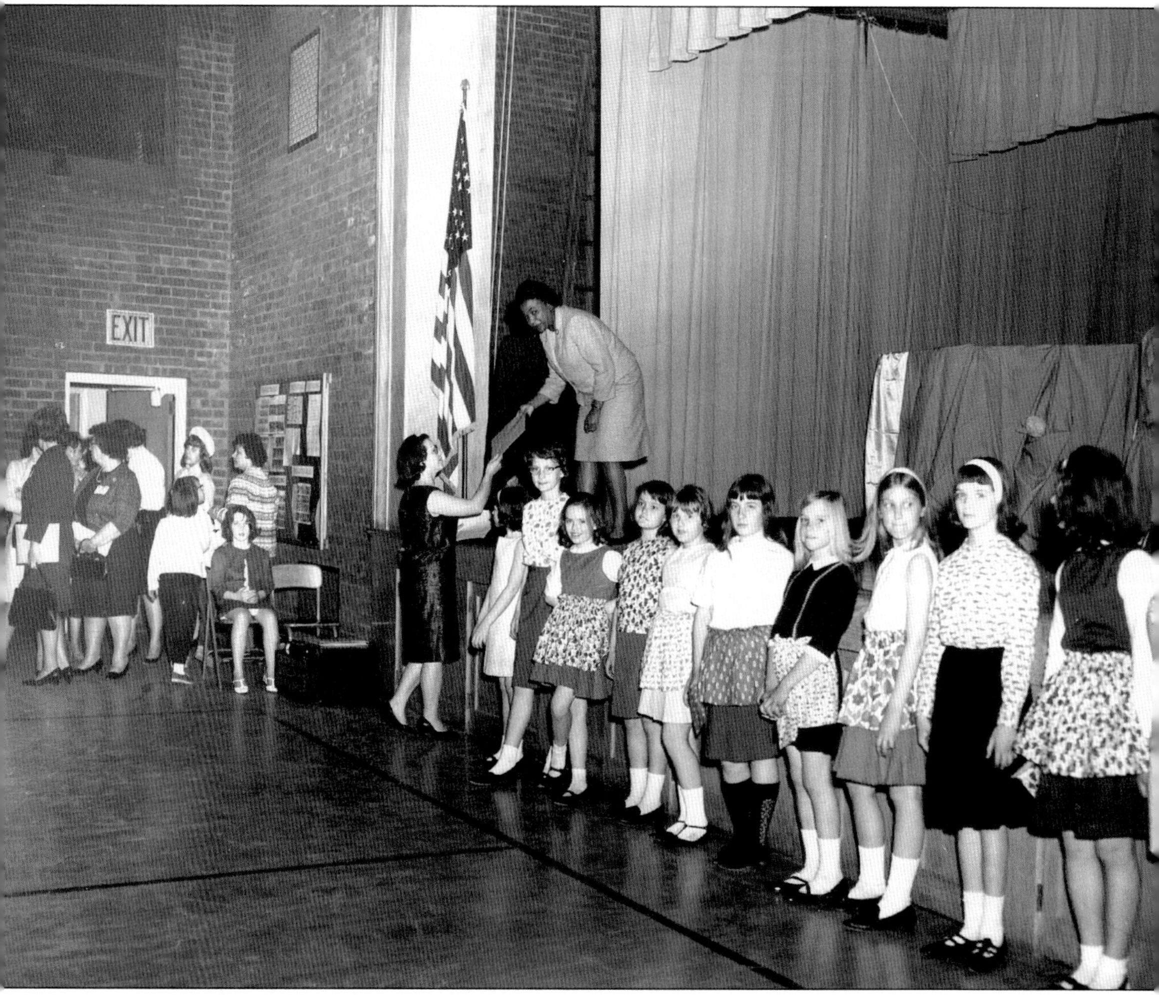

Students of 4-H at Marbletown Elementary School line up to show off their sewing prowess. Each girl was asked to create an apron and fashion it from start to finish. Mrs. Abbaghita hands results of the contest to be announced during the 4-H dress review on May 5, 1966. (Courtesy Marbletown Elementary School.)

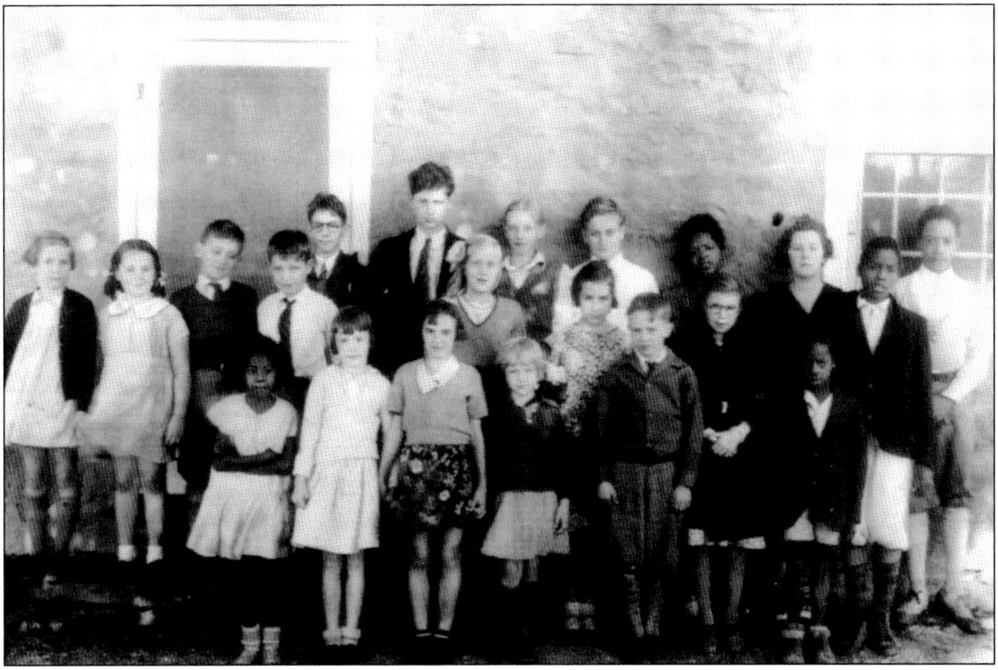

This photograph shows students from a class in the early 1930s standing in front of the Marbletown Stone School. Included are Lorraine ?, Evelyn Krom, Gloria Sacher, Kenneth Cole Sr., Camilla DeWitt, Roberta Newman, John DeWitt, John Warren, Grace Vanderly, Martha Miller, Regina Krom, Victor Sacher, John Kowal, Lillian Miller, and Robert Vandermark. (Courtesy Ed Croswell.)

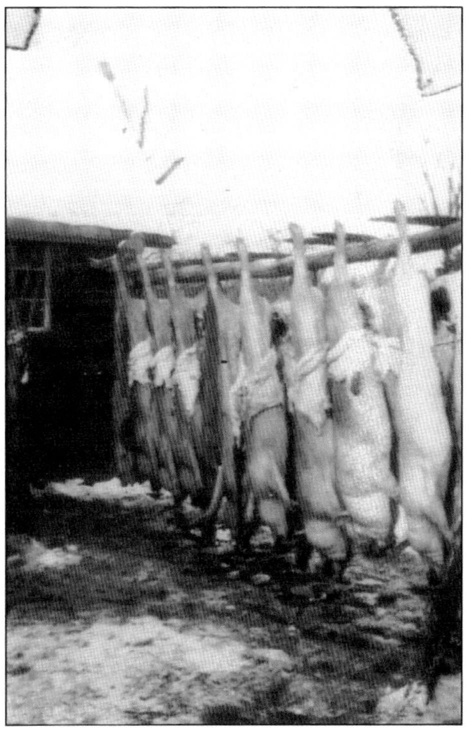

Most farms raised their own meat for consumption during the 1940s. Farmers got together and brought animals to neighborhood farms to be butchered. Each farmer specialized in certain animals they were better at butchering. The pigs in this picture were butchered on the Cole farm in Marbletown. (Courtesy Ed Croswell.)

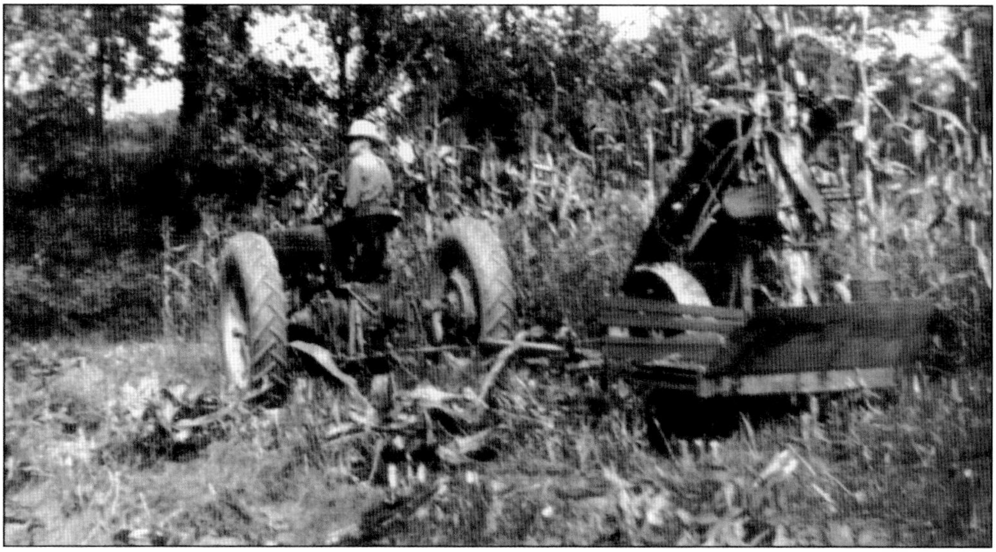

Robert Terwilliger, a local farmer, uses his farm tractor to harvest corn on the Cole farm in Marbletown around 1945. Terwilliger was known for his custom harvesting techniques. (Courtesy Ed Croswell.)

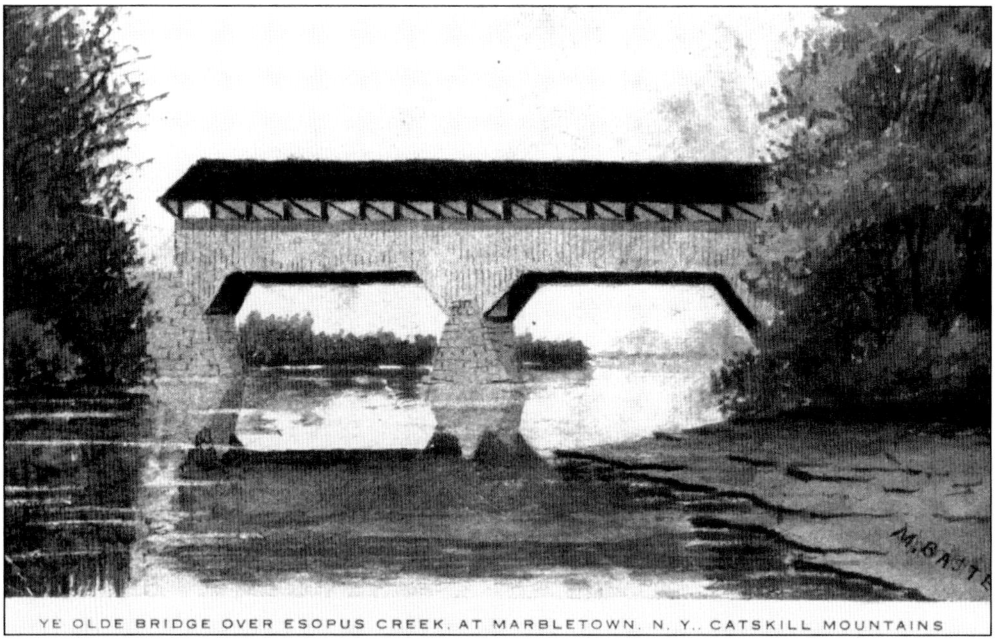

This postcard depicts the original covered bridge that was erected over the Esopus Creek on Hurley Mountain Road, off Tongore Road. Built sometime in the mid-1800s, the bridge served well, eventually being replaced by the iron bridge. (Courtesy George K. Van Sickle.)

Hunting and trapping have always been an integral part of life for many Marbletown families. Here, in this *c.* 1950 photograph, John Krom (left) and Danny Mihm pose with the pelts of a successful raccoon hunt. Coon dogs were utilized to help locate and flush raccoons from their dens. (Courtesy George K. Van Sickle.)

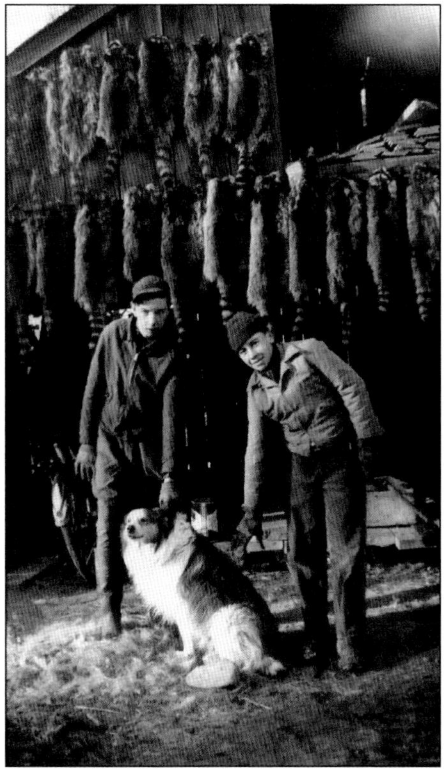

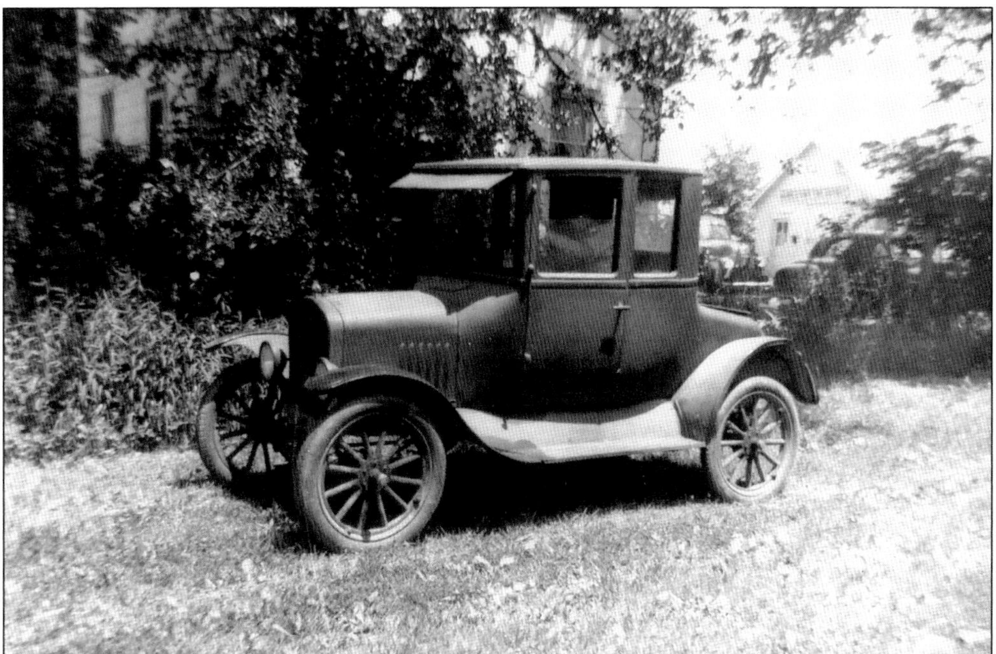

This 1923 Ford Model T coupe featured a four-cylinder, 20-horsepower engine. A front-mounted crank was used to turn the motor over. The top speed could reach as high as 50 miles per hour. (Courtesy George K. Van Sickle.)

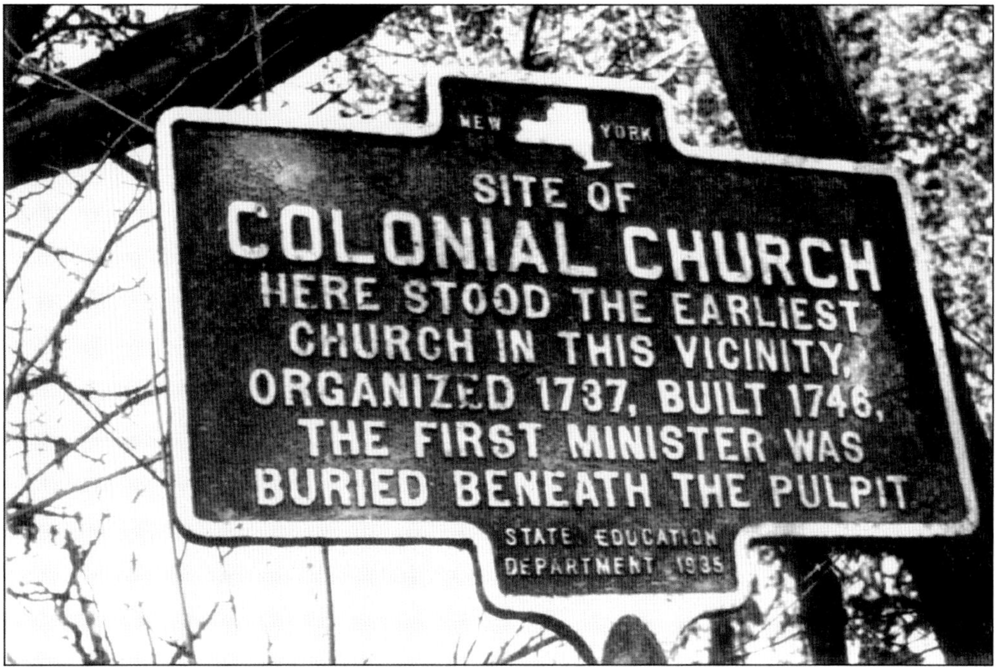

The Colonial Church, built between 1744 and 1746, was the first church in the northern area of Marbletown. It was built on the eastern side of the Old Mine Road, in what is now the old section of the North Marbletown Cemetery. As the sign points out, the first minister was buried beneath the pulpit. (Courtesy Charles Greene.)

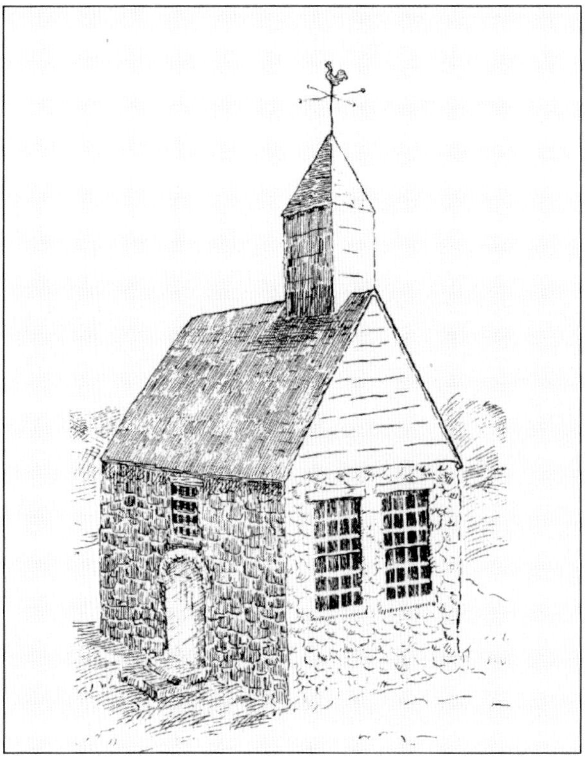

This sketch of the Colonial Church, done by S. N. Abbott, is a reproduction of the church edifice from an original drawing owned by Cornelius Oliver of Marbletown. The church was 54 feet by 44 feet and could seat as many as 250 people. In 1851, a replacement church was built alongside the cemetery. (Courtesy Jody Ford, Stone Ridge Library.)

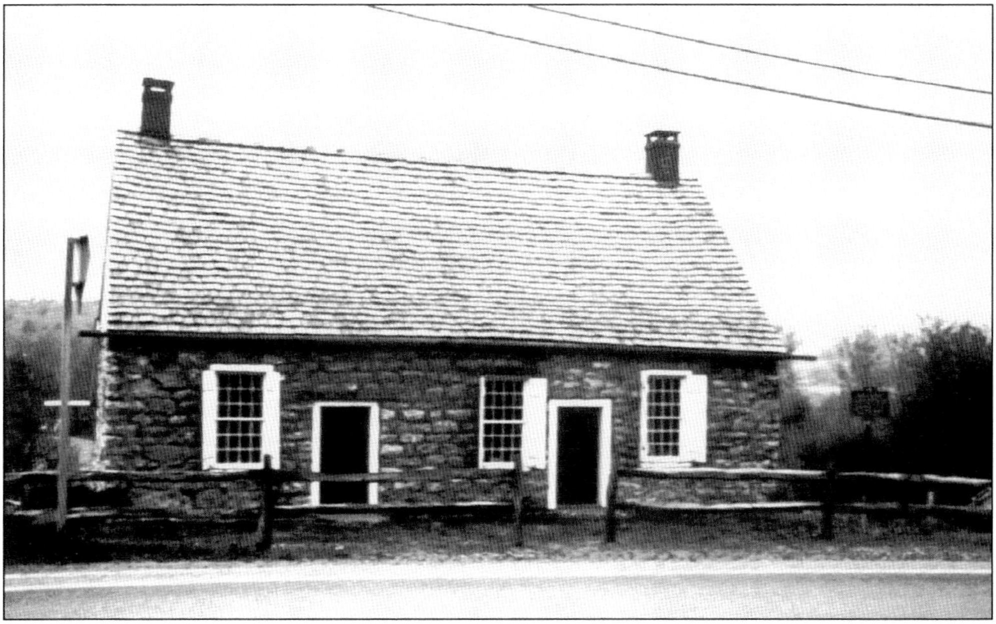

The Widow Davis Tavern sits directly on the Old Mine Road, now State Route 209. It was built by Isaac Davis. Its original use was a blacksmith shop. Presumed to be the oldest building in Marbletown, it held town archives and was the annual meeting place of residents. Public business of the Marbletown patent was conducted here. One writer, Willis Nash, speaks of it as being a place of public resort in 1680. Ownership of the tavern transferred to James Oliver and then to John Andries DeWitt sometime before 1800. Church assistants from the Marbletown church used the residence until 1815, and freed slaves of the Oliver family lived there after the Civil War. (Courtesy Stone Ridge Library.)

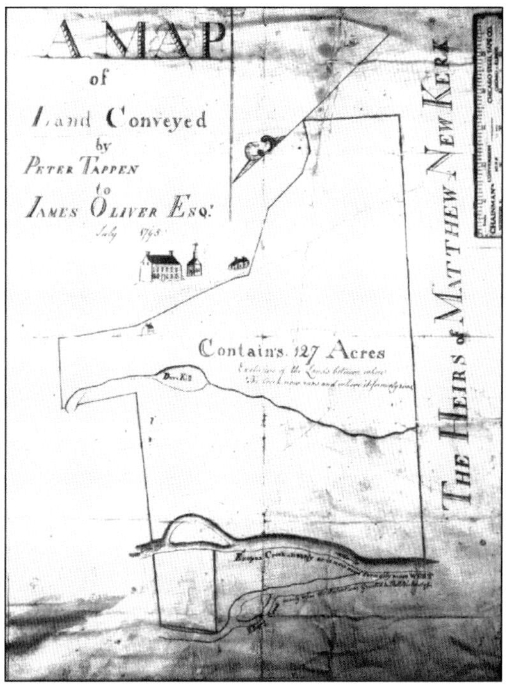

This old map is a copy of the original surveyors' map conveyed unto James Oliver, Esq., from Peter Tappen in 1705. The drawing of the larger stone house on the map represents the Oliver house. The church is the original Colonial Church, and the smaller stone house represents a smaller stone home that originally stood on the corner of the Old Mine Road and what is now Marcott Road. The small stone house just below the Oliver house represents the Widow Davis Tavern. James and his brother John later left the house and 127 acres to John Clifford Cole, who was named after John Oliver. (Courtesy Barbara Cole.)

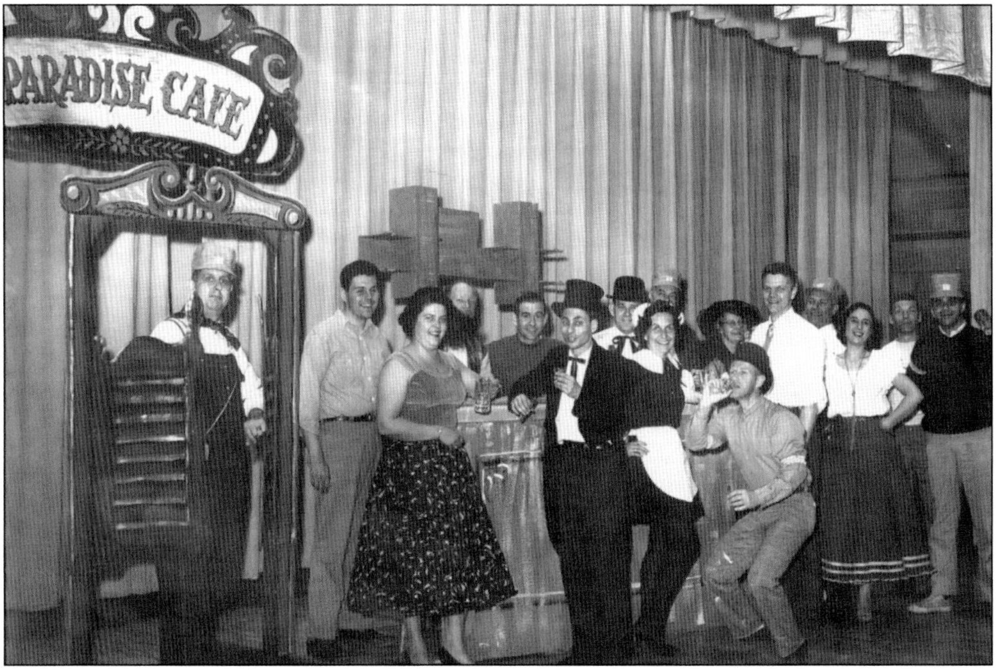

Teachers at Rondout High School show their school spirit during a performance of *Love Rides the Rails* on the high school stage in the early 1960s. Pictured are, from right to left, unidentified, Dixon McGrath, unidentified, Frank McCann, Bob Grupe, Hale Russ (in front), unidentified, Marsha Krom, Chick Meehan, Mickey Million, Arnold Gottesman, Ronald Mapstone, unidentified, Phyllis Jackson, Peter Zegel, and Roland Mayberry (standing in the swinging door). (Courtesy Beverly Bennett.)

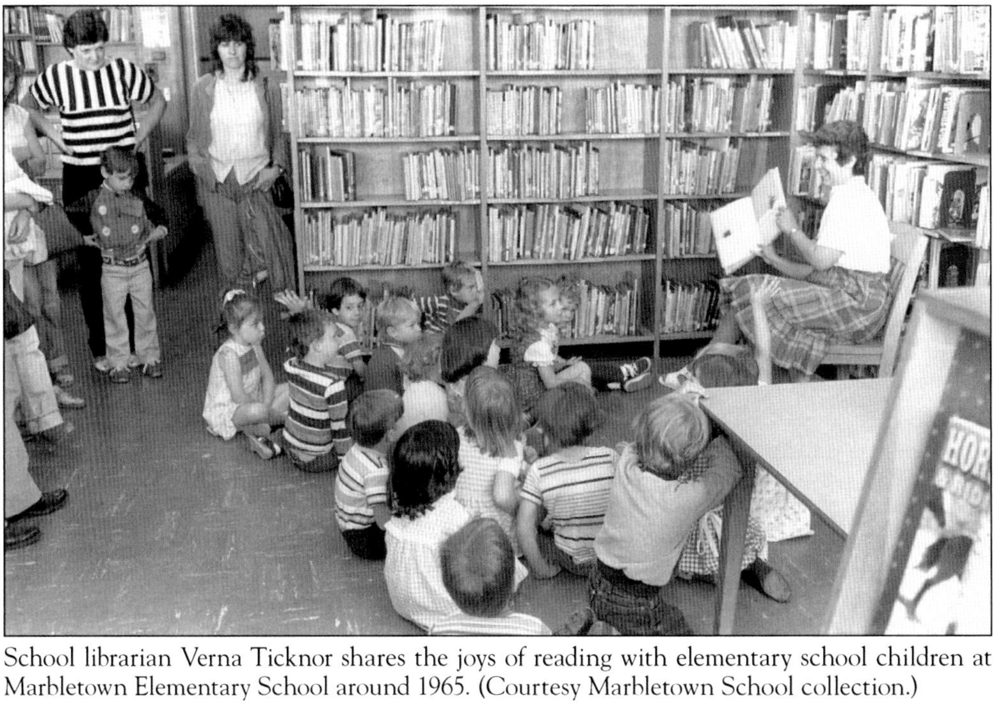

School librarian Verna Ticknor shares the joys of reading with elementary school children at Marbletown Elementary School around 1965. (Courtesy Marbletown School collection.)

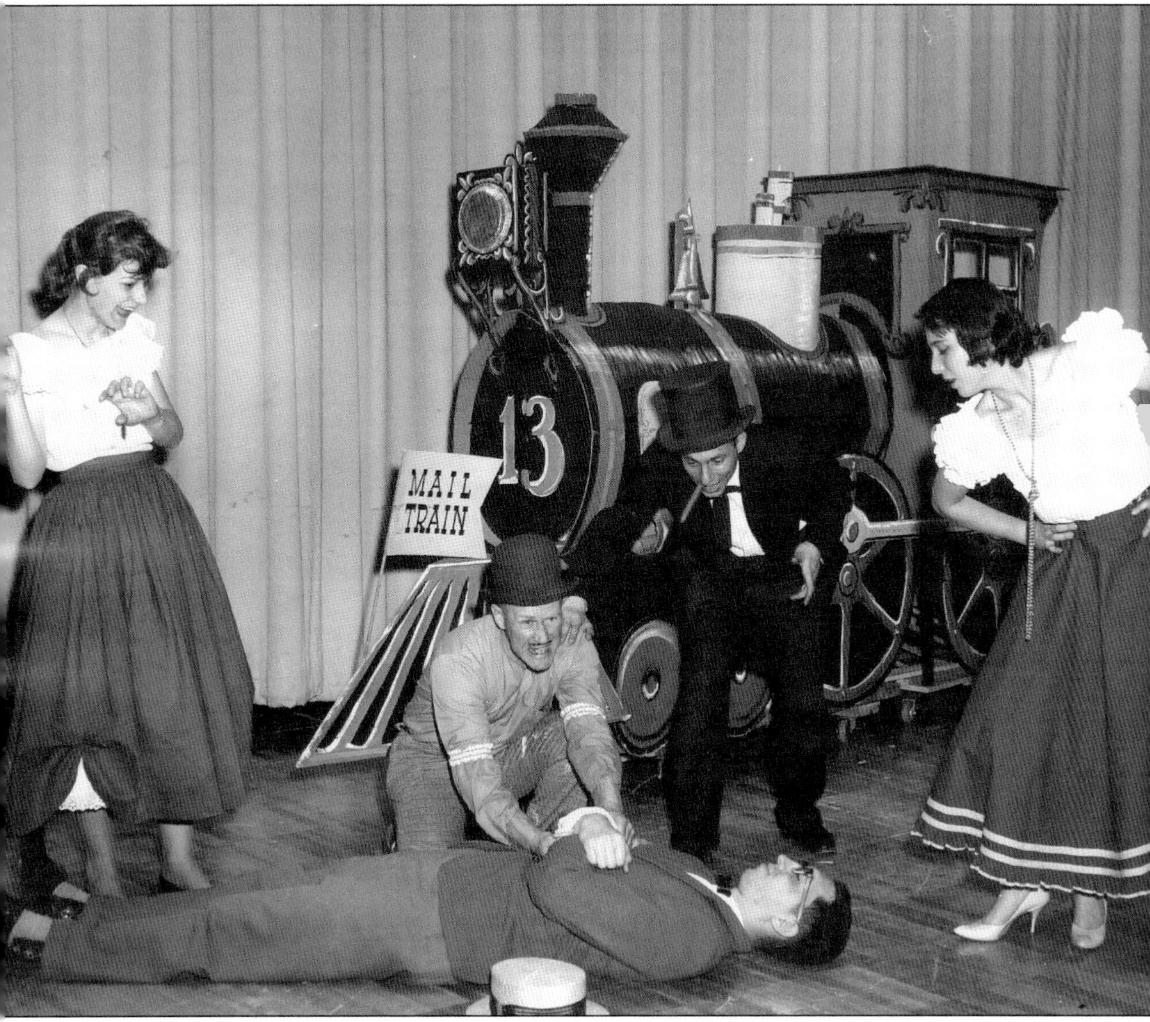

Hale Russ gives his all in the final act of *Love Rides the Rails*, a faculty play at Rondout High School. Looking on are Arnold Gottesman and two unidentified teachers. Math teacher Don Lee gives a convincing performance as the victim. (Courtesy Beverly Bennett.)

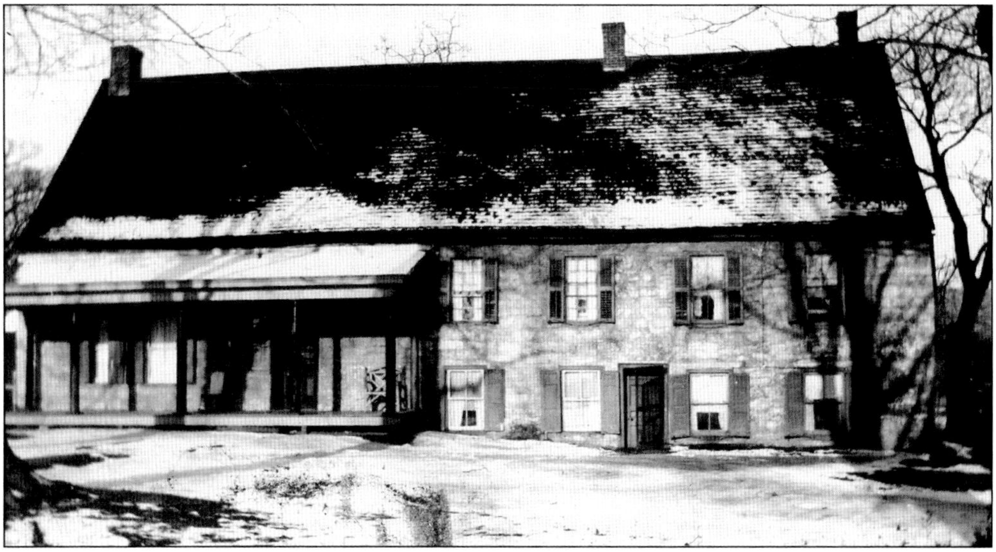

The DeWitt Cole house, built around 1800, was on the Marbletown/Hurley line along the Esopus Creek. It was originally known as the Pawling house. Levi Pawling was the first county judge of Ulster. Note the three chimneys on the roof. The middle chimney was actually directly on the border between Marbletown and Hurley. DeWitt Cole and his wife Minnie (Bush) Cole ran the active farm. DeWitt passed away after being gored by a bull, before the physician could make the trip to the house to tend to his wounds. DeWitt's son was the owner of the Oliver house, near the Widow Davis Tavern. A fire caused by boiling sap on a gasoline stove destroyed the home in 1939. (Courtesy Barbara Cole.)

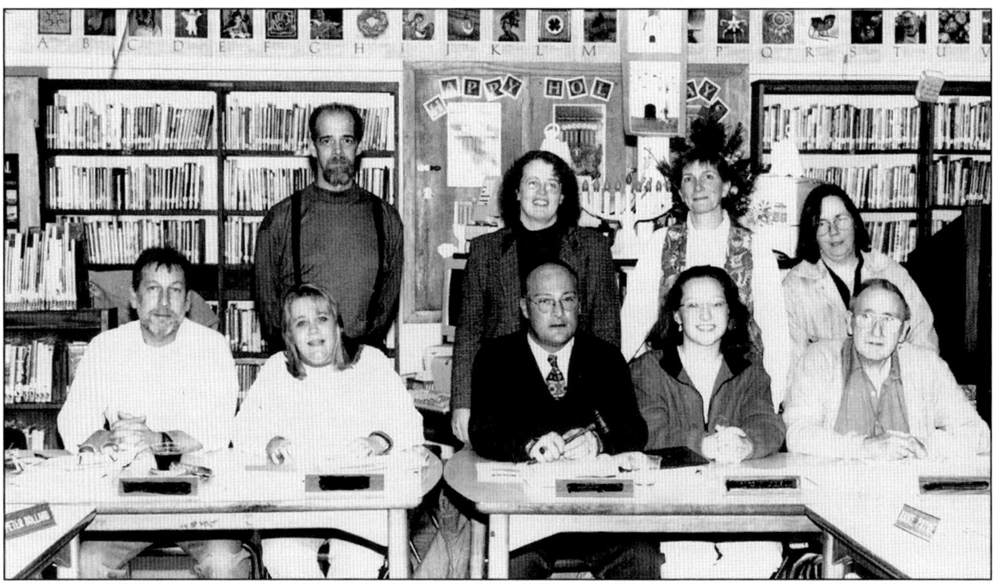

It takes true community spirit to run for a position on any school board. Members of the Rondout Valley Central School District Board of Education exemplify true dedication to the students of Marbletown. In this late-1990s photograph are, from left to right, (first row) Louis Costa, Maureen Sheehan, Carl Chipman, student representative Katie Martyniuk, and William McMullen; (second row) Peter Dollard, Anne Payne, board president Nancy Taylor, and Penny Kunz. (Courtesy Beverly Bennett.)

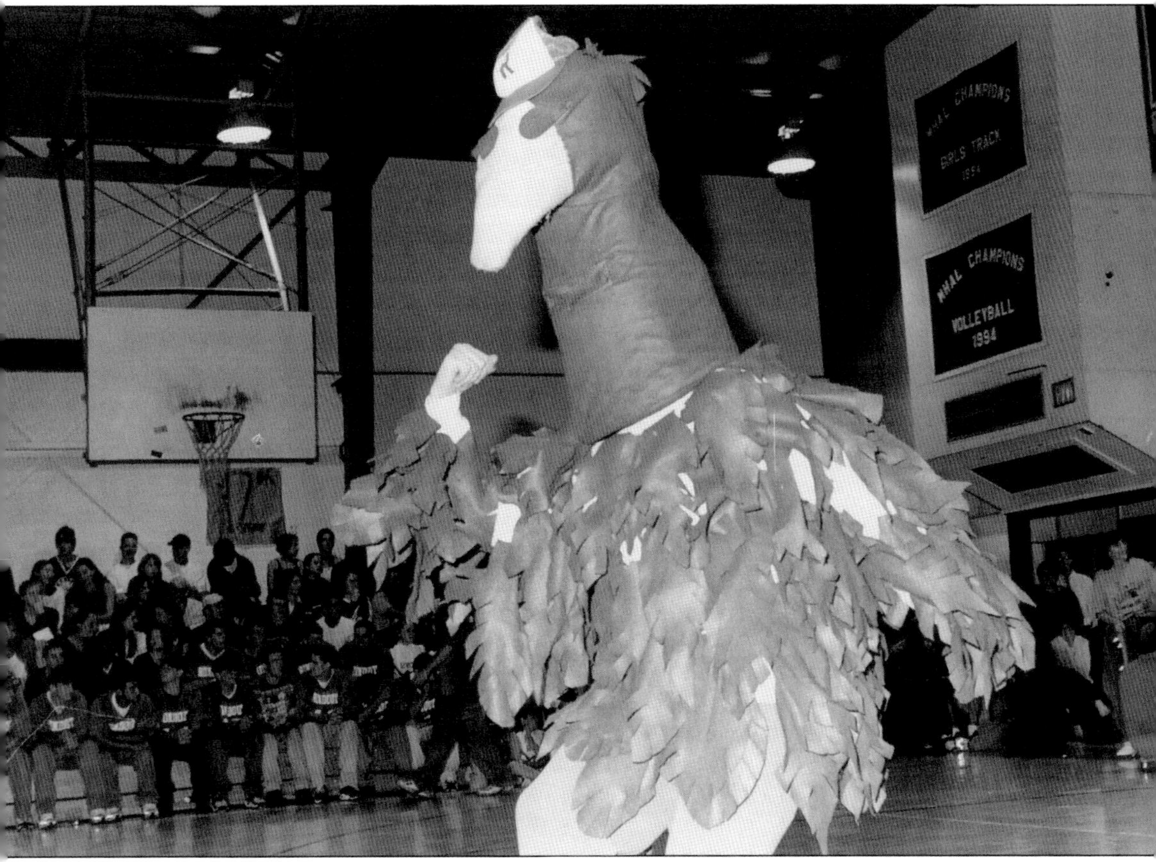

The gander is the mascot for all students in the Rondout Valley school system. This student, in a costume designed and constructed by art teacher William Hutcheon, struts his stuff during a pep rally in the 1990s. (Courtesy Beverly Bennett.)

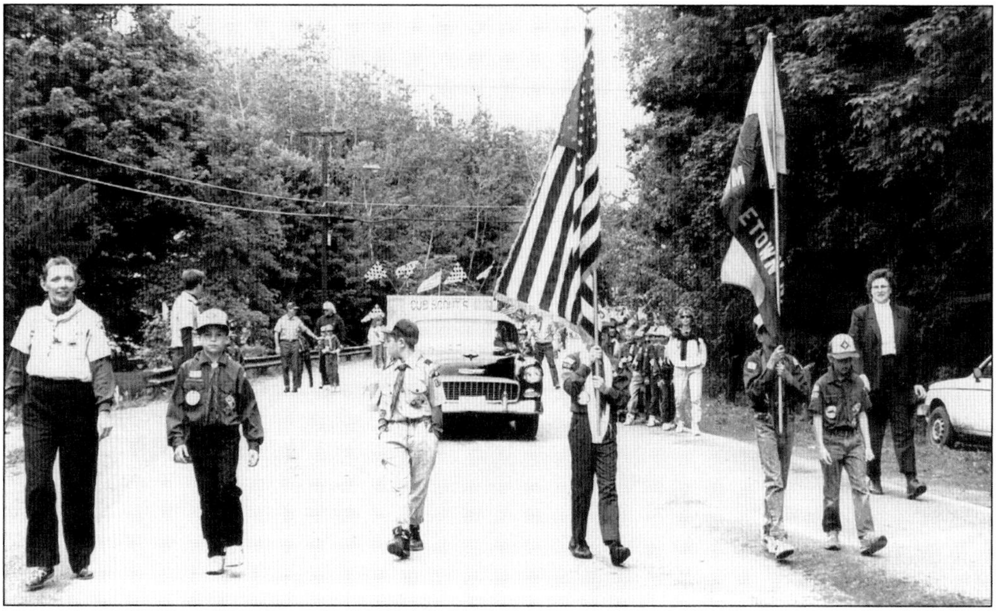

Boy Scouts from Troop 16 in Stone Ridge show their patriotism while marching in the annual Memorial Day parade on Main Street. From left to right are leader Roma Jane Simpson, leader Bill Doughman, Cub Scout Michael Knauer, four unidentified Scouts, and leader Gail Cassens. (Courtesy Jeff Schussler, Troop 16.)

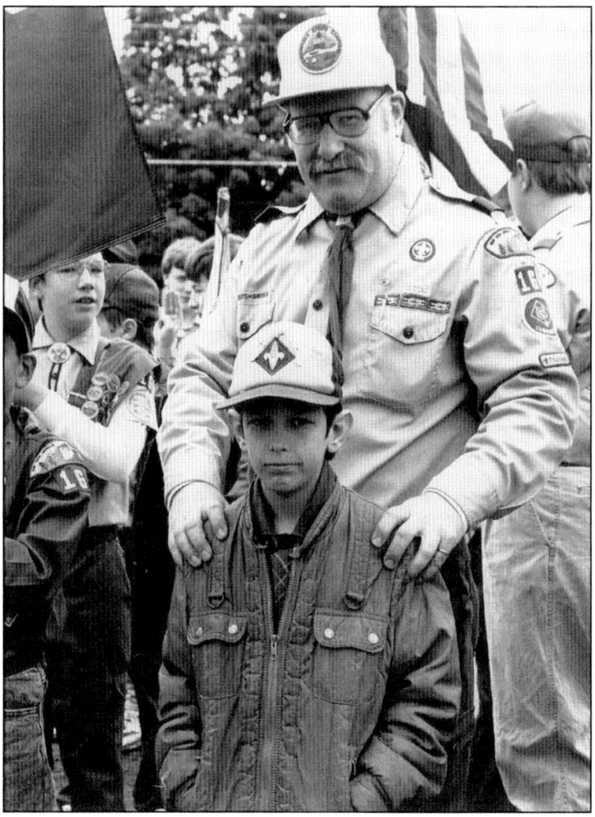

Troop leader Dave Simpson gives encouragement to Cub Scout Joey Pagliaroni during a Scout gathering, while Adam Scheringer looks on under the flag. Paul Giordano on the right helps coordinate the younger members of the group. (Courtesy Jeff Schussler, Troop 16.)

Involved in the Scouting program in Marbletown for many years, Roma Jane Simpson (left) confers with Karen Williams during the annual award ceremony held at Marbletown Park following the Memorial Day parade. Simpson and her husband Dave were instrumental in creating the high-quality Cub Scout and Boy Scout Troop 16 program. (Courtesy Jeff Schussler.)

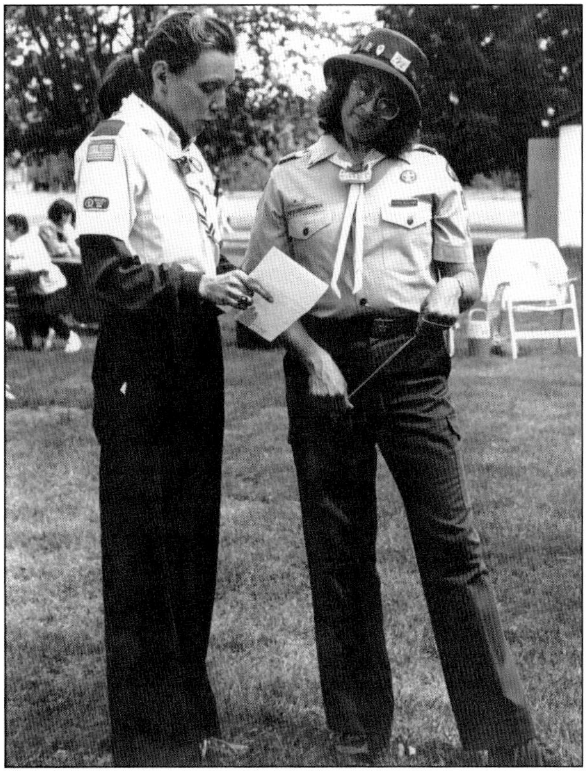

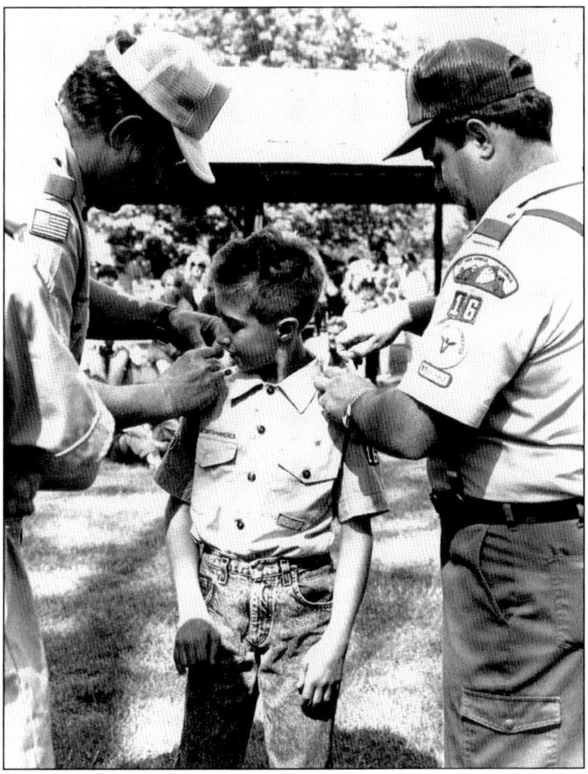

Here Michael Gagnon participates in the "bridging up" ceremony, where a Cub Scout officially becomes a Boy Scout. Leaders Ken Scherringer (left) and Walt Gill pin on the red epaulettes that signify the transfer at the troop's annual awards ceremony at Marbletown Park. (Courtesy Jeff Schussler.)

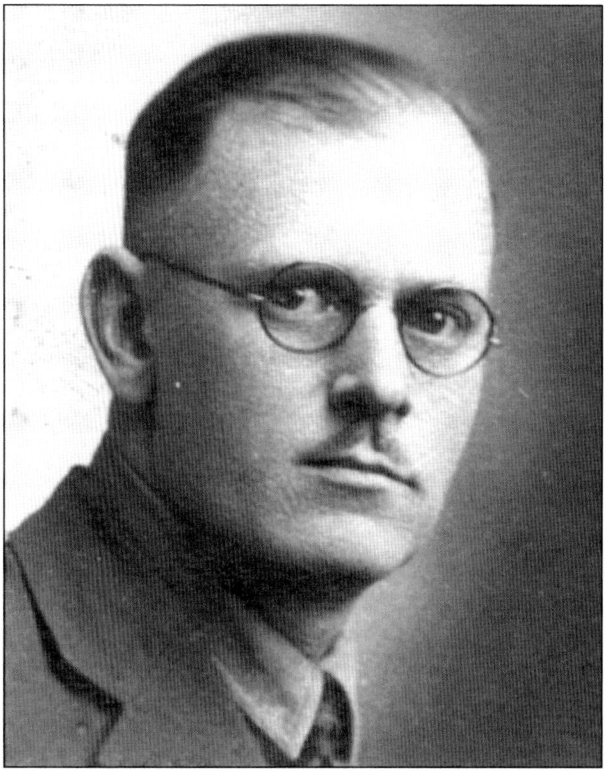

This picture is of John Clifford Cole, who inherited and lived in the Oliver house. He was named after John Oliver. He was a well-known dairy farmer. Cole's son Kenneth Sr. and Kenneth's wife Lois still live in the Oliver house today. (Courtesy Kenneth Cole Sr.)

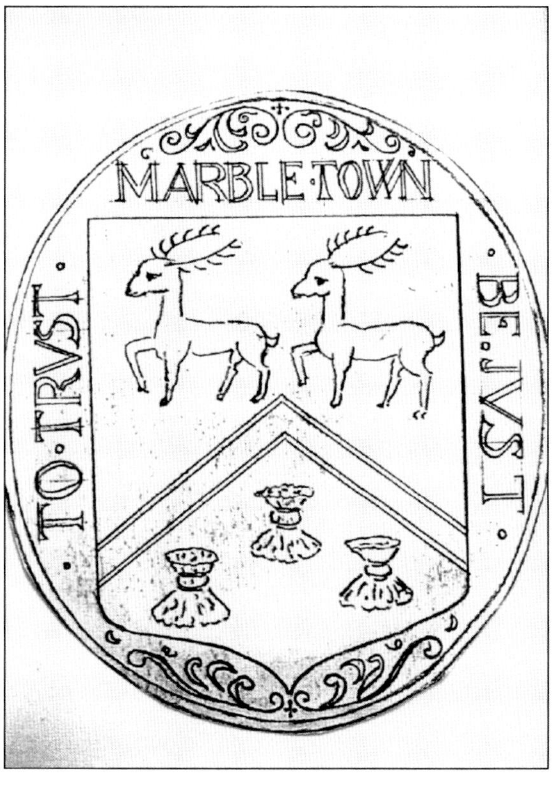

The great seal of the Town of Marbletown is derived from a patent given by Queen Anne on June 25, 1703. The motto To Trust, Be Just flanks the sides. The three wheat sheaves on the bottom represent the fertility of the lower lands, while the deer on top speak to the hunting grounds so prevalent in the area. The original seal was made of silver and is just under three inches in length. It is displayed in the Metropolitan Museum of Art in New York City. It generously made a replica that was presented to the Town of Marbletown and is kept in the town hall. (Courtesy Jody Ford, Stone Ridge Library.)

Two

HIGH FALLS

In its heyday, High Falls was an industrious village. The cement mines and the D&H Canal brought prosperity and work to the people who lived there. Canal traffic brought money to the area, goods, and a stable way of life until the railroad usurped the efficacy of the canal for transportation of goods. The Rondout Creek was a favorite place for children as well as adults to swim in the summer and skate in the winter. Boarders flocked to the area from more urban cities. It was a wonderful way of life in the clean air of the country. The village boasted the usual staple businesses such as a blacksmith shop, a gristmill, hardware stores, bakeries, and a variety of churches. The one-room schoolhouse taught many levels of children together. Life was good.

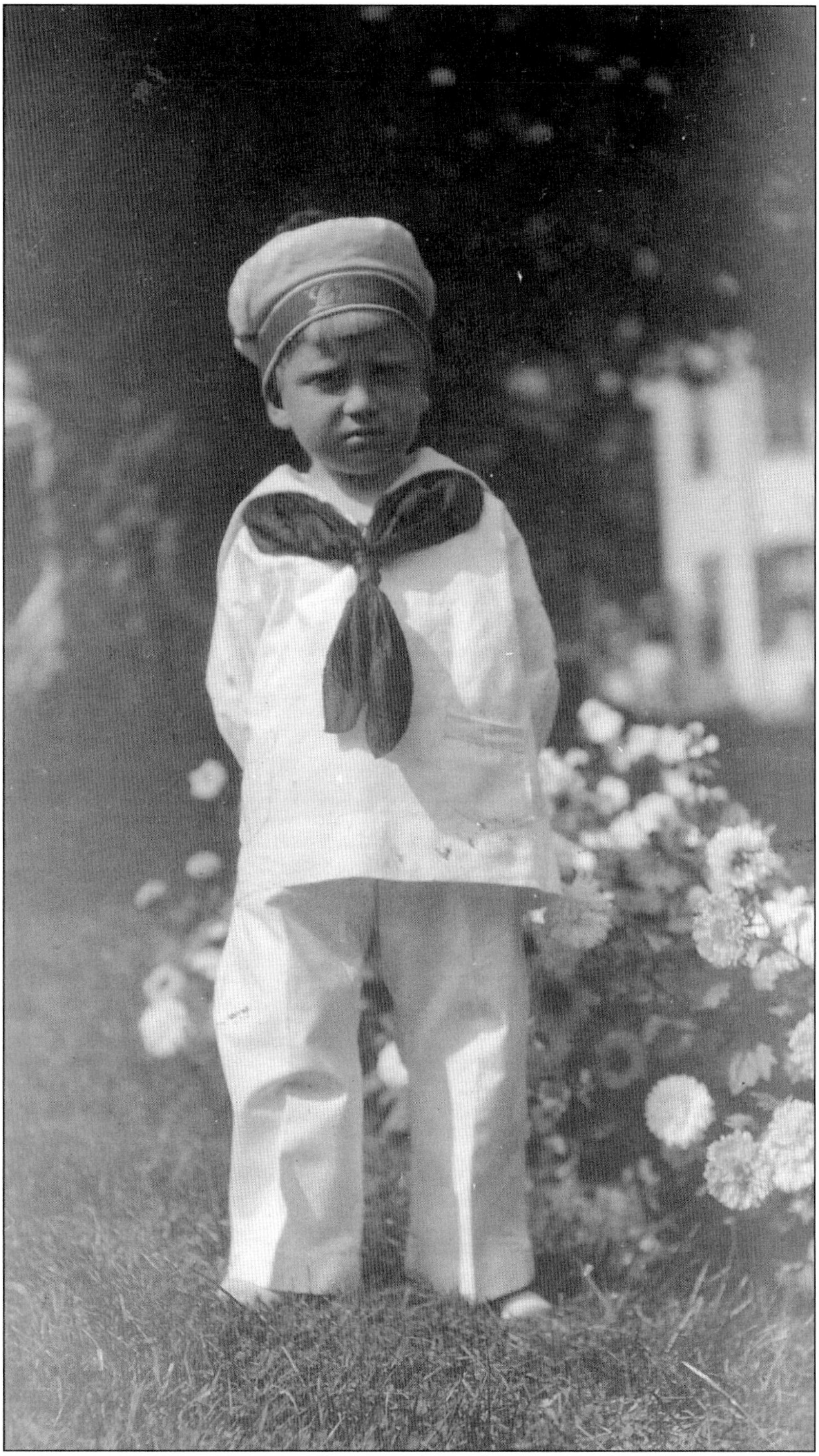

Junior Quick of High Falls poses in his crisp white sailor suit in this c. 1910 photograph. (Courtesy Charles Greene.)

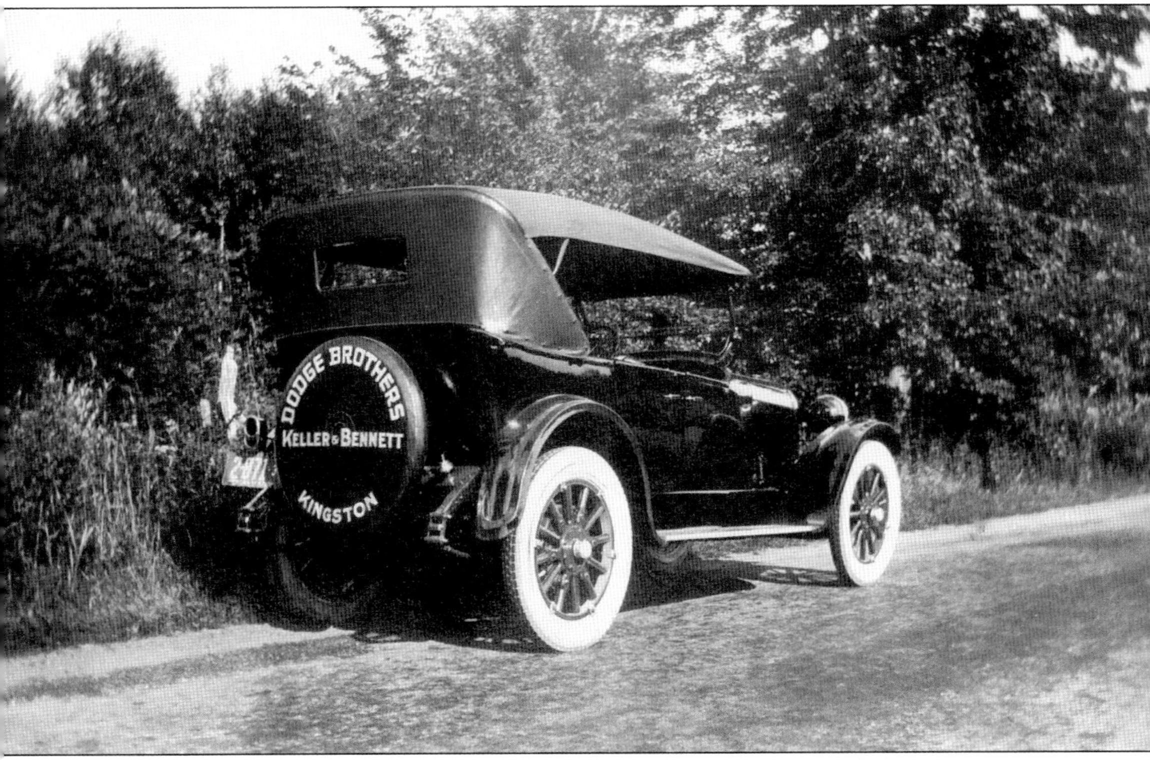

Dodge Brothers of Kingston, Keller, and Bennett took this vehicle to the Ashokan Reservoir to take promotional pictures around 1890 for their dealership. Note the extra wide whitewalls that were popular on the first cars. (Courtesy Charles Greene.)

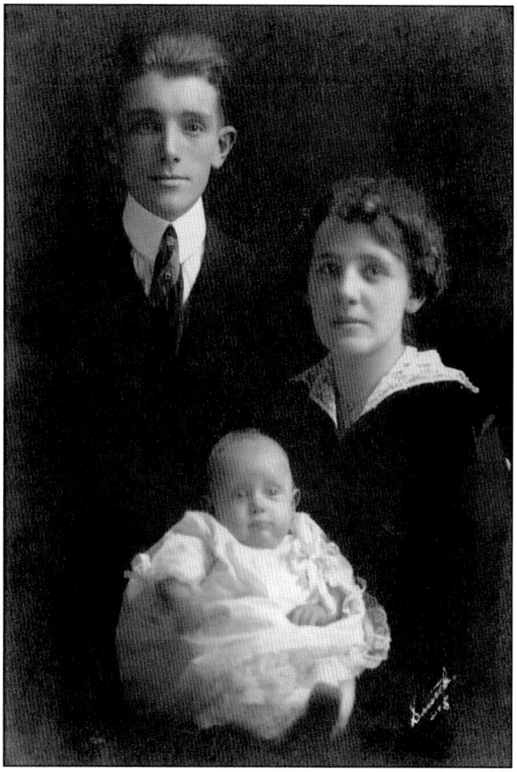

Eva (Grant) Quick and her husband, Joseph, pose with their infant son, James Jr., in this c. 1916 family portrait. The Grants were a prominent family in the High Falls/Accord area. (Courtesy Charles Greene.)

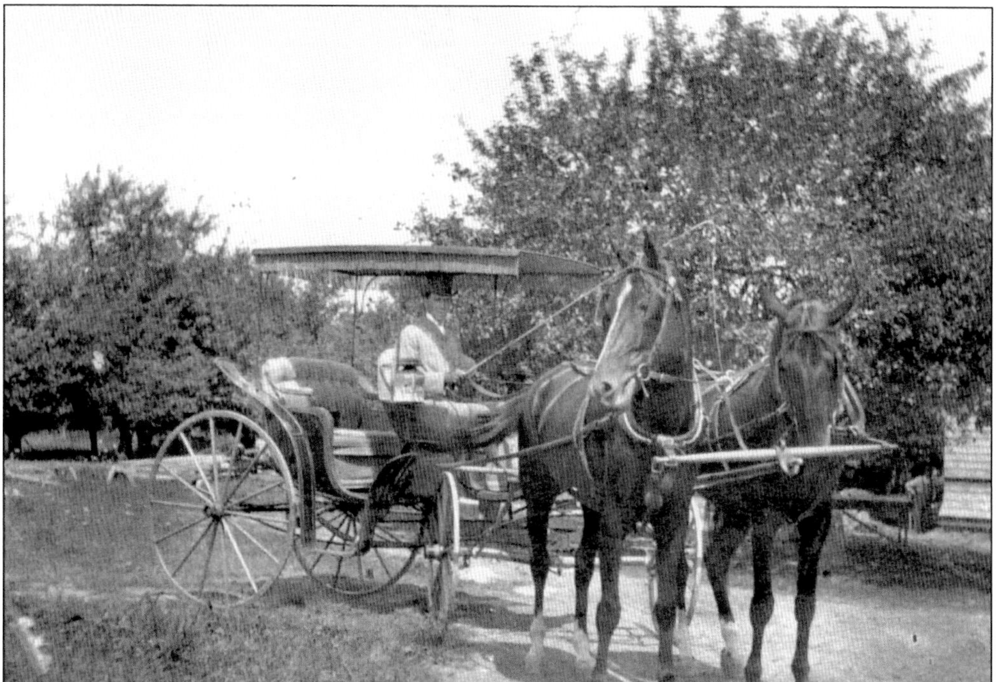

George Grant takes the Mc Neir horses, Dimples and Dotty, for a spin in his covered carriage around 1869. (Courtesy Charles Greene.)

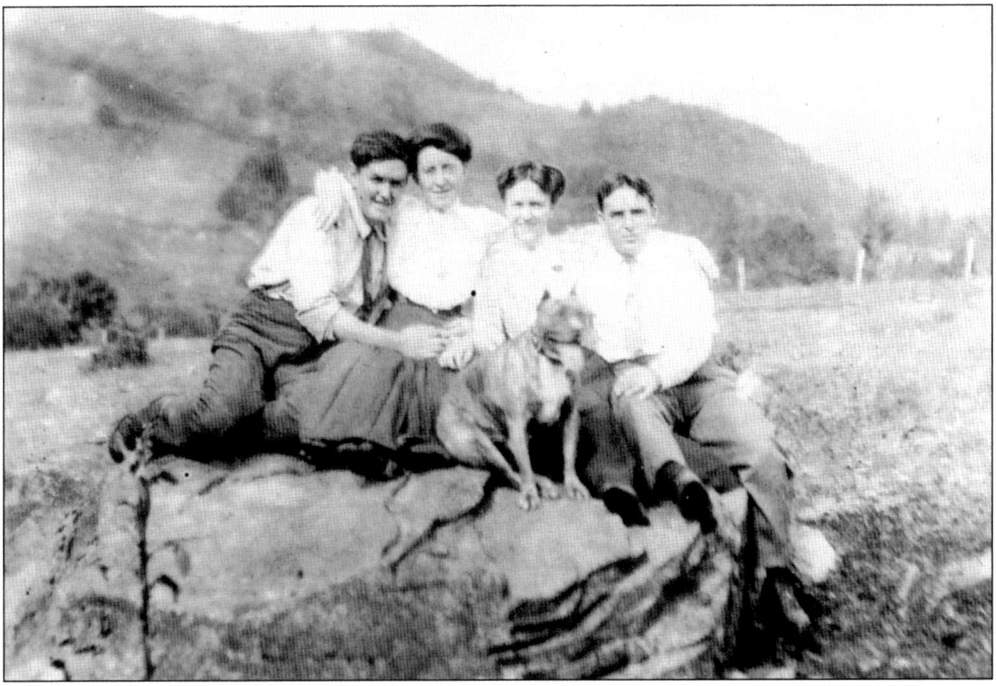

From left to right, Clarence and Bertha Krom enjoy the outdoors with Earl Grant and his wife, Catherine. They are pictured around the late 1800s near the Ashokan Reservoir. (Courtesy Charles Greene.)

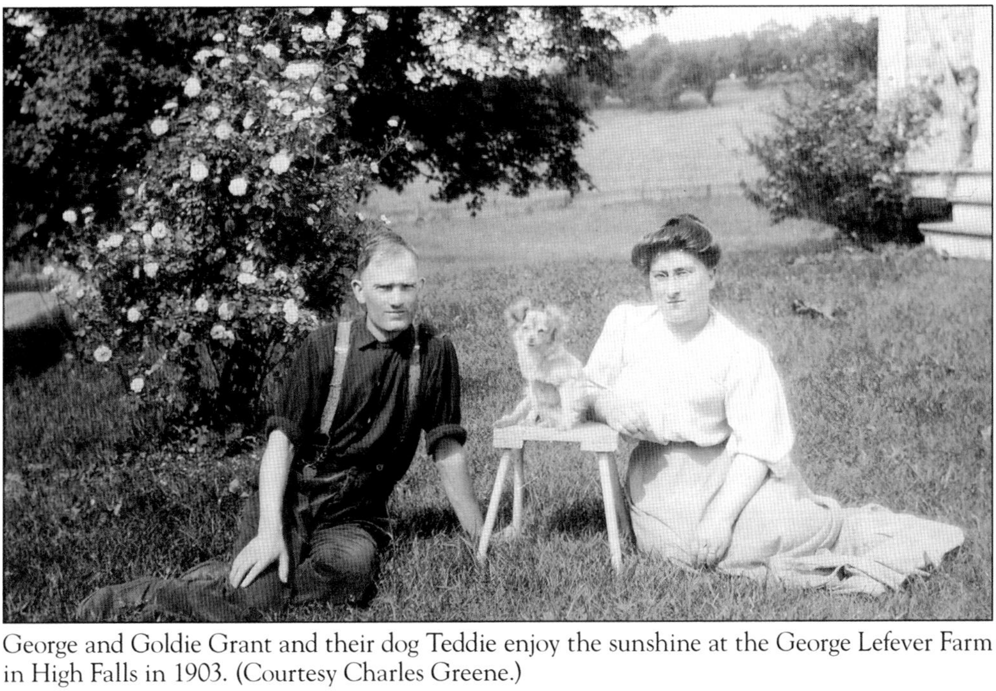

George and Goldie Grant and their dog Teddie enjoy the sunshine at the George Lefever Farm in High Falls in 1903. (Courtesy Charles Greene.)

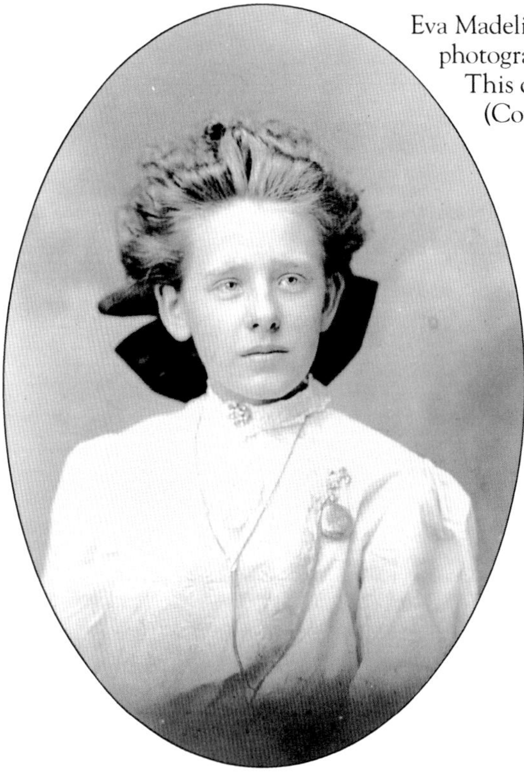

Eva Madeline (Quick) Grant was 16 when this photograph from around the late 1800s was taken. This classic pose exemplifies the dress of the time. (Courtesy Charles Greene.)

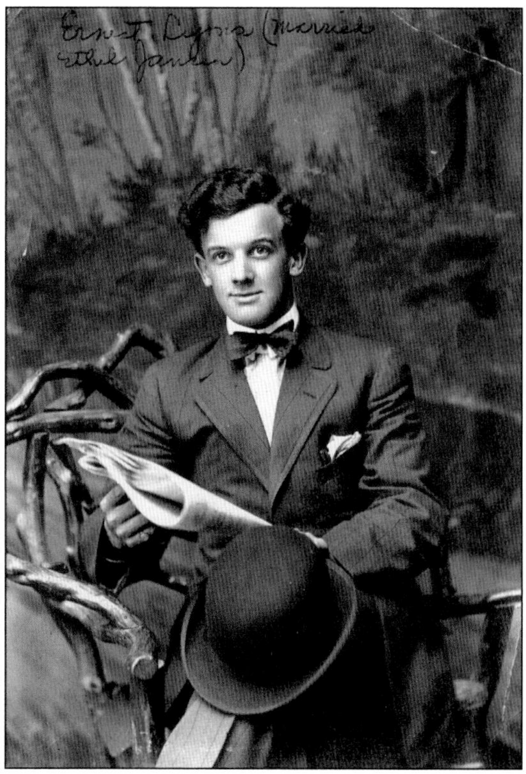

Ernest Lyons, who was married to Ethel Jameson of High Falls, was a railroad station agent in Fallsburg. He is pictured here around 1900. (Courtesy Charles Greene.)

Merton Grant, of High Falls, was a cook for the Ontario and Western Railroad. He is pictured in this *c.* 1890 formal portrait. (Courtesy Charles Greene.)

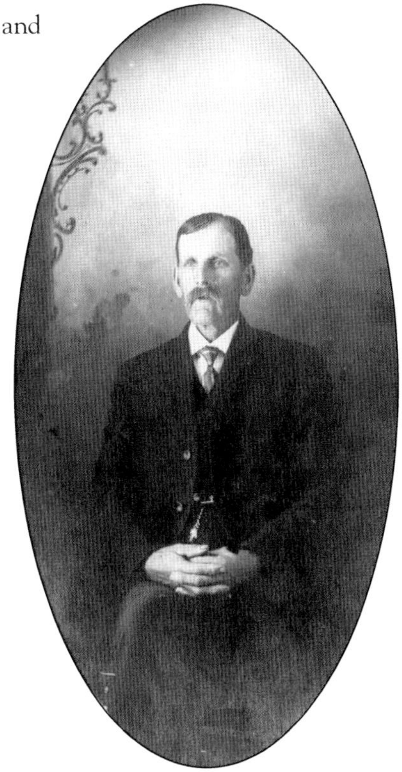

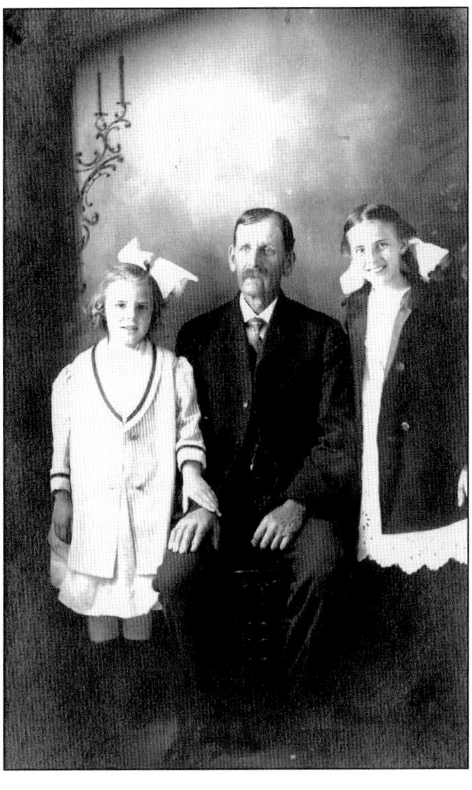

Merton Grant is shown with Vi Barley, left, age 10, and Bea Barley, age 7. The large bows in the girls' hair were very popular in the late 1800s and early 1900s. (Courtesy Charles Greene.)

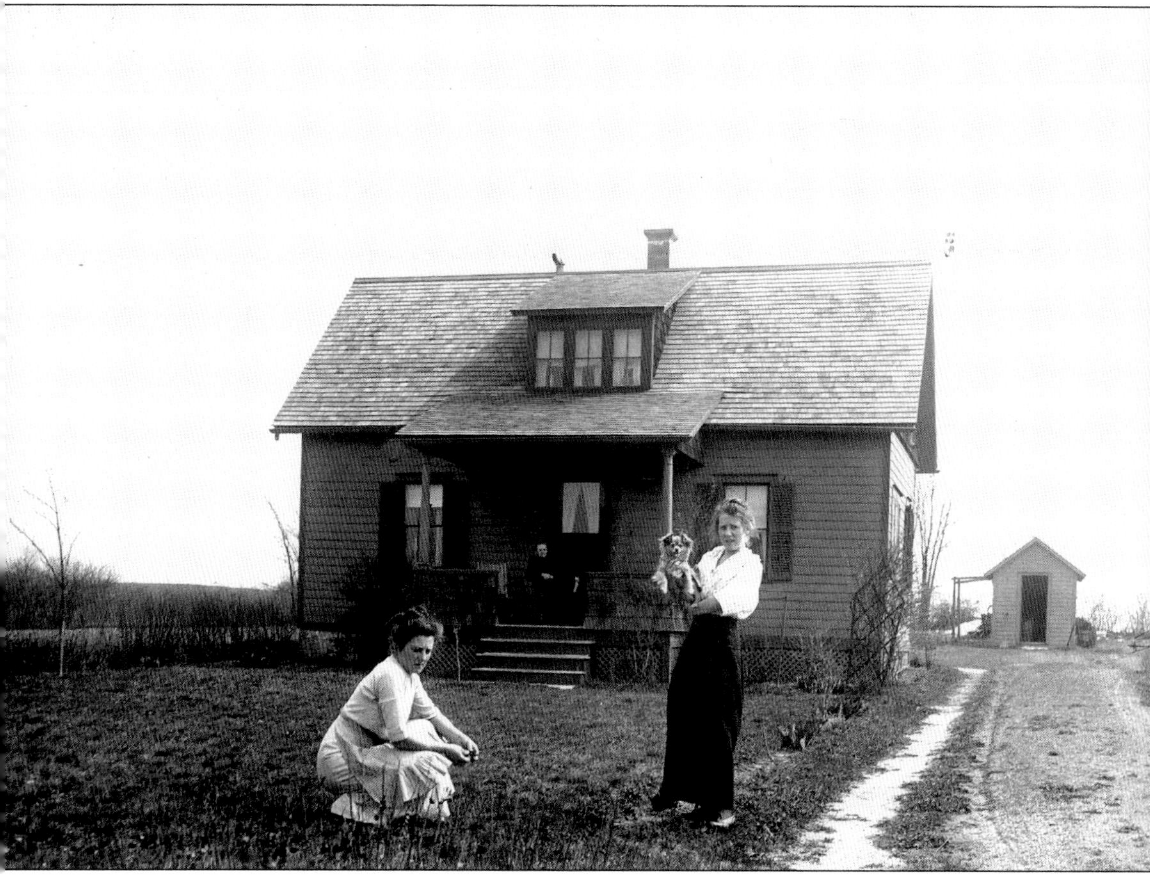

Taken in 1915, the Barley homestead in High Falls is pictured with Myra and Eva playing with Teddy in the foreground. Grandma Barley, who was confined to a wheelchair, watches from the porch. (Courtesy Charles Greene.)

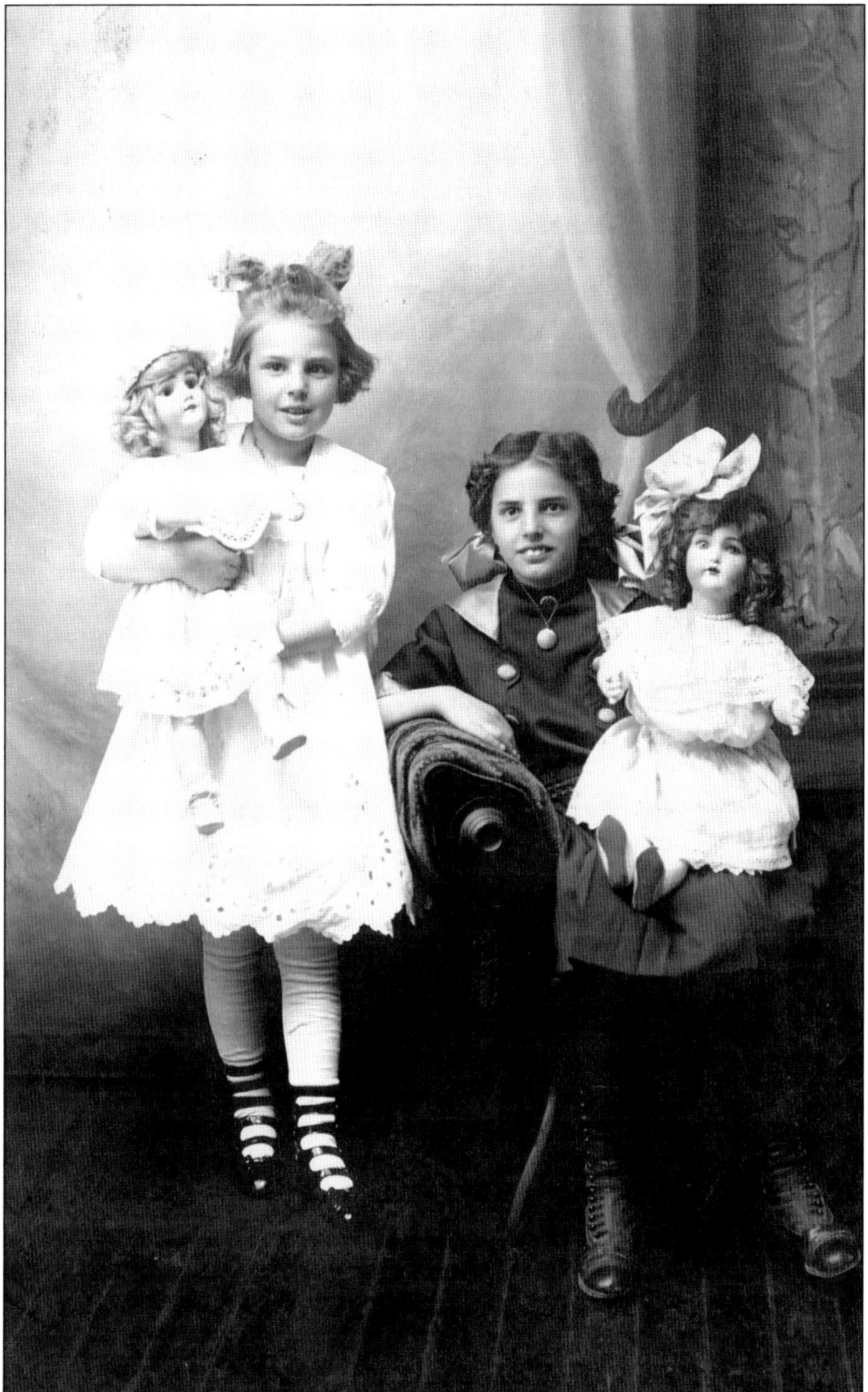

Note the similarities of the dress between Bea Barley, left, and Vi Barley with regard to their dolls around 1900. Each button on Vi's shoes had to be buttoned using a special hook. The dolls sport lace bonnets and dresses. (Courtesy Charles Greene.)

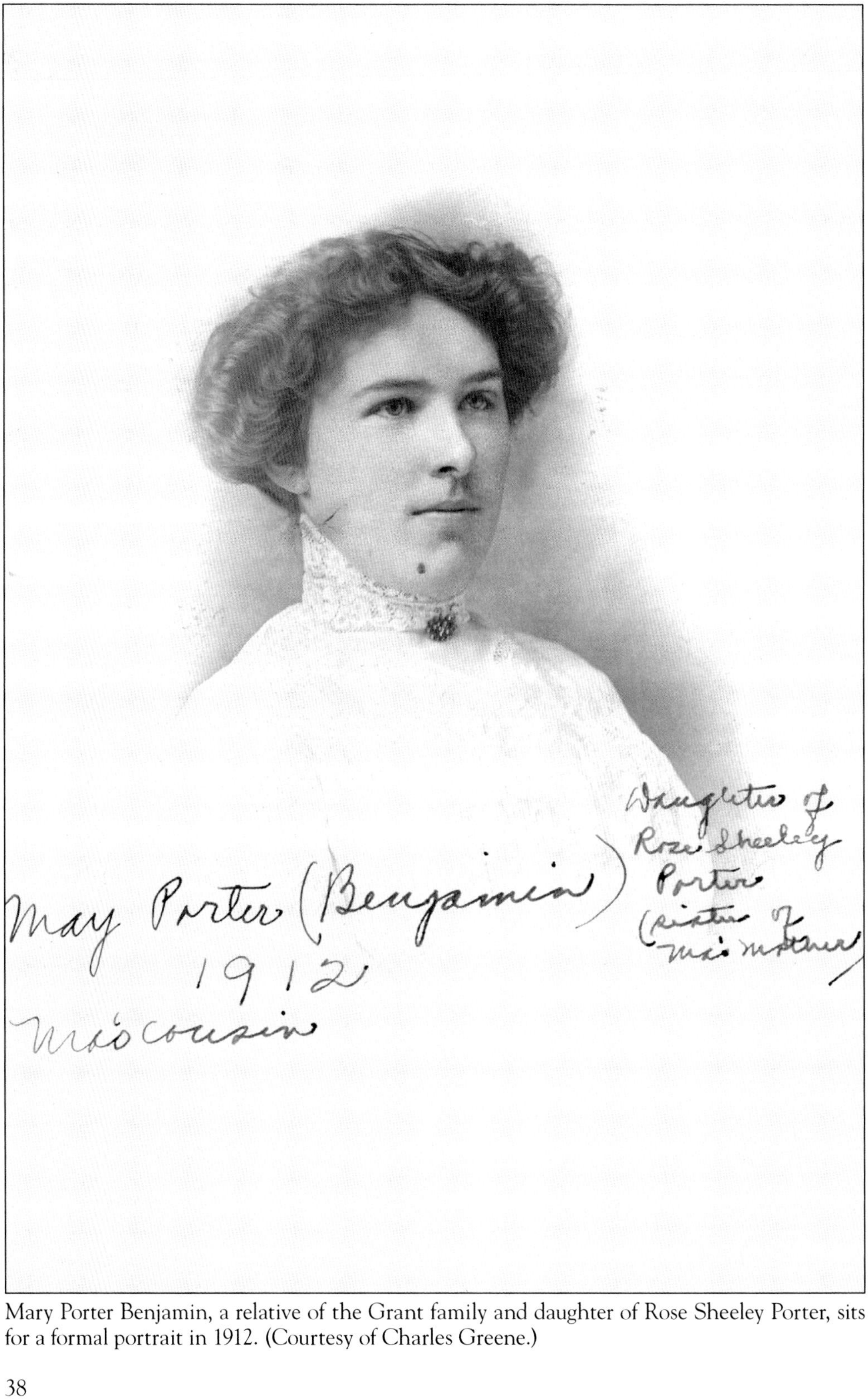

Mary Porter Benjamin, a relative of the Grant family and daughter of Rose Sheeley Porter, sits for a formal portrait in 1912. (Courtesy of Charles Greene.)

Pictured here around 1921 is Bea Barley at approximately 16 or 17 years of age. The Barley family had a large farm in the Kyserike/Accord area. (Courtesy Charles Greene.)

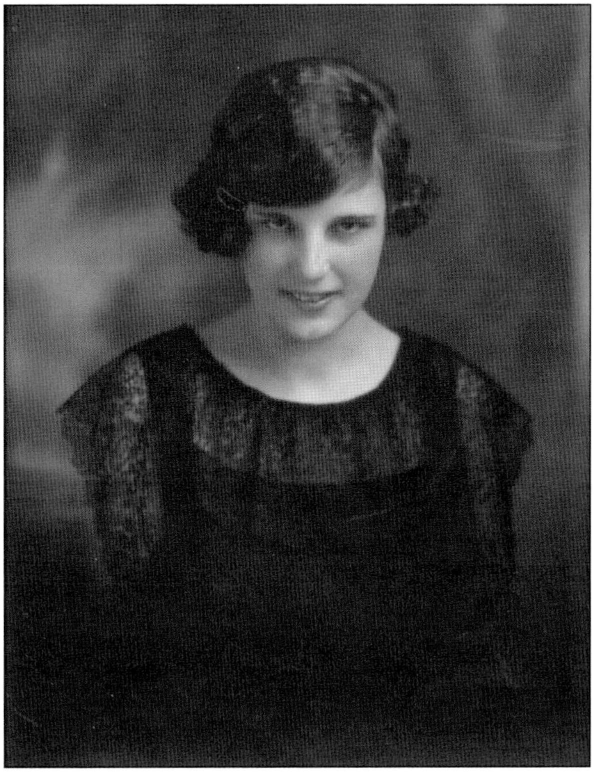

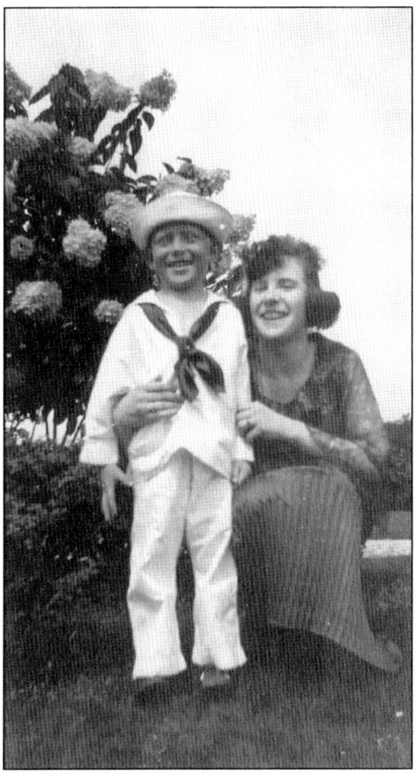

Junior Quick of High Falls poses in his sailor outfit with Mary Castle at Orange Lake around 1910. (Courtesy Charles Greene.)

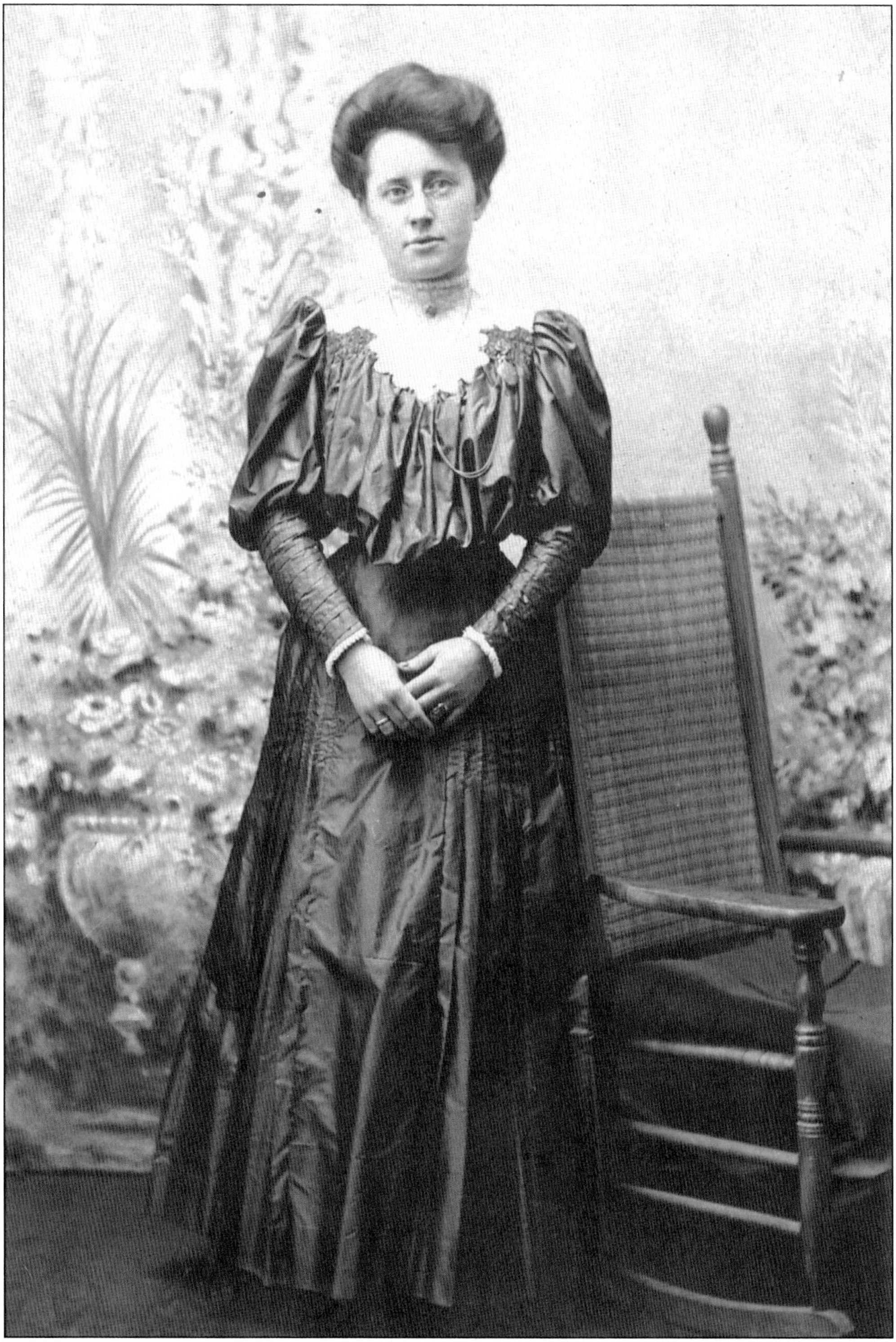

Kate Grant, whose family resided in High Falls, is pictured in her wedding dress in the early 1900s. Many brides chose darker colors for wedding gowns. (Courtesy Charles Greene.)

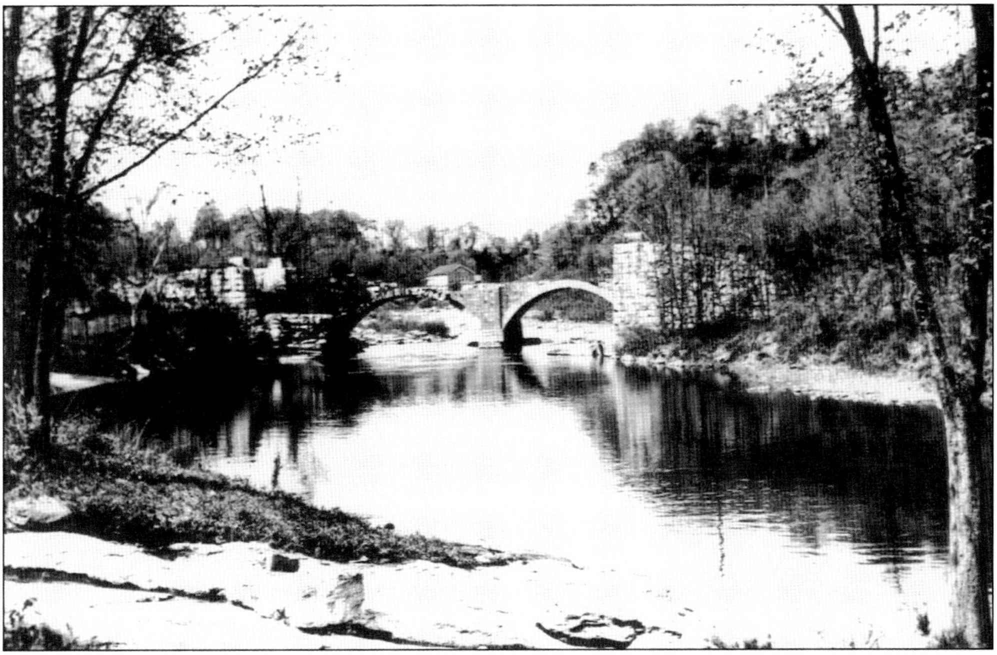

The High Falls Aqueduct was built by the D&H Canal Company in 1828. Stone native to the area was used to construct the 116-foot-long structure. It carried canal boats across the Rondout Creek for at least 20 years. It was finally demolished in 1956. (Courtesy Jody Ford, Stone Ridge Library.)

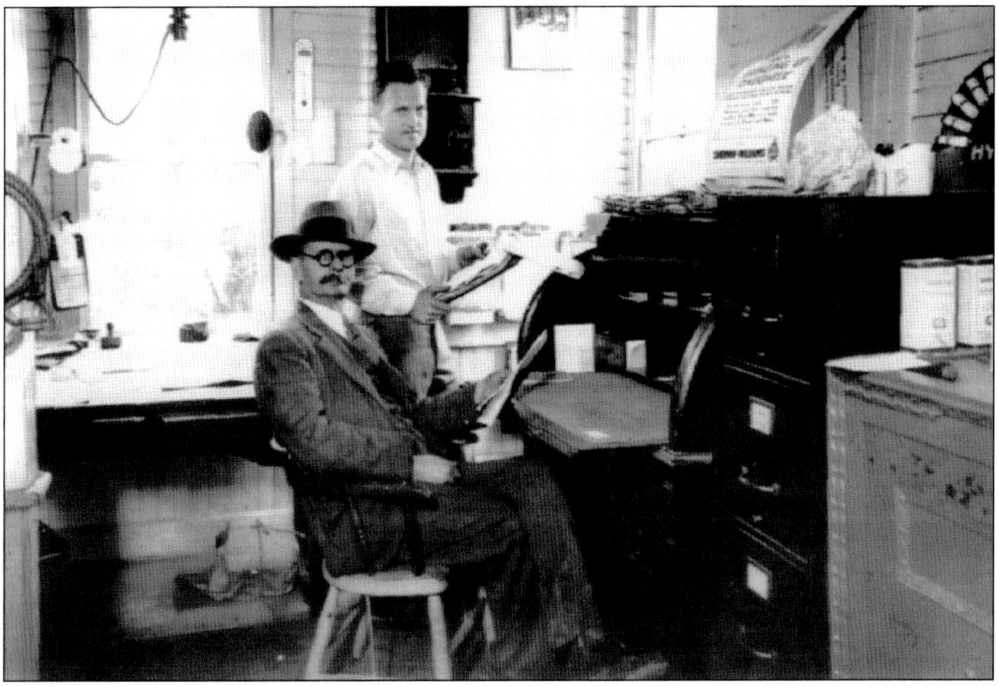

Pictured in the office of Walter Davenport are Walter Davenport (left) and his brother Morris Davenport. Note the old-time office fixtures such as the large safe in the foreground. Computers were nonexistent in those days. (Courtesy Ed Croswell.)

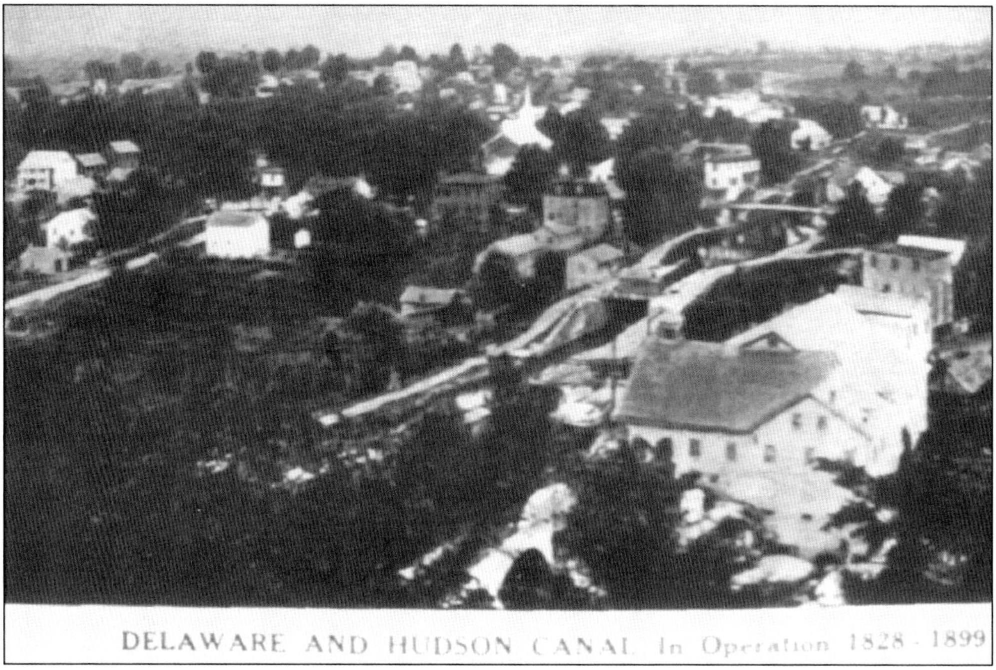

This excellent overhead view shows the bustling village of High Falls. The D&H Canal transected the center of town. The canal was 108 miles long and had 108 locks. It served to bring coal from mines in Pennsylvania to New York City. (Courtesy Betty Croswell.)

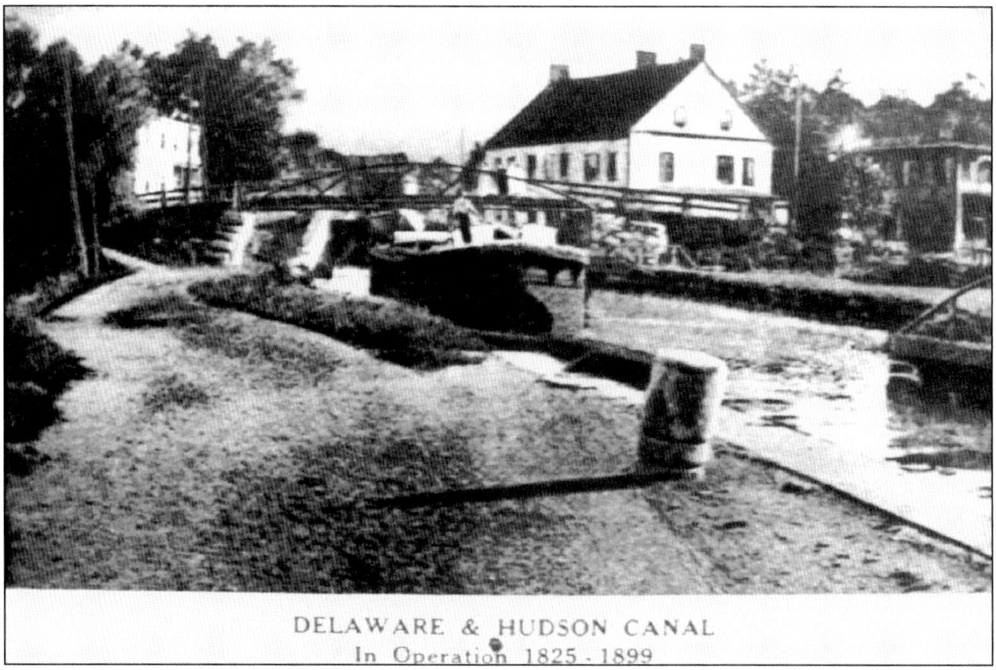

This c. 1902 colored postcard pictures the D&H barge canal, in operation from 1825 to 1899. The building at the extreme right was the High Falls Hardware Company. The development of the railroads caused the canal to become less profitable to use. It ceased to operate in 1899. (Courtesy Betty Croswell.)

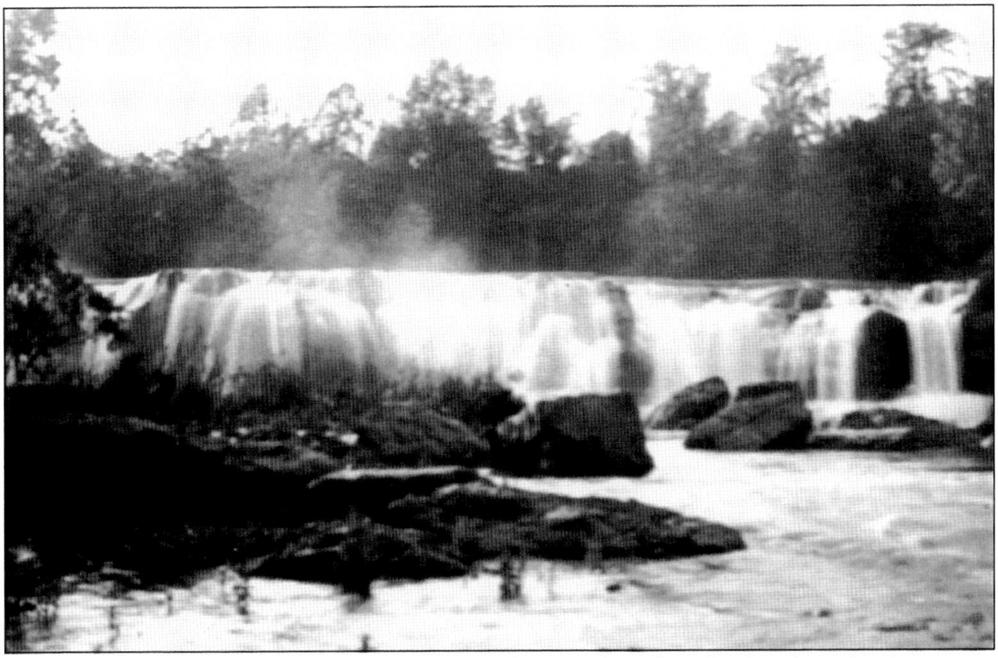

Pictured is an early-1900s photograph of the falls at High Falls. The Rondout Creek was not navigable in this area, hence the D&H Canal system. Later on, waterpower was harnessed at these falls by the Central Hudson Electric Company. (Courtesy Jody Ford, Stone Ridge Library.)

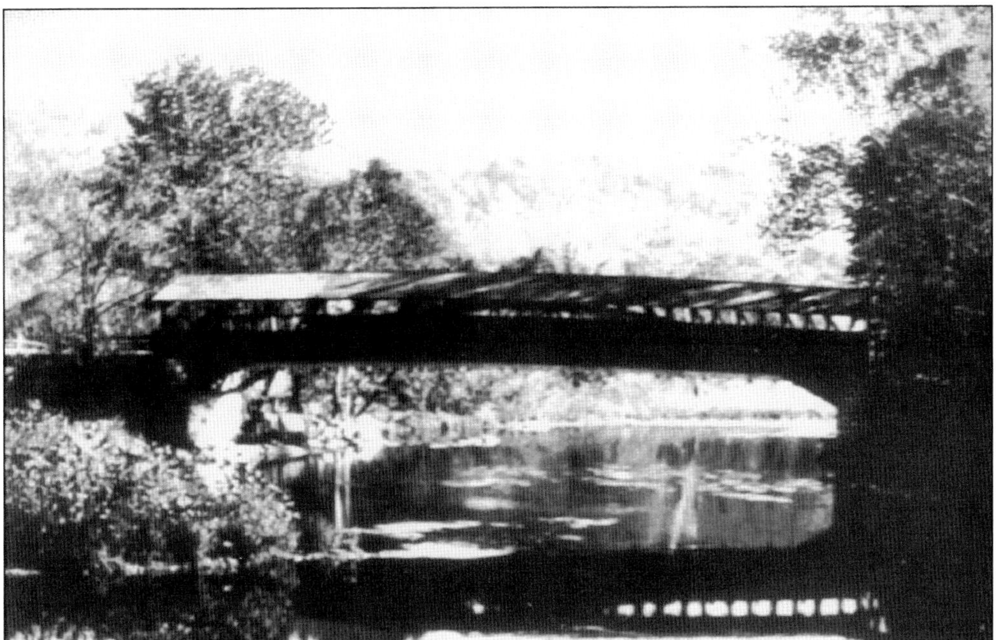

Pictured is the Coxing Bridge, which crossed the Rondout Creek just east of the village of High Falls. Covered bridges served to keep the bridge flooring from getting wet, which caused rotting. This bridge is an example of the Burr arch truss design that was patented in 1804 by Theodore Burr. (Courtesy Jody Ford, Stone Ridge Library.)

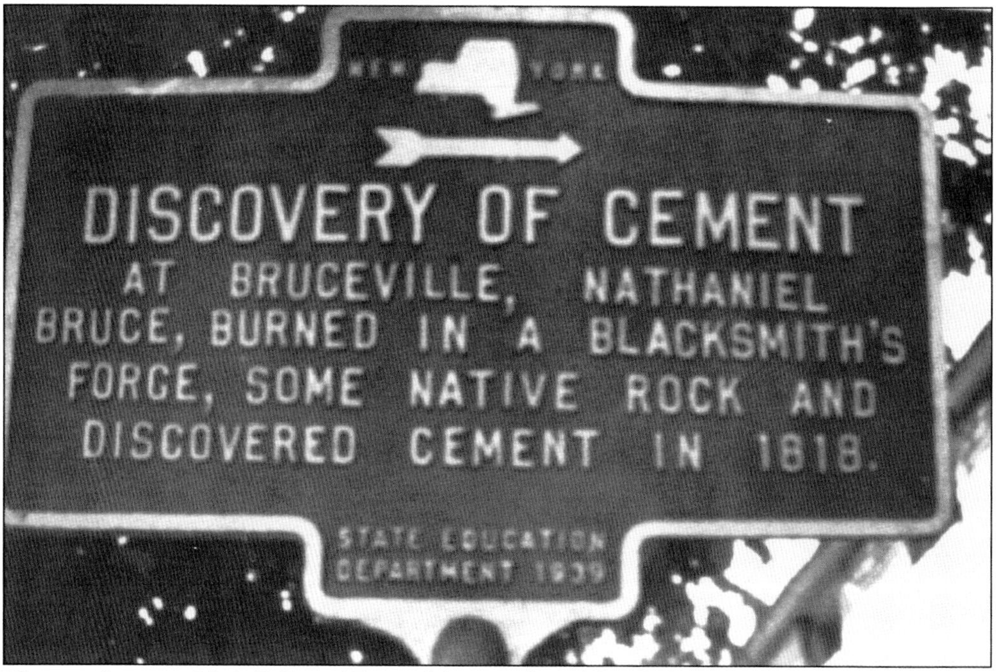

The area between High Falls and Rosendale was plentiful with limestone caves. Limestone is a key ingredient in the production of cement. The D&H Canal needed hydraulic cement (which hardens underwater) to complete work on its canal locks. In 1825, limestone was quarried and taken to kilns for burning. The industry peaked in 1899 with over 5,000 local men employed. (Courtesy Jody Ford, Stone Ridge Library.)

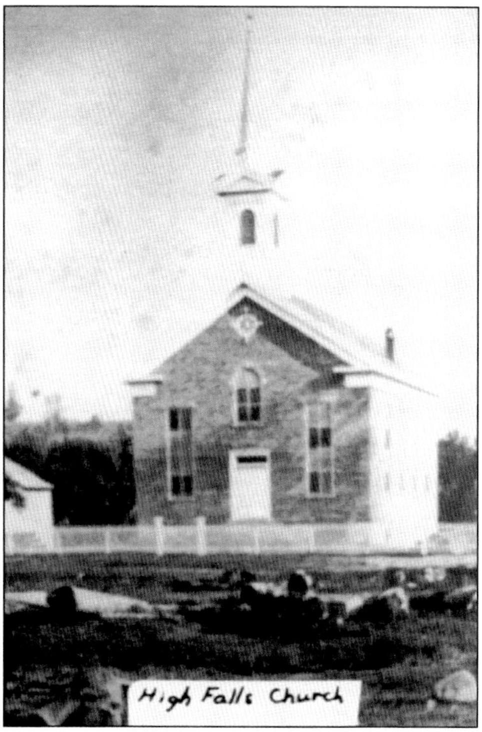

The High Falls Community Church, built in the mid-1800s, sits close to the center of the High Falls community. (Courtesy Stone Ridge Library.)

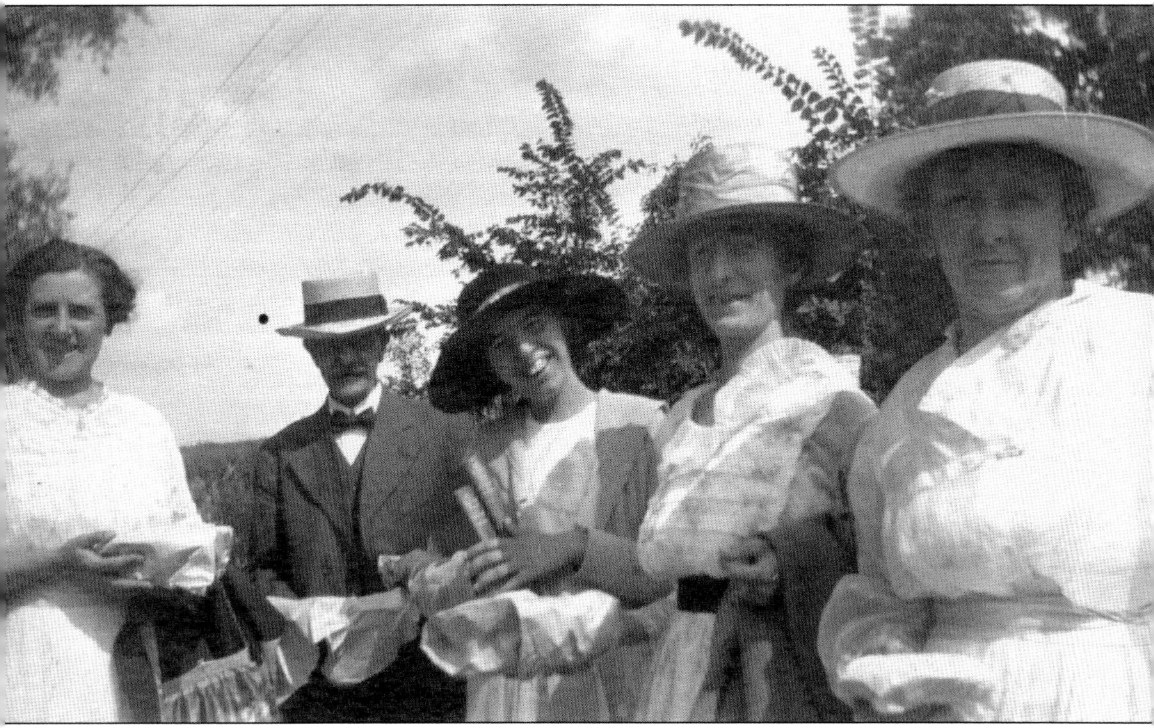

Members of the Relyea family pose in High Falls on their way to visit a friend in August 1919. Pictured from left to right are Myra, Mr. Relyea, Violet, Lucille, and Mrs. Relyea. Note the Sunday finery common in those days. (Courtesy Charles Greene.)

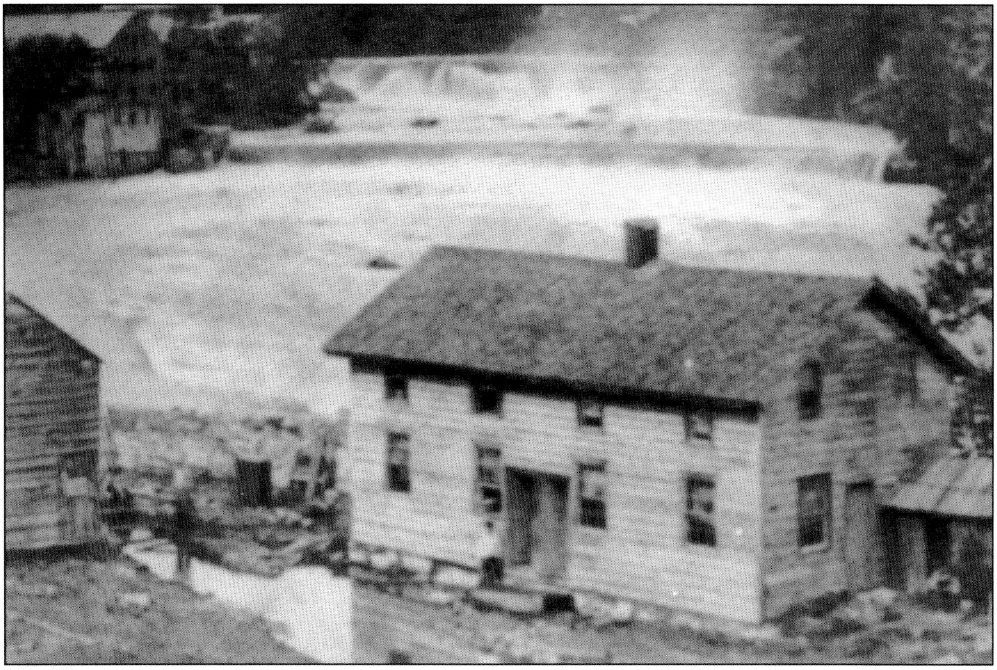

This late-1800s home was located below the Rondout Creek falls in High Falls. Many workers on the D&H Canal system, as well as cement factory workers, lived in the village. (Courtesy Stone Ridge Library.)

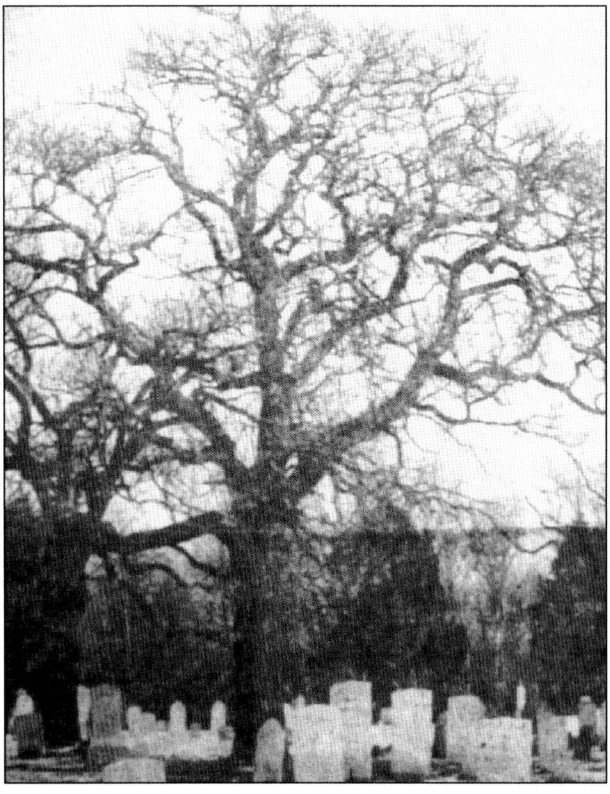

This sassafras tree, growing in the Benton Bar Cemetery, was reported to be the largest of its species by the New York State Department of Agriculture. The circumference of the trunk was four feet, and the crown spread was 57 feet. The tree's age at the time of the photograph was estimated to be at least 33 years old. The previous record sassafras tree had been in Wyoming County, New York. (Photograph by Bob Haines.)

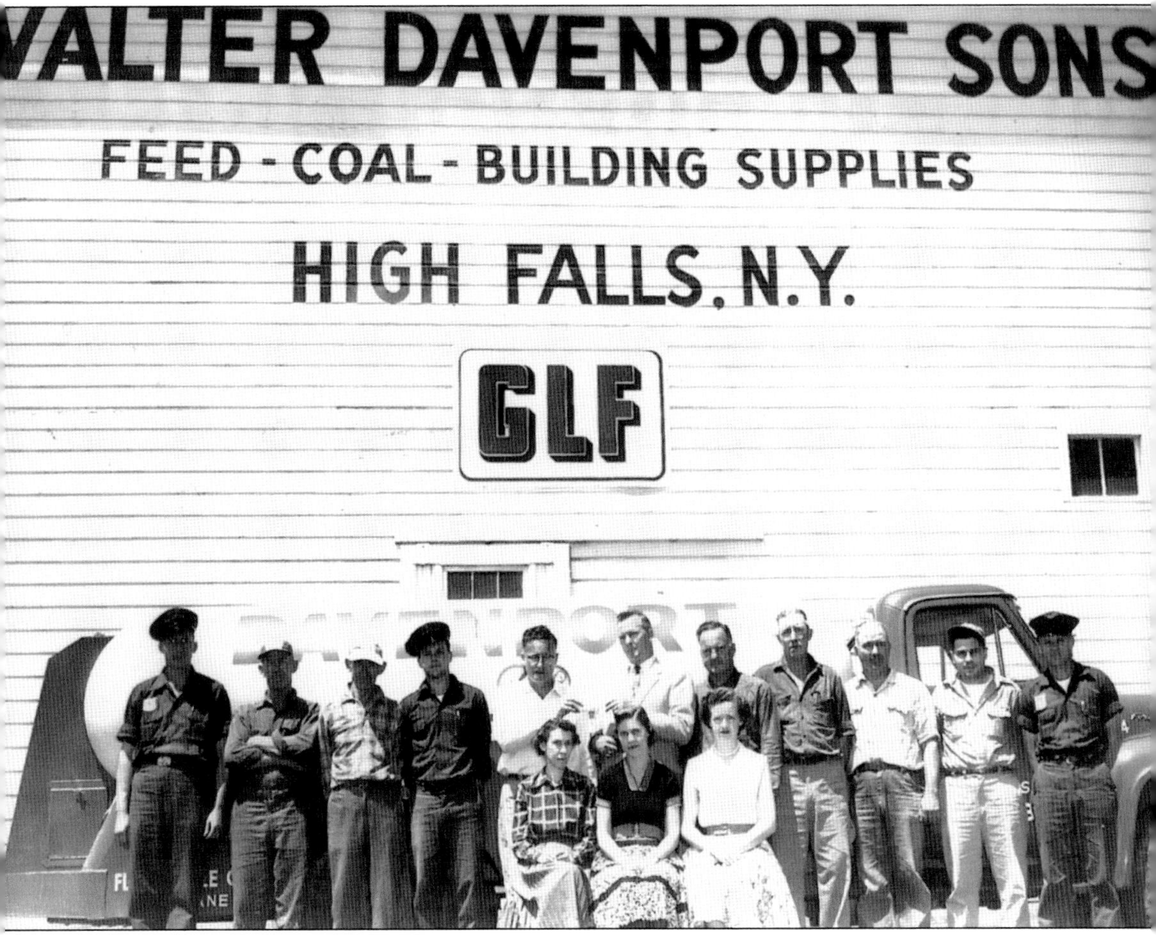

Walter Davenport employees happily pose outside the office for a company picture in 1954. Pictured are, from left to right, (first row) Ann Trowbridge, Anne Vandemark, and Eleanor Connor; (second row) Bob Hornbeck, Bill Connor, Roscoe ?, Ernie Beesmer, Kenneth Davenport, unidentified, Morris Davenport, Jim Robinson, Elmer Osterhoudt, Buzz Lockwood, and Ray Nichols. (Courtesy Ed Croswell.)

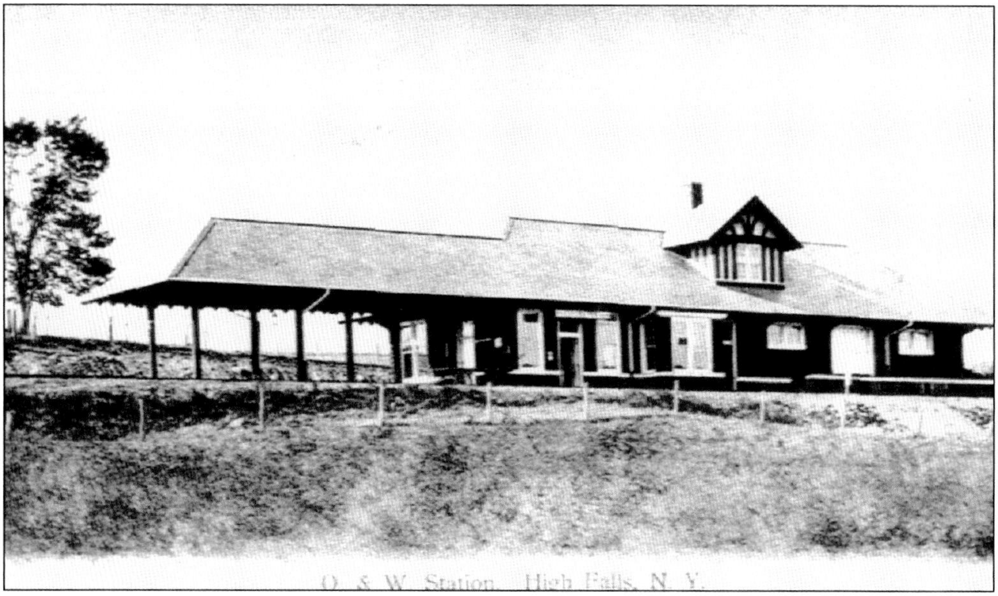

This wonderful postcard shows the New York, Ontario and Western Railway station in High Falls. Located high above the Rondout Creek in High Falls, the station was a busy destination for early travelers. Today it has been converted into a private home, and the railroad bed serves as a well-utilized footpath for hiking and biking. (Courtesy George K. Van Sickle.)

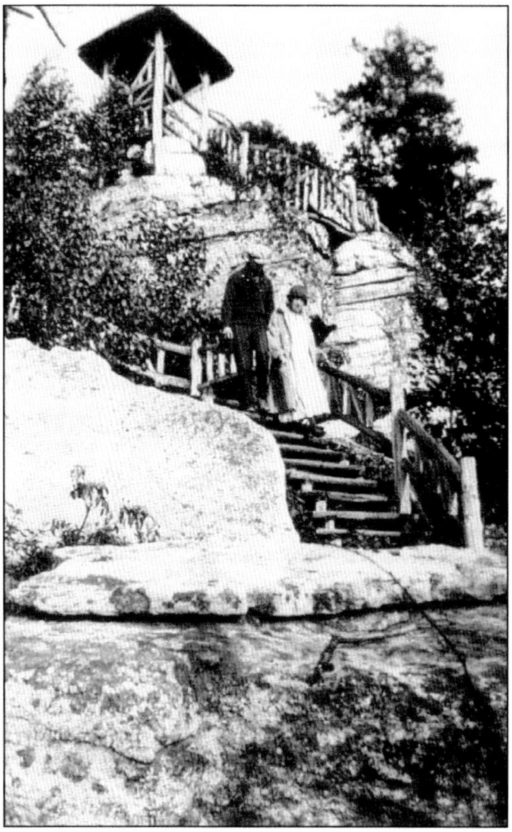

Taken on May 31, 1924, this photograph of Gladys Ford and Al Weingarten is from one of the winding wooden stairways at Mohonk Mountain House. Mohonk Mountain House was a well-known resort of that era. Many traveled from long distances to enjoy the wonderful ambiance of the Smiley family resort. (Courtesy Charles Greene.)

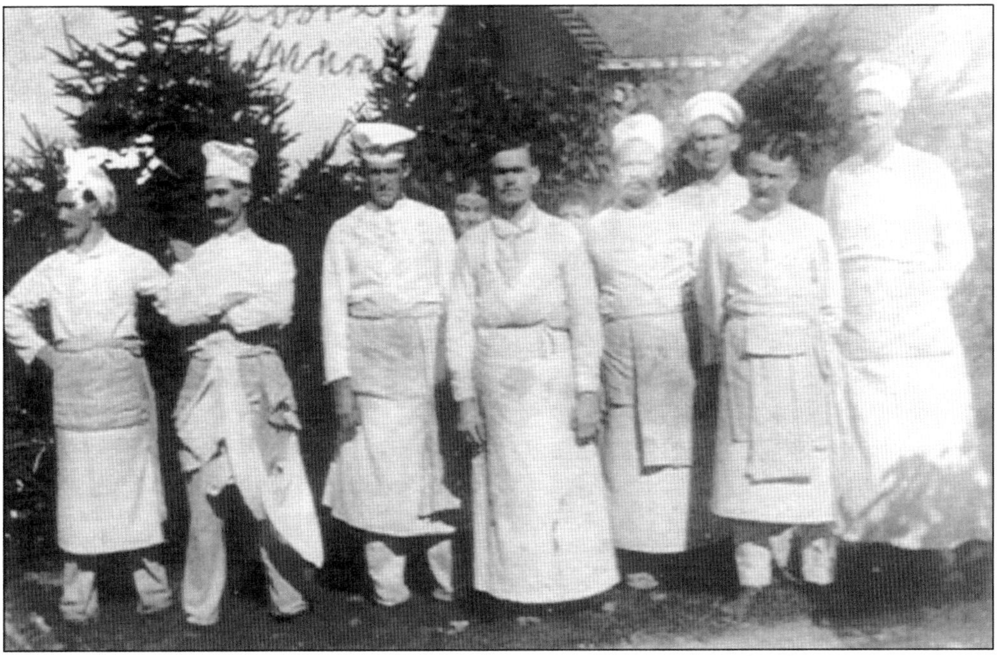

This wonderfully old, *c.* 1898 photograph is of the cook staff at Mohonk Mountain House. The "Mountain House" was well known for its superb cuisine then as well as today. The formal dining room offers full-course meals to guests and is a sought-after destination by many locals. (Courtesy Charles Greene.)

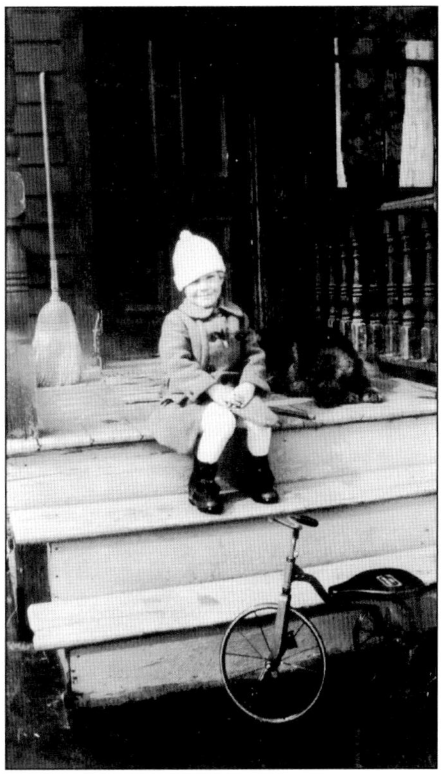

Simple pleasures such as a "no frills" tricycle were important to children like Kathryn Quick, pictured here sitting on the front stairs of her High Falls home during the winter of 1922. (Courtesy Charles Greene.)

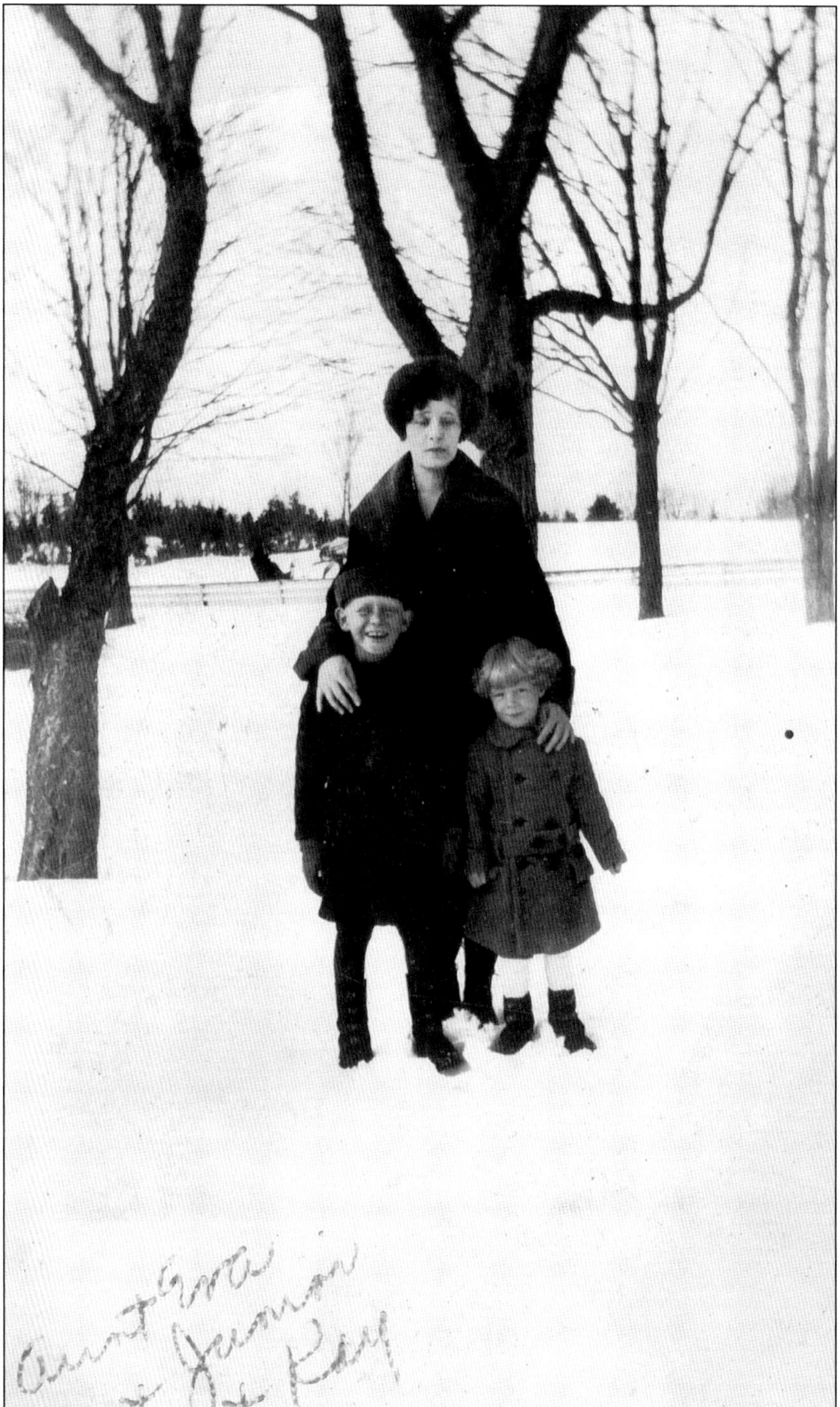

Eva Quick and her children Junior and Kay pose outside their High Falls home during the winter of 1922–1923. Winters were colder, and it was not uncommon to be ice-skating by Thanksgiving. (Courtesy Charles Greene.)

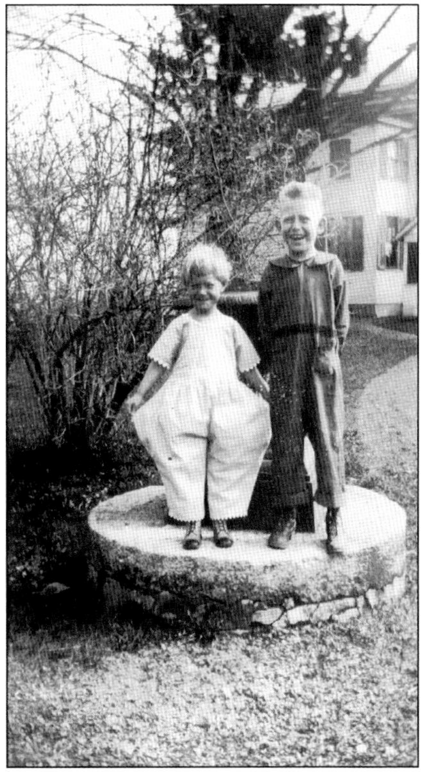

Kathryn and Junior Quick pose on the well cover of their High Falls home in the spring of 1923. (Courtesy Charles Greene.)

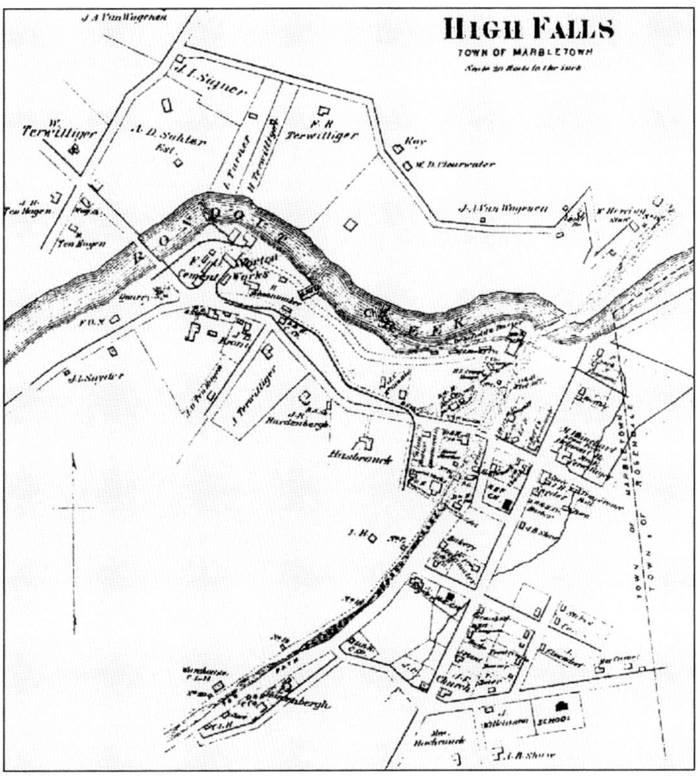

This 1875 tax and property map shows all the property owners in the hamlet of High Falls. One can see how important the Rondout Creek was to this hamlet. Each property owner's name is shown. (Courtesy Jody Ford, Stone Ridge Library.)

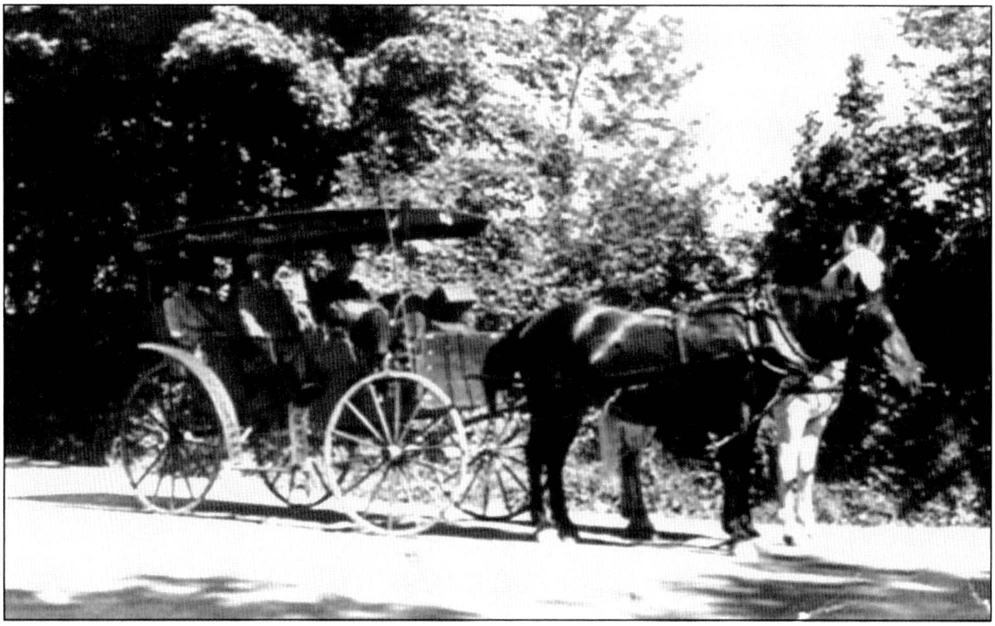

Guests at Mohonk Mountain House enjoy an afternoon carriage ride on the miles of well-manicured carriage roads that traverse the property. Driver George Grant handles the well-matched pair of horses from the resort's stables in 1941. (Courtesy Charles Greene.)

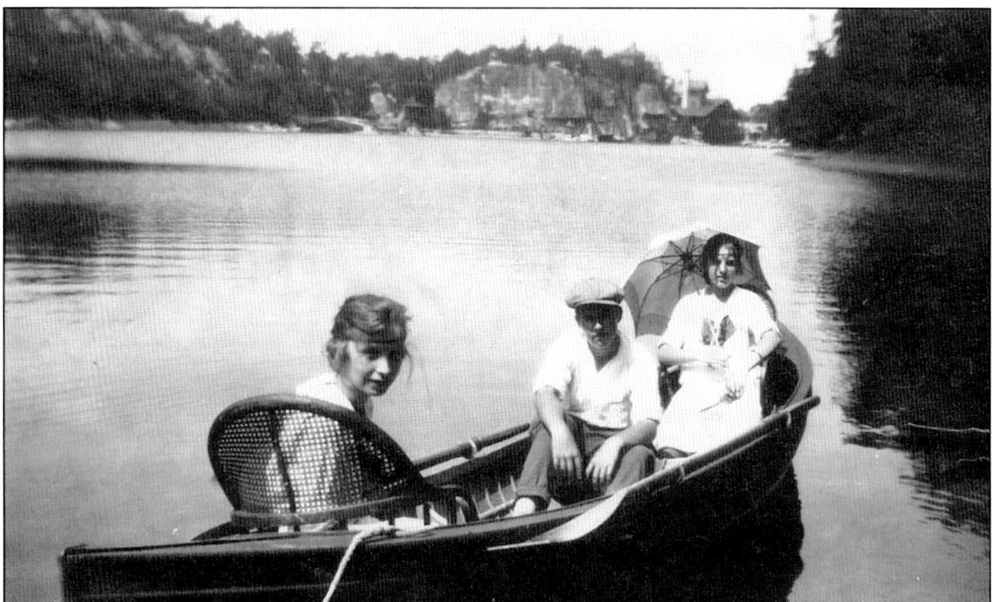

Mary Evans, Cliff Sherman, and Bea Barley take a wonderful canoe ride on Lake Mohonk at Mohonk Mountain House in July 1918. Note the vintage cane back supports in the boat. (Courtesy Charles Greene.)

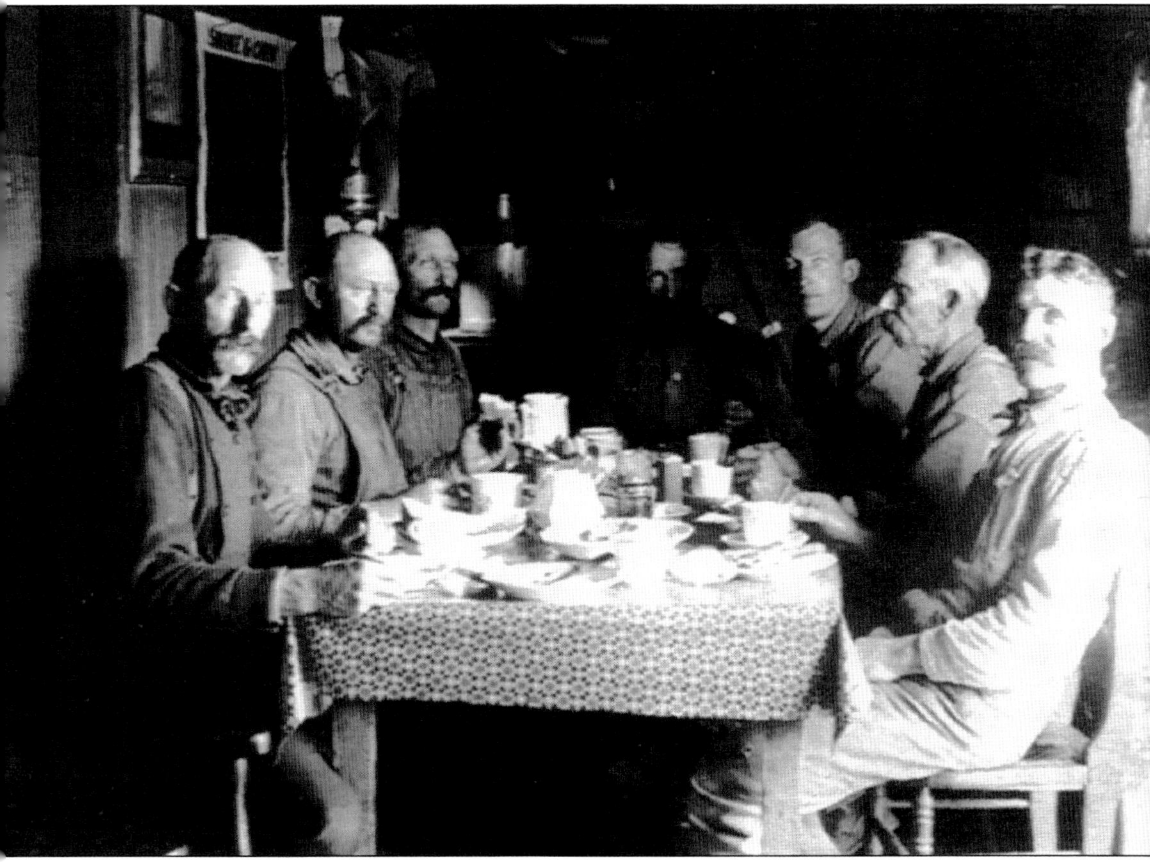

Merton Grant, seated third from left, worked as a cook on the New York, Ontario and Western Railway, based out of the High Falls station. He is shown in this *c.* 1912 photograph with other railroad workers enjoying a well-earned meal. (Courtesy Charles Greene.)

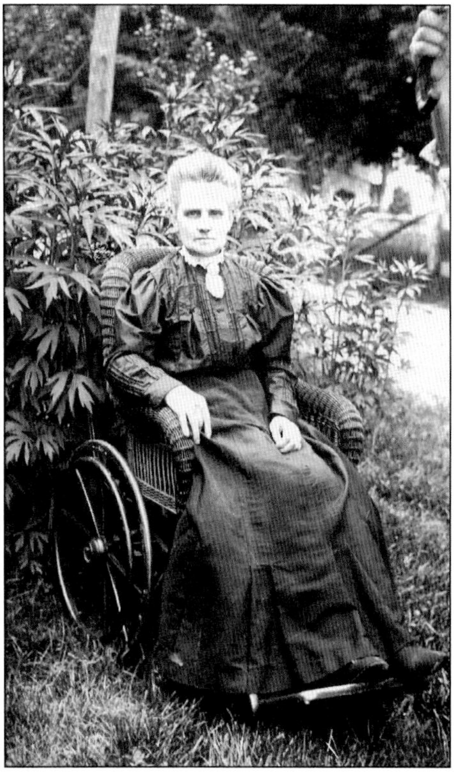

Catherine Grant posed for this photograph at the Corner House in Kyserike. Note the wicker seat on the wheelchair, and the Victorian dress of the era. (Courtesy Charles Greene.)

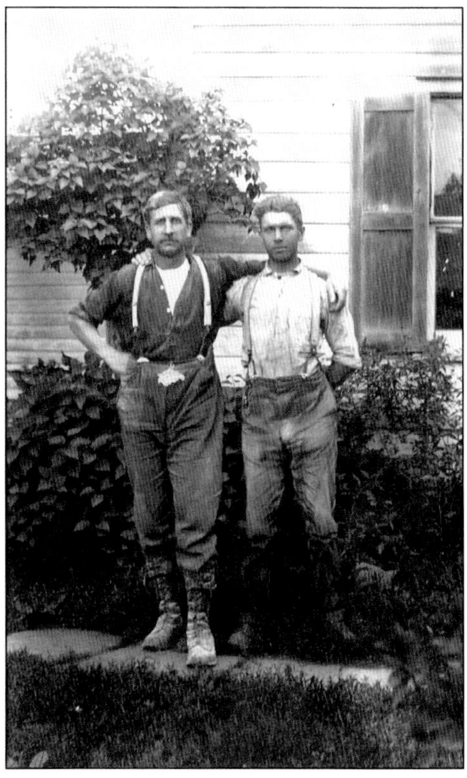

Bill Dale (left) and Alfred Rider pose outside the Trowbridge Farm house. Located in the Kyserike area, the farm offered boarding facilities for families looking to vacation far away from New York City. (Courtesy Charles Greene.)

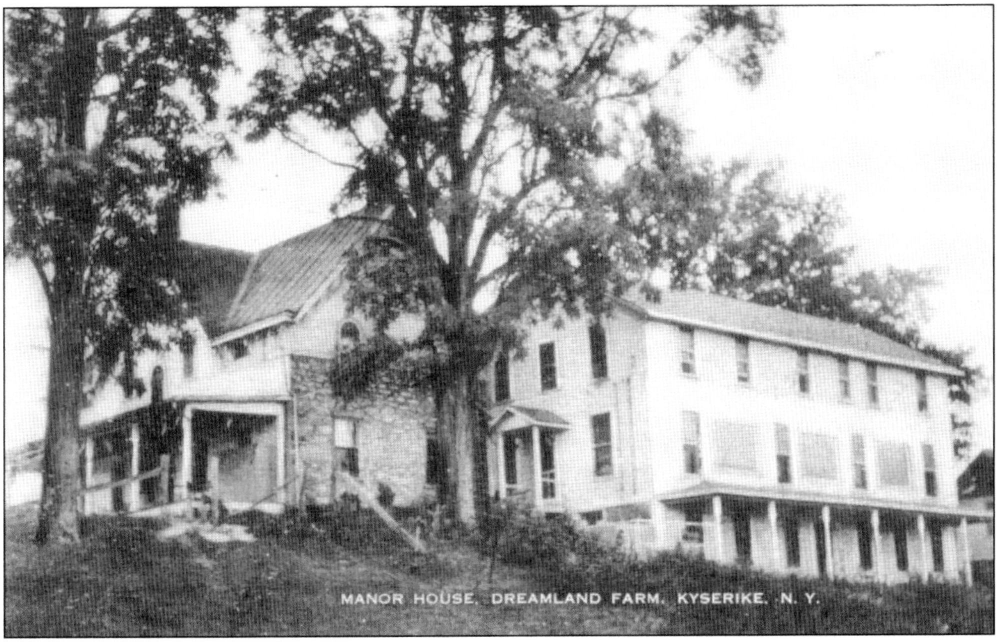

Dreamland Farm was a well-known boardinghouse and summer resort for families from New York City in the 1930s and 1940s. Originally owned by the Kortwright family as a working farm, the Kristeller family purchased the property in the late 1920s and turned it into a resort, complete with music and dancing. The large wooden wing that was added to the stone house featured a casino-type area on the lower floor. In the 1950s, the resort was converted to a children's camp, which it remains today, known as Camp Epworth. (Courtesy Paul Wikane.)

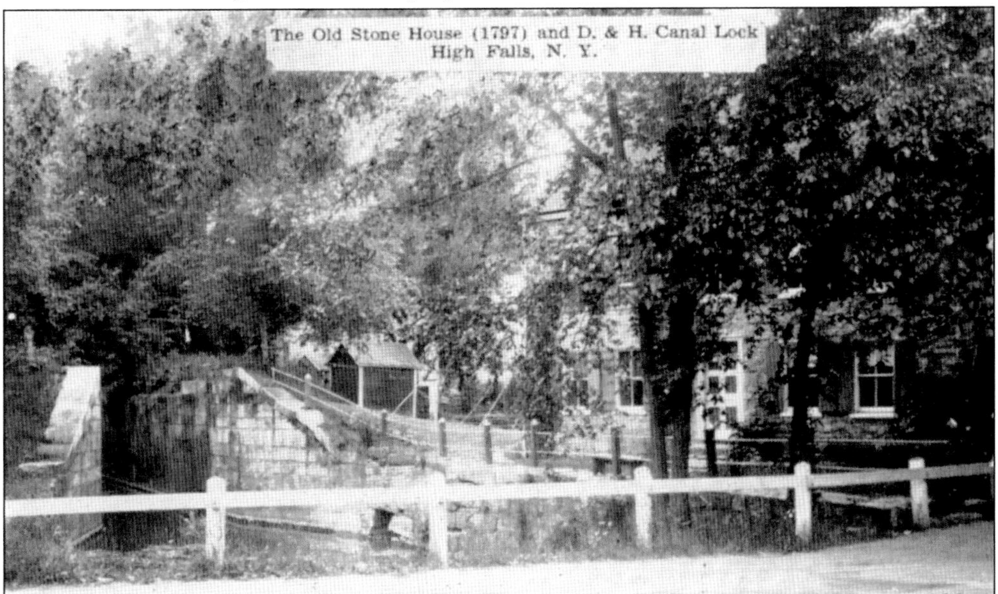

Lock 16 of the D&H Canal sits preserved in front of the DePuy Canal House in High Falls. Located on the D&H Canal "Five Locks Walk," one can see the expert stonework that was so precise mortar was not requited to keep the stones in place. From this lovely postcard, one can almost imagine watching the barges traveling on the canal. (Courtesy Paul Wikane.)

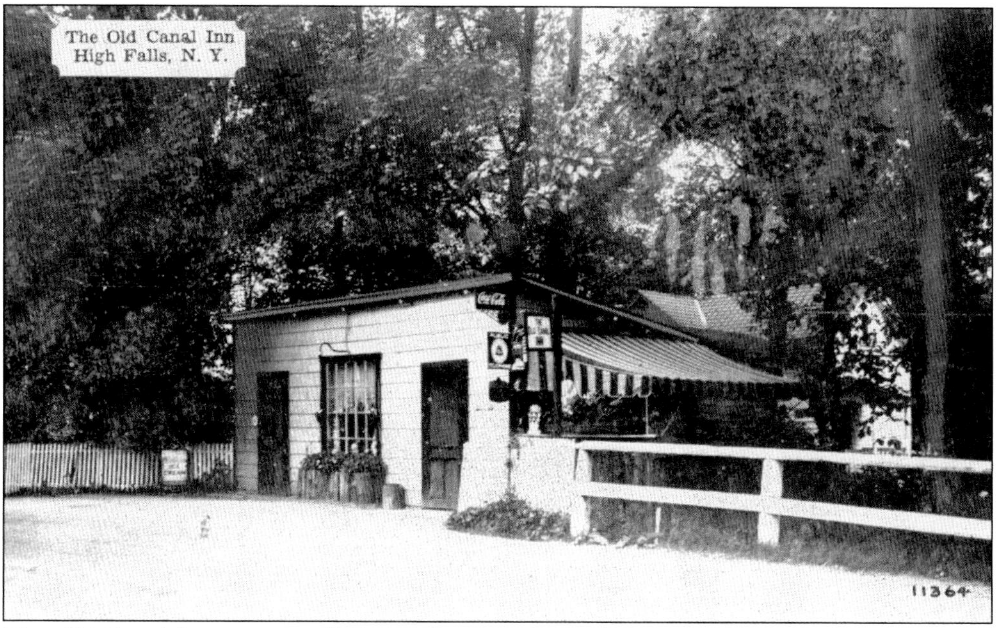

The Old Canal Inn was actually located across the road from the DePuy Canal House, just below lock 16, and near the banks of the Rondout Creek. This c. 1920 postcard shows the old inn with the lock tender's cottage behind it. (Courtesy Paul Wikane.)

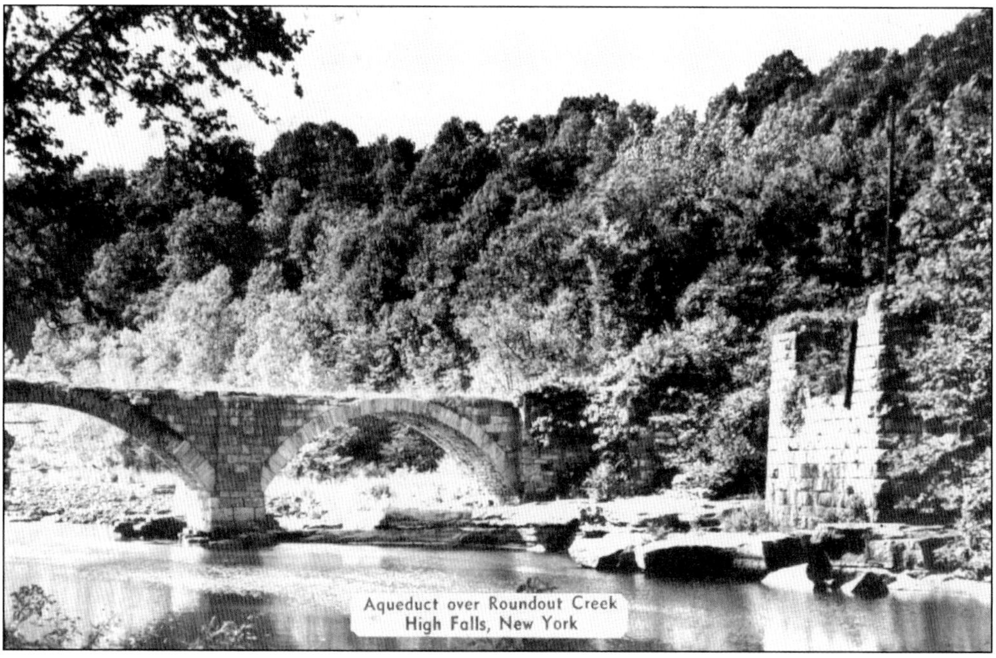

Here is a great c. 1930 photograph of the old canal aqueduct that was built over the Rondout Creek in High Falls. Barges bypassed the falls in the creek by traversing the old stone aqueduct. (Courtesy Paul Wikane.)

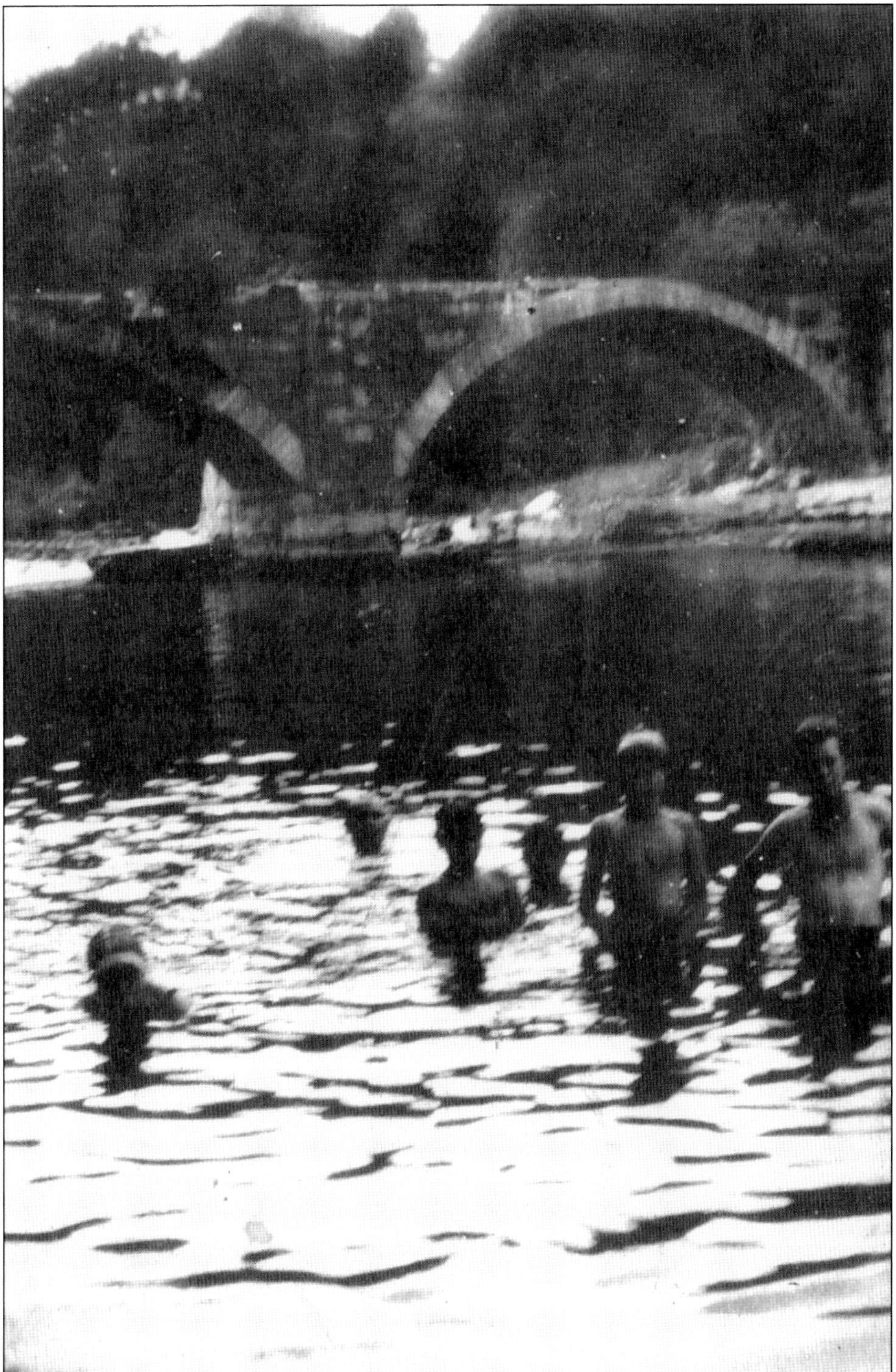

The Rondout Creek was a popular swimming hole in the 1940s. Access was easy from either Main Street or Bruceville Road in High Falls. Here local children enjoy a refreshing dip. (Courtesy Paul Wikane.)

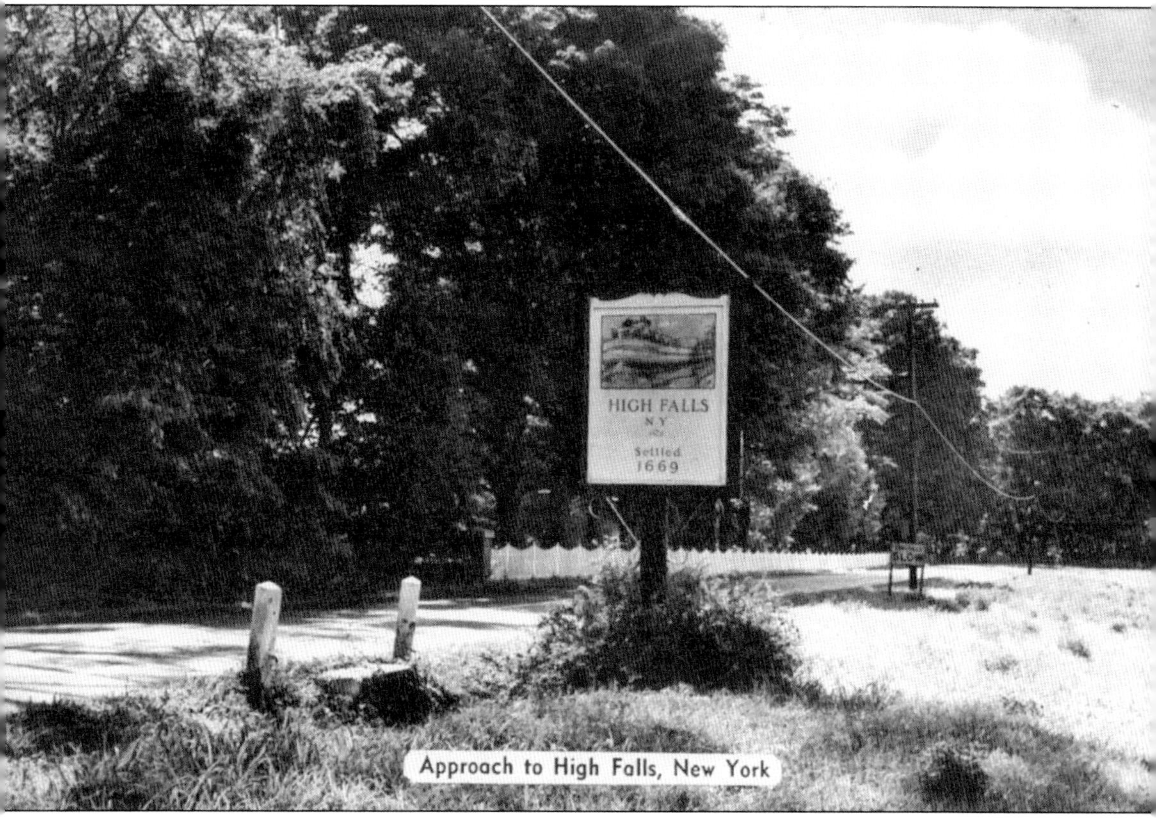

Town pride shows in the hamlet of High Falls, with the installation of signs showcasing its canal history. The D&H Canal was instrumental in putting High Falls on the map in the 1800s. (Courtesy Paul Wikane.)

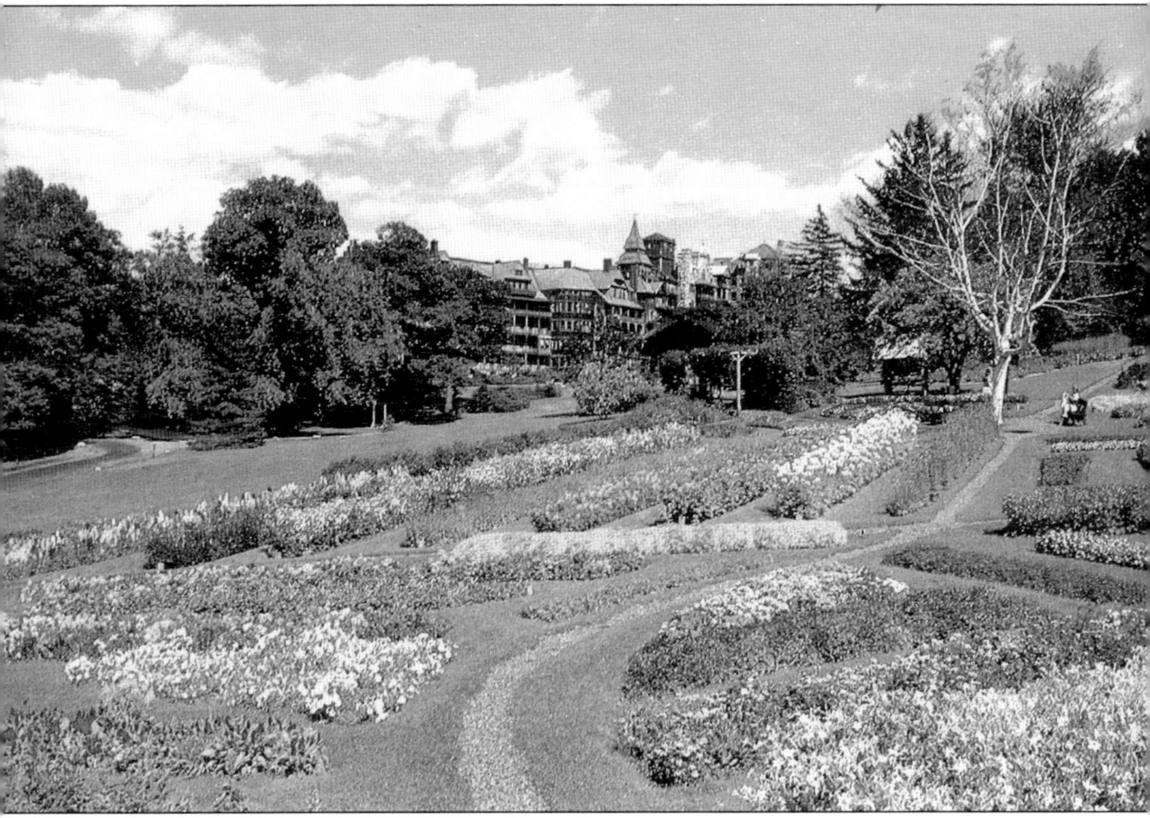

Pictured here are the lovely formal gardens of Mohonk Mountain House. Located on the Marbletown–New Paltz border, the well-tended gardens are a popular place for guests to stroll and take in the grandeur of an era gone by. (Courtesy Paul Wikane.)

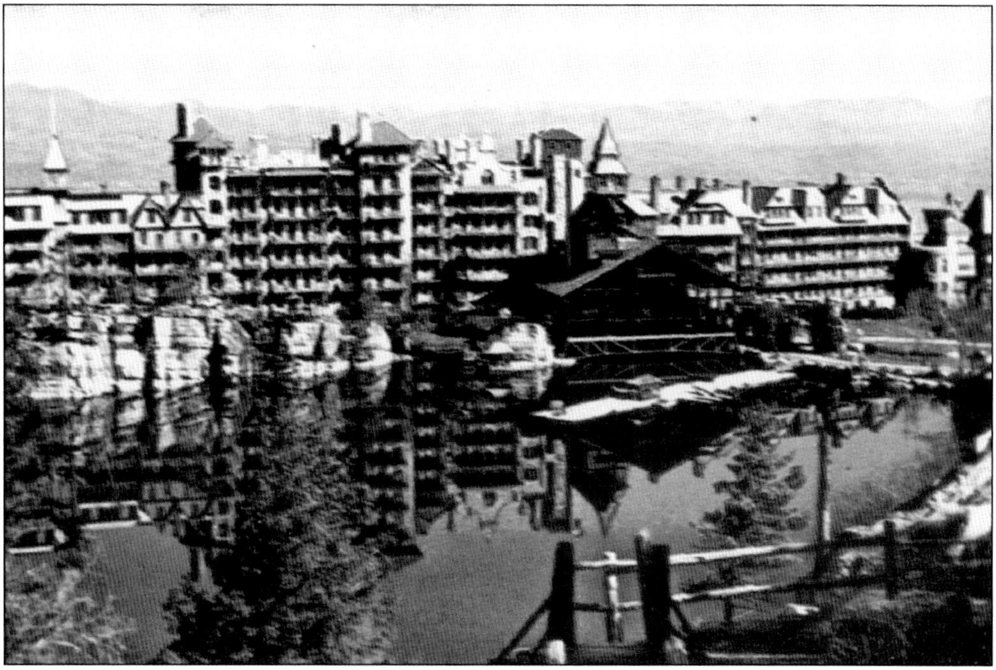

Looking across Lake Mohonk, this photograph shows the 19th-century Mohonk Mountain House, built by the Albert K. Smiley family in 1869. The 265 rooms of the Victorian resort offer a distinguished respite from life in the 21st century. Designated as a national historic landmark, the resort was once used as a movie site for the movie *The Road to Wellville*, starring Anthony Hopkins and Matthew Broderick. (Courtesy Paul Wikane.)

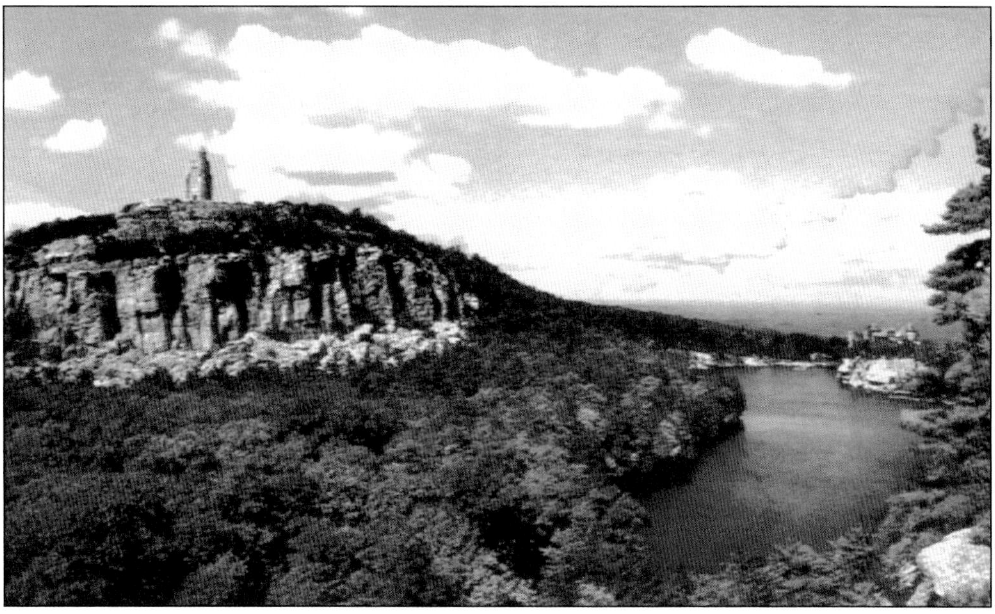

Overlooking some of the 2,200 acres of Mohonk Mountain House, the Skytop Tower prominently stands out. One can see the Mountain House on the right side of the picture with the lake in between. The beautiful Shawangunk Mountain ridge makes a spectacular place to visit, especially in the autumn months. (Courtesy Paul Wikane.)

Three

Cottekill, Kripplebush, and Vly-Atwood

Cottekill holds an important place in local history. The New York, Ontario and Western Railway provided a direct path for travelers to reach the area. Charles Brodhead, one of the first trustees of Marbletown, lived in the area. His house eventually descended to the Snyder family. Boarders came by steamer to Kingston and then by rail to Cottekill. The home's driveway is all that remains of the first road from Kingston to High Falls. That road can also be found near the Bevier house in Marbletown. It is possibly the Cocksinck Wagon Path. It roughly follows the old rail bed. Kripplebush was also known as the Yaugh Crepel Bush, meaning a large area of crooked trees. Settlers came to the area as early as 1704. Barrel-hoop making was the main industry in the area. Farms were an integral part of life, providing most goods needed to survive. Vly-Atwood, locally known simply as the Vly, occupies most of the upland area of Marbletown. The meaning of *Vly*, or *vley*, is "a depression with water in it," or, simply, a swamp. A number of lumber mills operated in the Atwood area. Some were water powered. In times of drought, these mills closed down until Mother Nature provided heavy rainstorms, when they would reopen. The one-room schools continued to be integral parts of daily life.

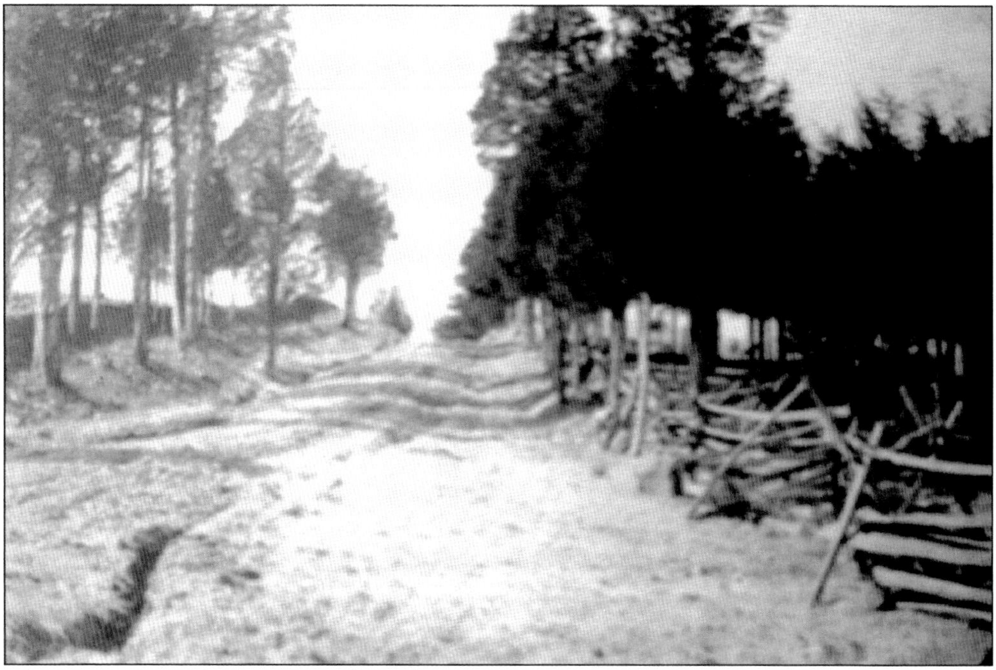

This unique fence, known as a stake and rider fence, sits at the corner of Cottekill Road and the Old Mine Road. This picture is from around 1900. Today this dirt roadway has been replaced by busy State Route 209. (Courtesy Jody Ford, Stone Ridge Library.)

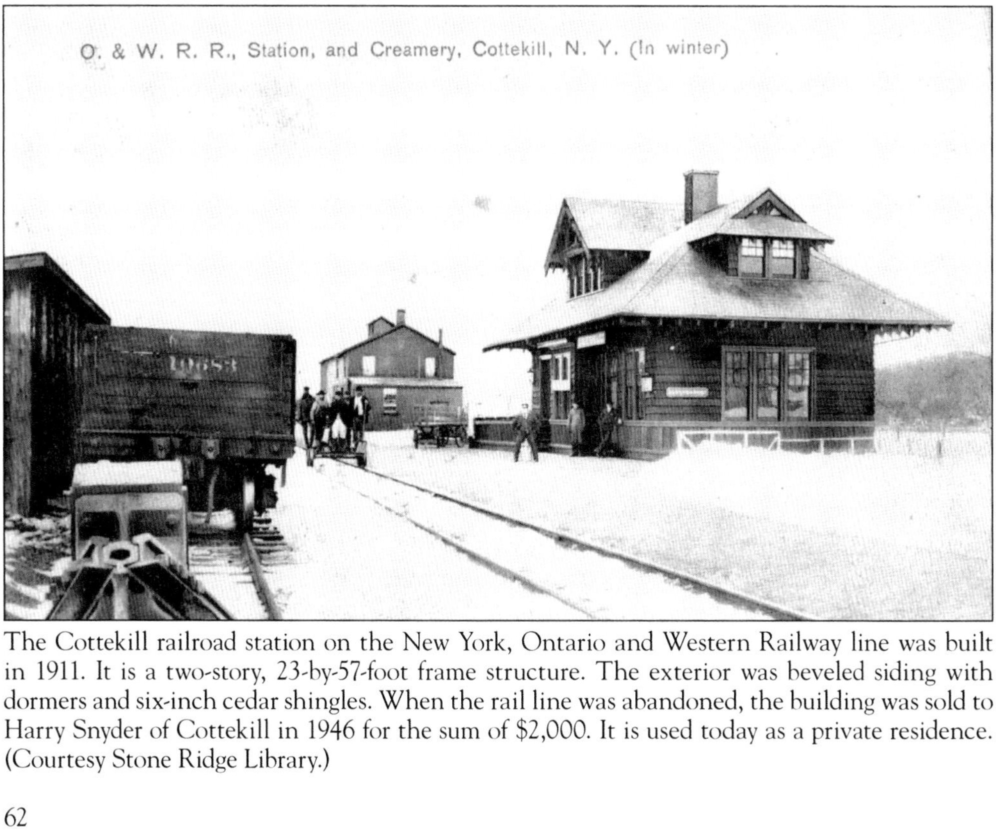

The Cottekill railroad station on the New York, Ontario and Western Railway line was built in 1911. It is a two-story, 23-by-57-foot frame structure. The exterior was beveled siding with dormers and six-inch cedar shingles. When the rail line was abandoned, the building was sold to Harry Snyder of Cottekill in 1946 for the sum of $2,000. It is used today as a private residence. (Courtesy Stone Ridge Library.)

Muriel Vreeland, at age 15, happily poses in her Camp Fire Girls uniform while shoveling snow. The photograph was taken after a large winter storm at her Cottekill home. (Courtesy Charles Greene.)

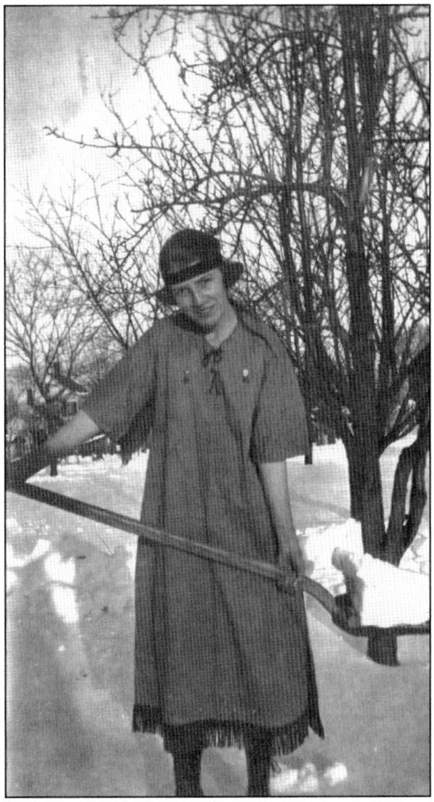

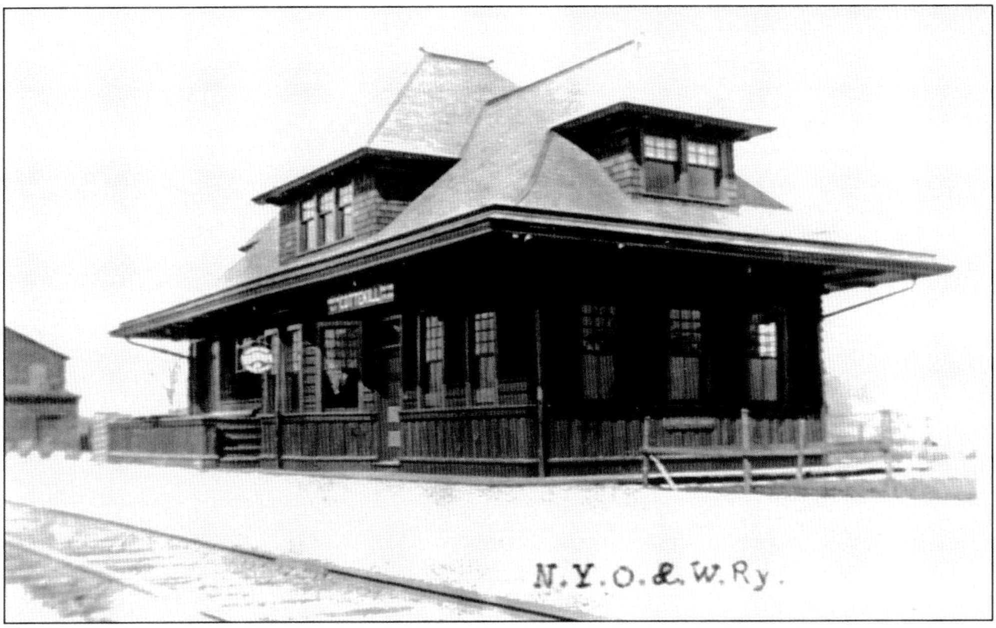

This c. 1920 photograph is of the Cottekill train station, operated by the New York, Ontario and Western Railway. The station was later used as the first meeting place of the Cottekill Fire Company before its firehouse was built almost directly behind it. (Courtesy New York, Ontario and Western Railway Historical Association.)

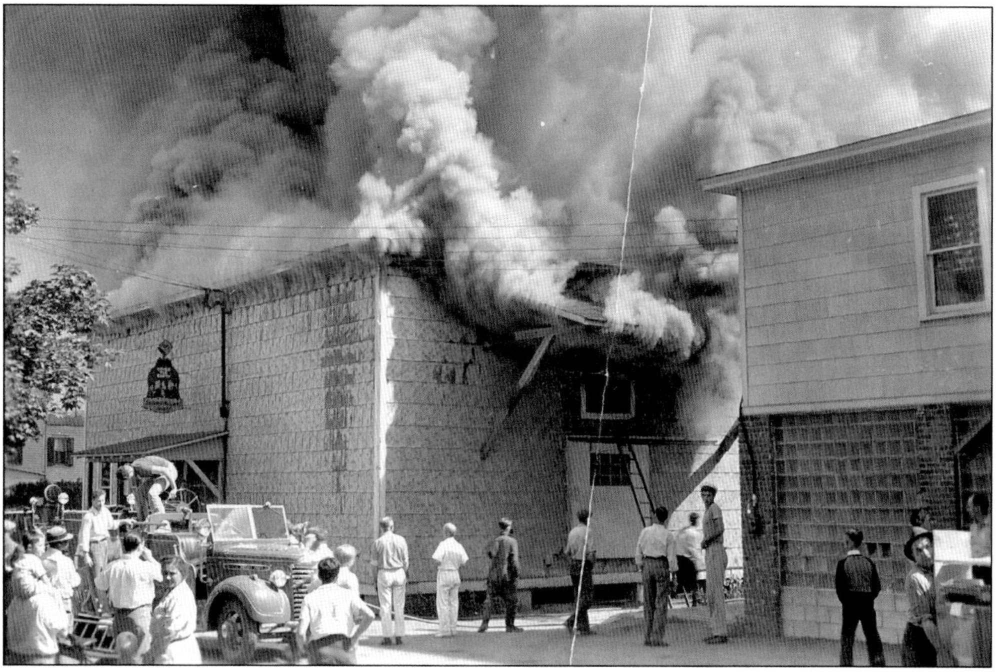

The Harry Snyder Feed Mill, located on Cottekill Road, caught fire and burned on July 20, 1941. The first call for help came into Kingston Fire Company at 3:25 p.m. Note the large amount of black smoke coming from the windows. By 4:10 p.m., the entire building and contents were destroyed. (Courtesy Brad Fiore, Cottekill Fire Company.)

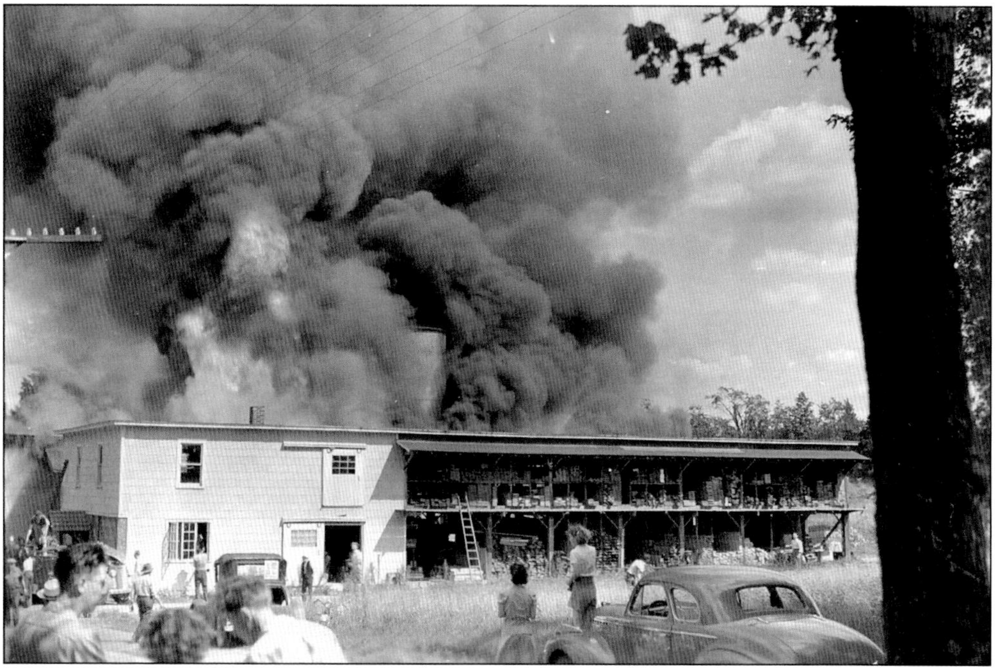

Local Cottekill residents watch in horror as the fire creeps toward the outdoor storage area of the Harry Snyder Feed Mill. Cottekill received mutual aid from companies as far away as Kingston to fight this enormous fire. (Courtesy Brad Fiore, Cottekill Fire Company.)

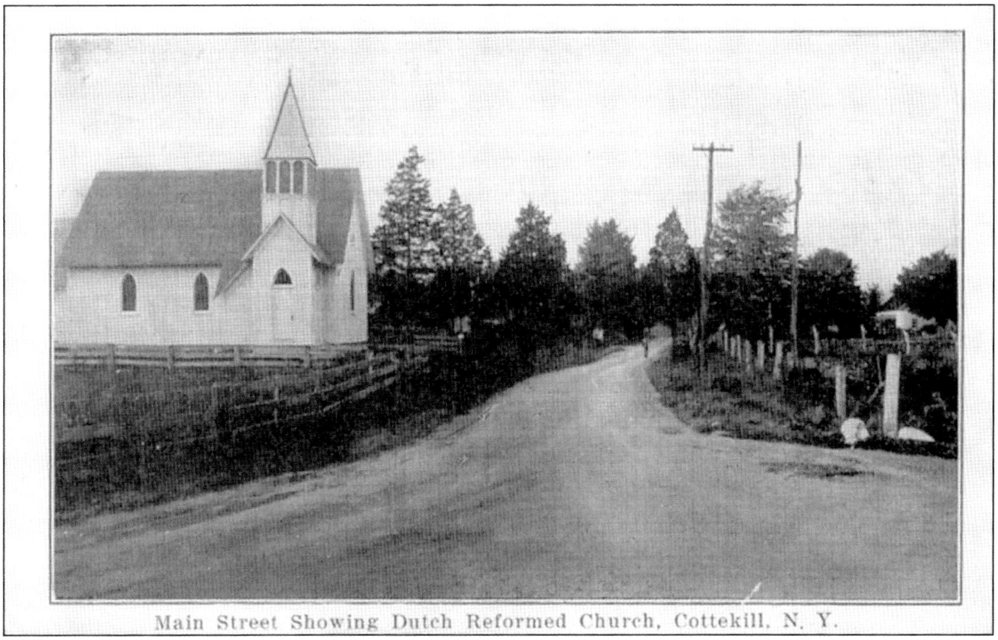

This is a rare *c.* 1910 photograph of the Dutch Reformed church that stood at the corner of Cottekill and Coxing Roads in Cottekill. All that remained of the church was a set of stone steps.

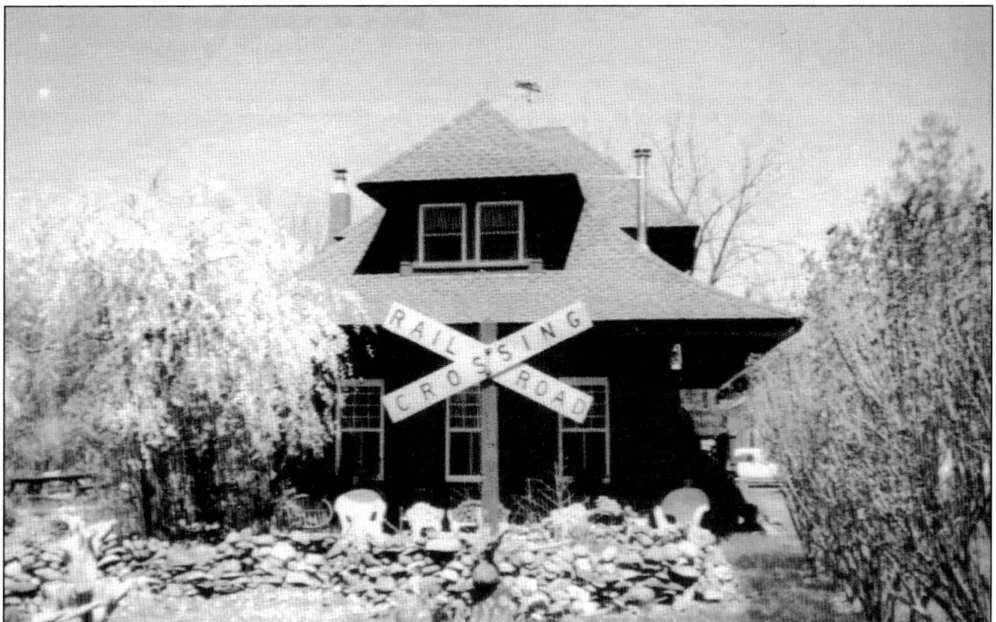

The Cottekill railroad station, once a stop on the bustling New York, Ontario and Western Railway, was converted to a private residence. It still maintains its railroad heritage, as the once abandoned train tracks are now a well-used "rail trail," offering visitors a safe place to walk, run, or ride bikes. (Courtesy Brad Fiore, Cottekill Fire Company.)

Kripplebush District School

June 1918

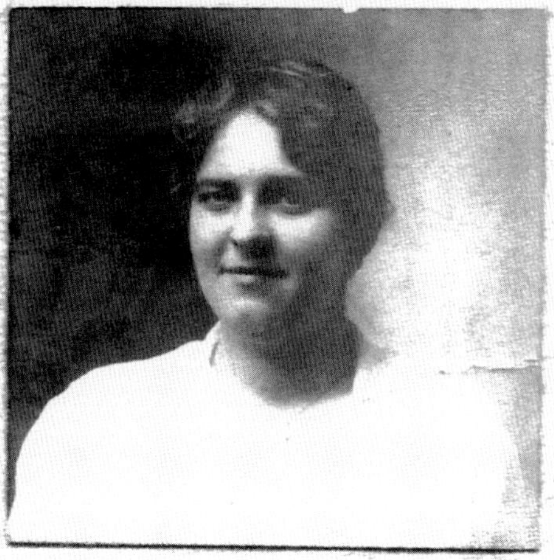

Ellen L. Appley, Teacher

Pupils	Pupils
Earl Christiana	Gladys Van Demark
William Hornbeck	Burnice Van Aken
Rodney Johnson	Melvena Van Aken
Lewis Lounsberry	Dorothy Davis
Rowland Osterhoudt	Theresa Davis
Royalston Osterhoudt	Vera Davis
Kenneth Osterhoudt	Dora Hendricks
George Roosa	Esther Hornbeck
James Roosa	Hannah Hornbeck
Peter Roosa	Mary Hornbeck
Herbert Smith	Anna Lounsberry
Lester Van Demark	Esther Lyons
Archie Van Aken	Maud Lyons
Ross Van Aken	Ruby Miller
Granville Wood	Gertrude Osterhoudt
Pearl Roosa	Marjory Osterhoudt
Edith Sherman	Annie Quick
Murlie Smith	Beatrice Quick

One-room schoolhouses were located in every hamlet in Marbletown. Each school taught grades 1–12. The Kripplebush one-room school published a yearly booklet listing pupils who attended the school. Pictured here is a page from the 1918 school year. Teacher Ellen Appley's photograph sits above the class roster. Notable names such as Osterhoudt, Hornbeck, Christiana, Van Aken, and Davis are still commonly seen in Marbletown today. (Courtesy Lawrence Skalla.)

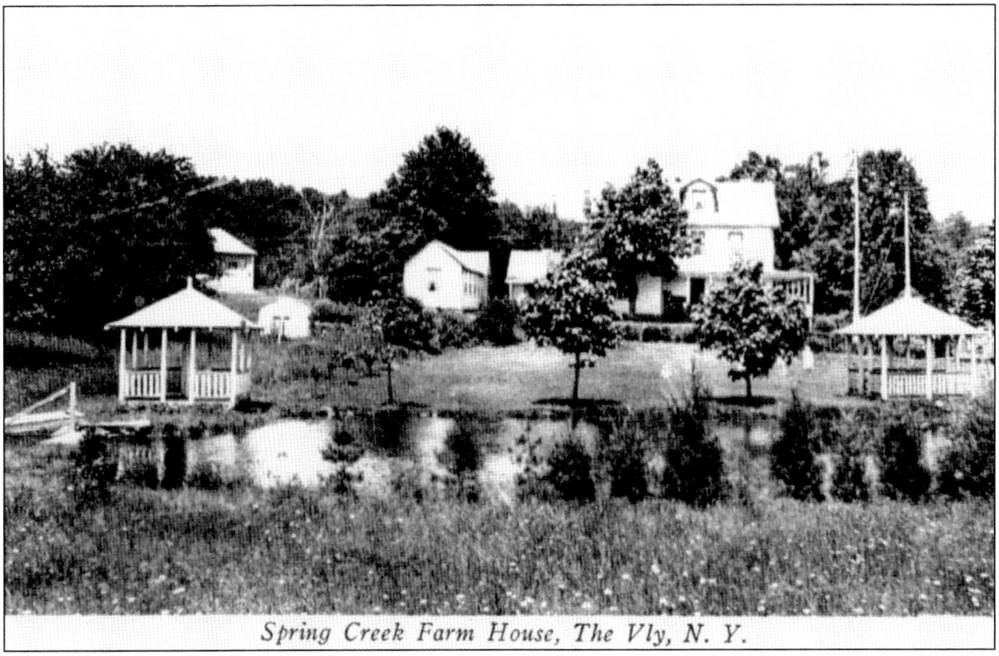

Thomas and Anna Olson (affectionately known as "Nanny" and "Pop" to family and neighbors) purchased this property in 1910 and ran the Spring Creek Farm boardinghouse until Thomas's death in 1954. The property was sold, and a small bar called the Page One Chateau remained in business throughout the 1960s. In the 1970s, it changed hands to become known as the Fertile Earth Farm. In the late 1970s, the main house was destroyed by fire. A new home was constructed and is known today as Goose Pond. (Courtesy Eric Fedde.)

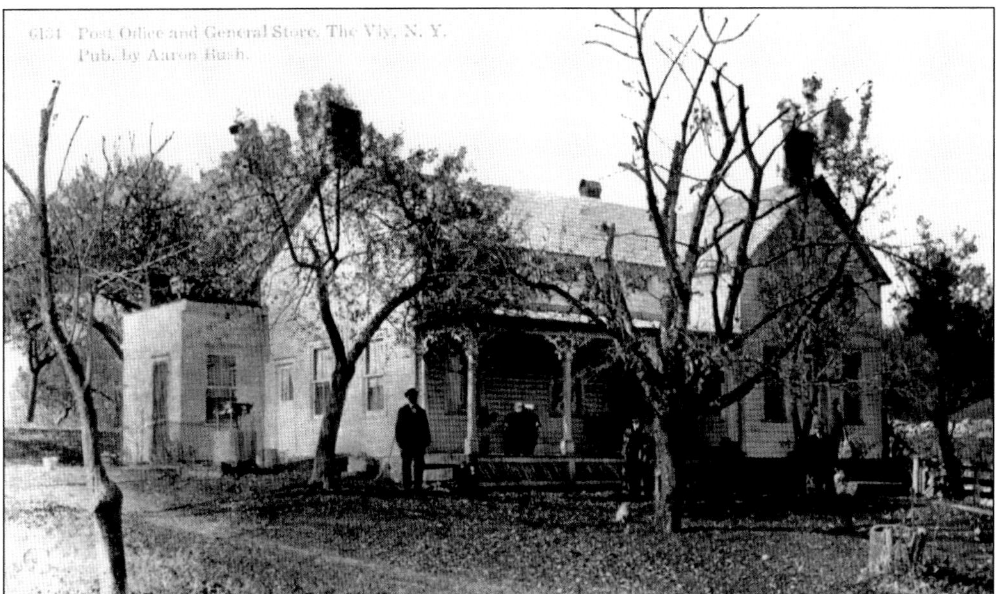

The Vly Post Office served this community from 1899 until 1917. Aaron Bush was the postmaster and also ran a store from his residence located on Mill Road near the intersection with Buck Road. (Courtesy Eric Fedde.)

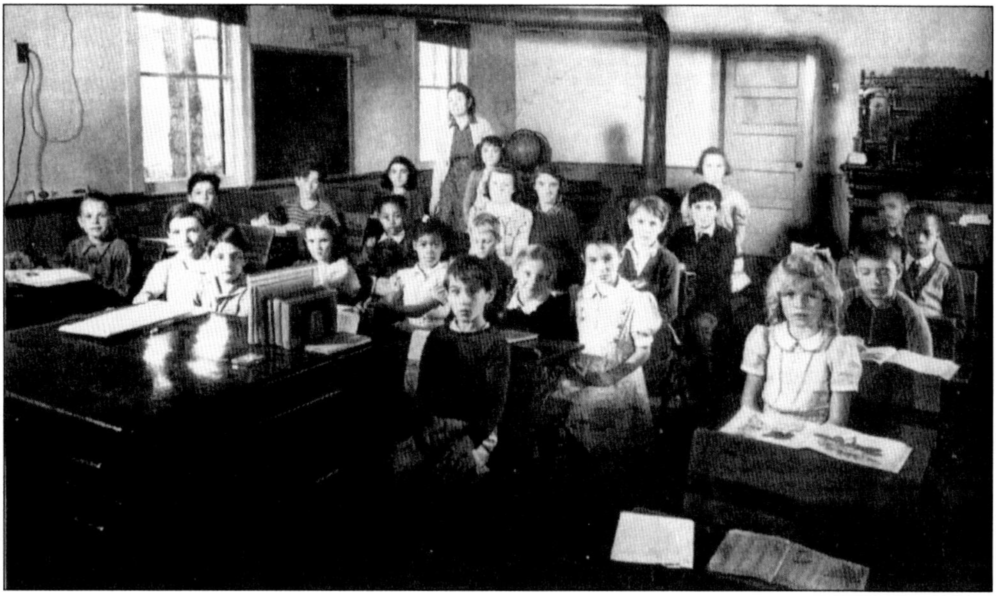

The Atwood school, located on Atwood Road, was one of many one-room schools located throughout the town of Marbletown. Here Mrs. Malone poses with one of her classes. Those students identified are Robert Johnson, Merritt "Sonny" Markle, Edie Brown, teacher Mrs. Malone, Margaret Brown, Nick Brown, Margery ?, Raymond Brodhead, May Smith, Dorothy Freer, Shirley Brodhead, Walter Wedvik, Sally Davis, Helen ?, Arthur Davis, Francis Freer, Edna ?, Ruth Johnson, Edward Alfanso, and Bray McLennan. (Courtesy Charles Greene.)

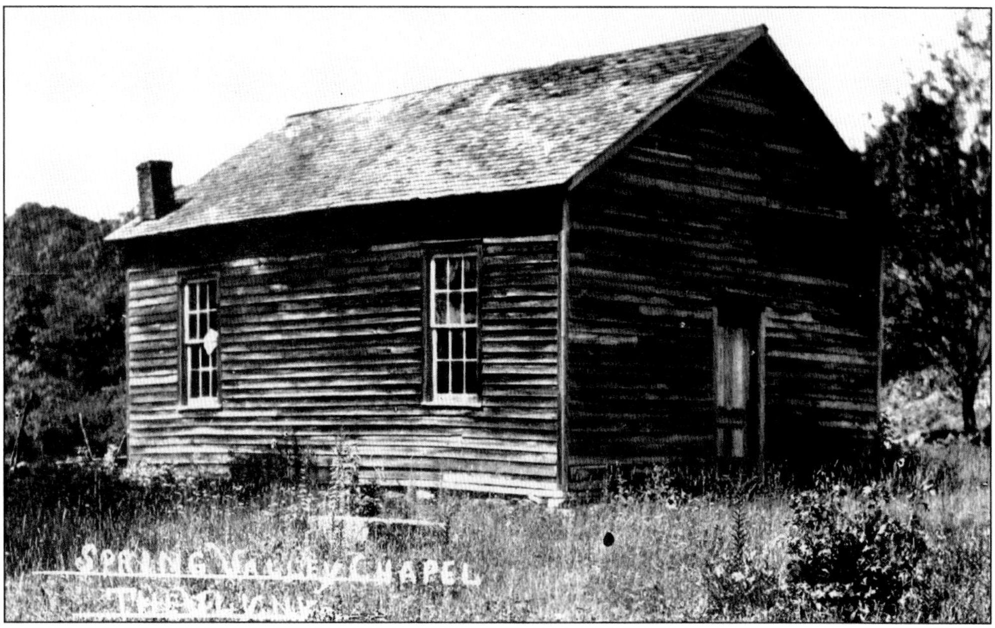

The Vly Chapel dates back to 1870. Thomas Olson Sr., who ran a boardinghouse, conducted services here for many years. The newly formed Evangelical Fellowship Church held services here from 1975 until 1978 when it moved to the former Vly Methodist Church. In the mid-1980s, the chapel was razed by the Marbletown Highway Department as it was deemed unsafe. This postcard is from around 1910. (Courtesy Eric Fedde.)

Built in 1893, the Vly Methodist Church remained open for worship until 1975 when it closed its doors due to dwindling membership. In 1978, the Evangelical Fellowship Church began holding services here after obtaining the deed for the church. (Courtesy Eric Fedde.)

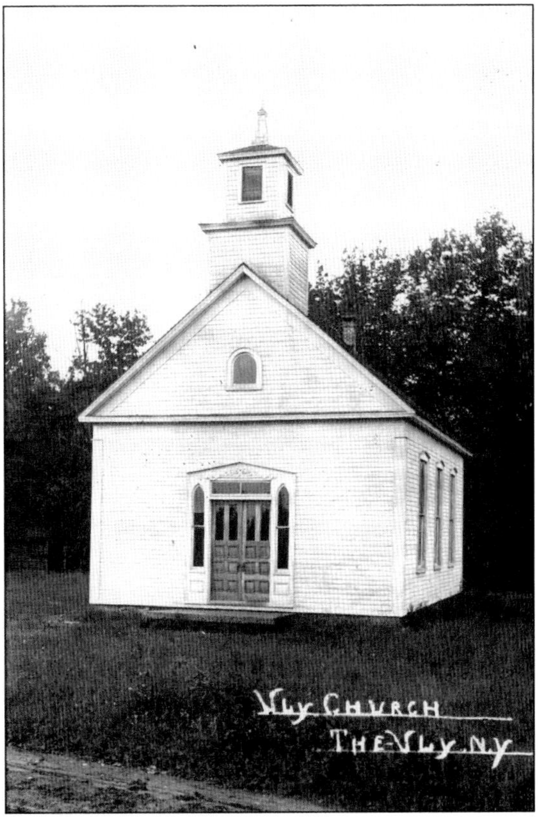

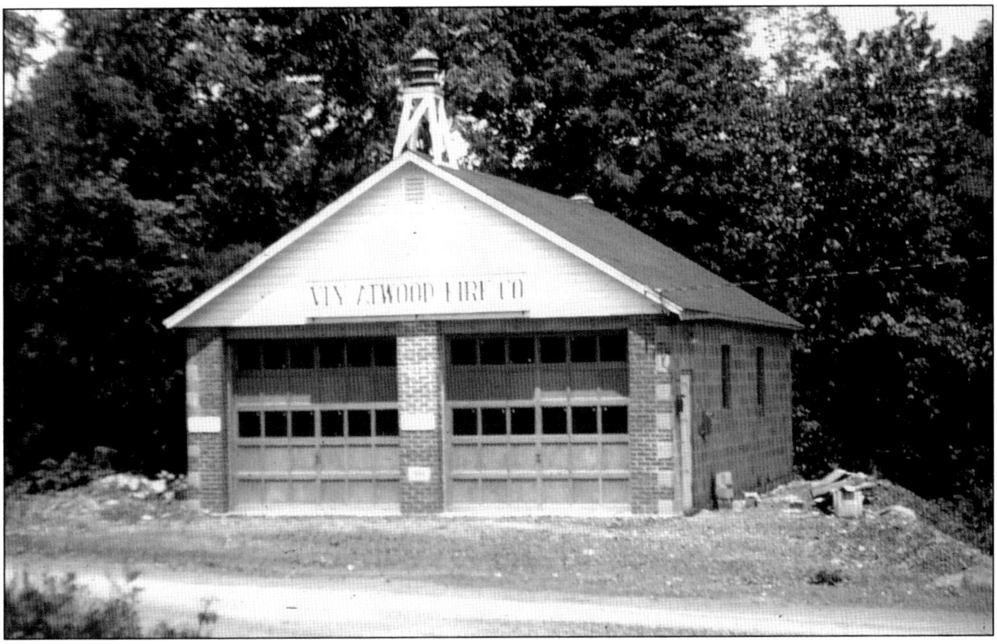

The Vly-Atwood Fire Company was formed in 1953. This 1955 photograph shows the newly constructed firehouse. In 1962, an addition was completed to house two trucks, and a meeting room was added in 1985. (Courtesy Eric Fedde.)

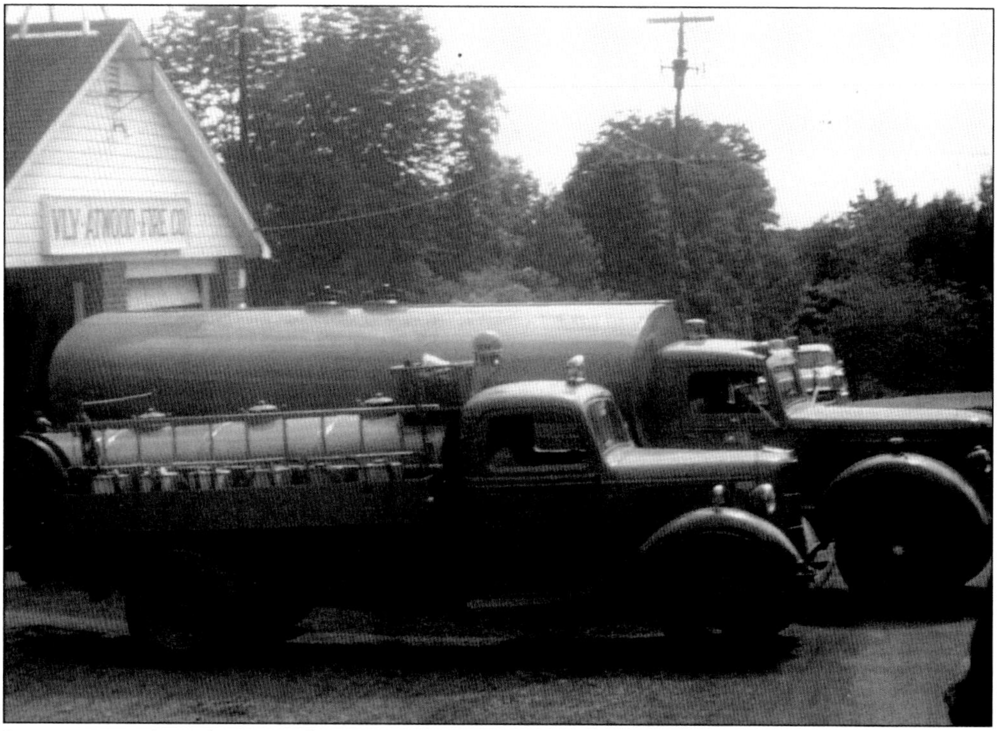

In service at the Vly-Atwood Fire Company in the 1960s were two tankers. One was a 1935 Ford and the other a 1937 Federal with a 3,500-gallon tank. Great care had to be taken when maneuvering this truck up and down the hilly roads in the Vly. (Courtesy Russell family.)

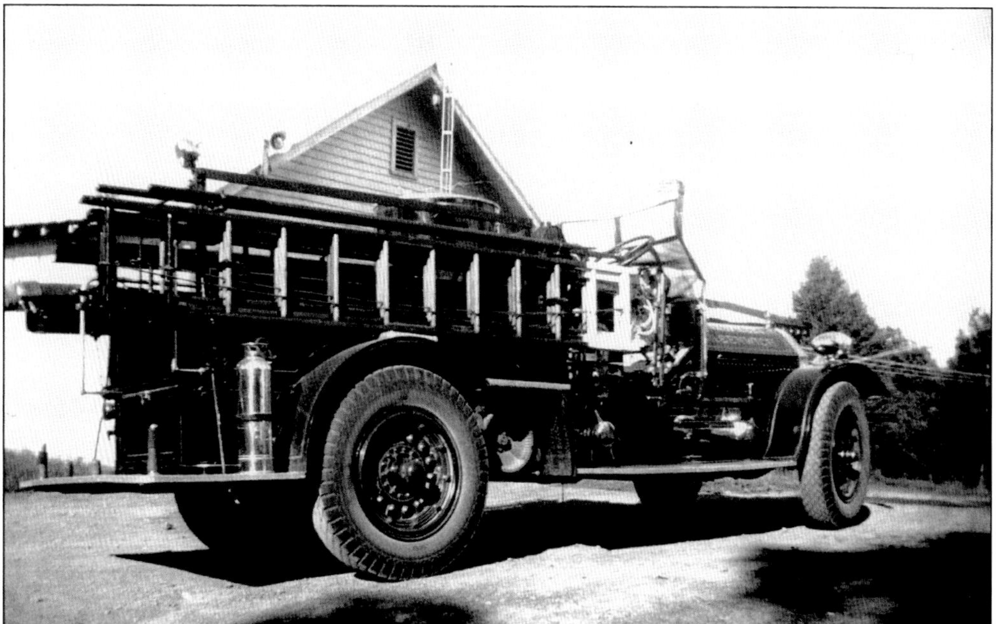

In 1954, the Vly-Atwood Fire Company purchased its first fire engine (a 1921 Seagrave) from a fire department in Connecticut for $200. Notice the steering wheel is on the right. Victor Merritt served as the first chief from 1954 to 1977. (Courtesy Russell family.)

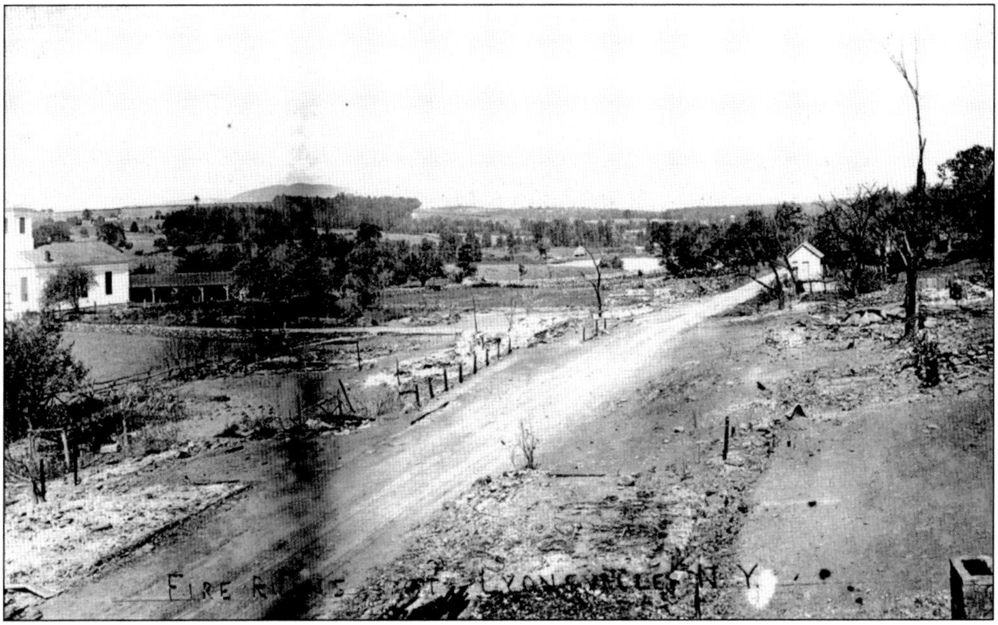

This postcard photograph showing fire ruins was taken about 100 years ago along the county road in Lyonsville. The Lyonsville Reformed Church and Lyonsville Pond are visible. Note how open the land is. (Courtesy Eric Fedde.)

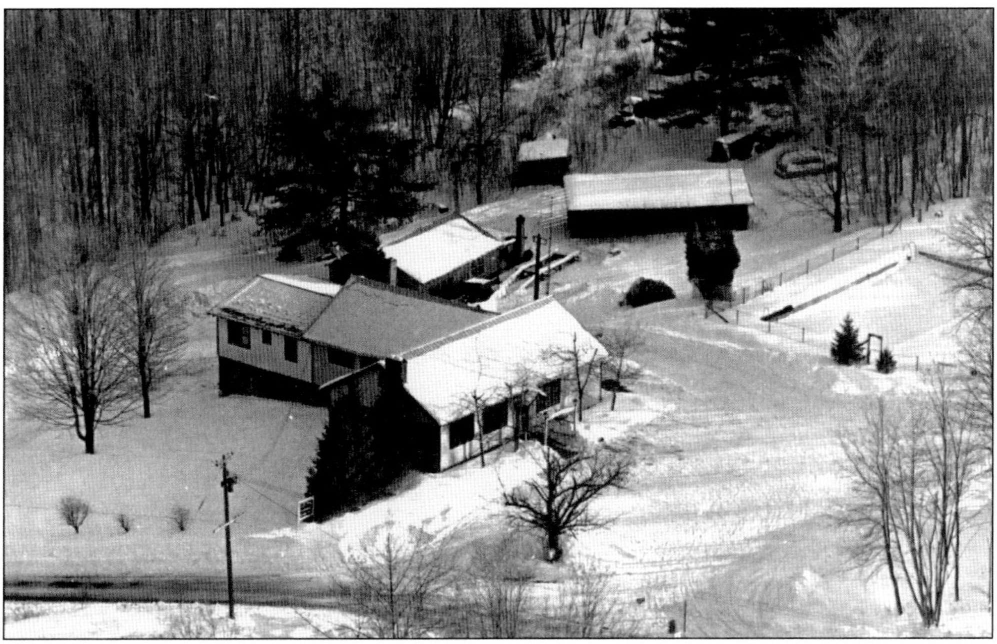

Vi Russell built the Blue Flame Tavern after World War II. She was the proprietor until the late 1960s when the business was leased until the late 1970s. At that time, it was sold and reopened under the name Atwood Inn. In the mid-1980s, it was sold again and now is a private residence. (Courtesy Eric Fedde.)

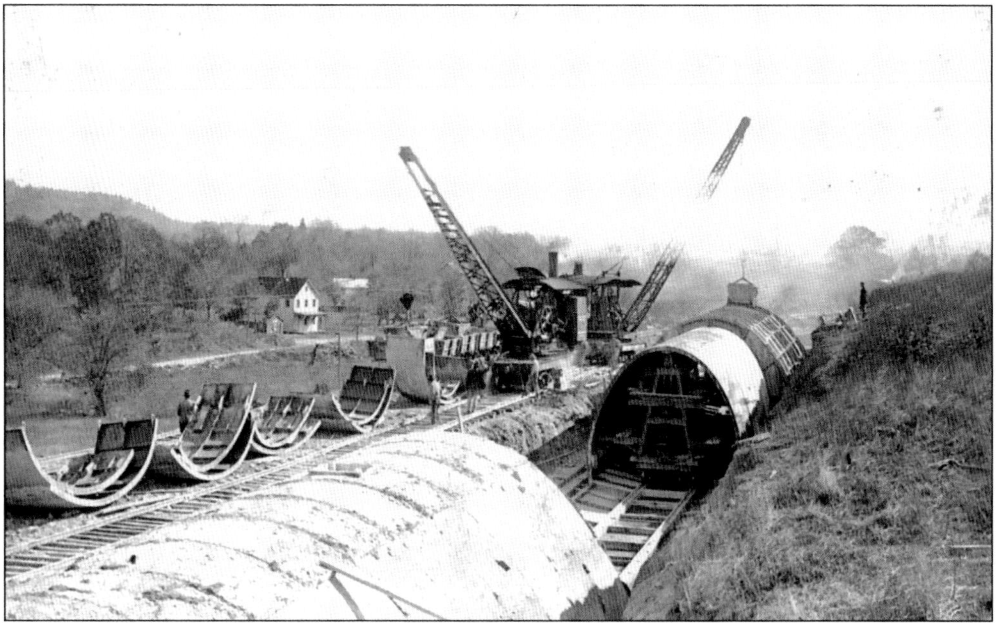

This postcard shows construction of the Catskill Aqueduct along Atwood Road (Route 213). Forms were used for the concrete walls of the pipeline, one section at a time. Dirt was then used to completely cover the pipeline. (Courtesy Eric Fedde.)

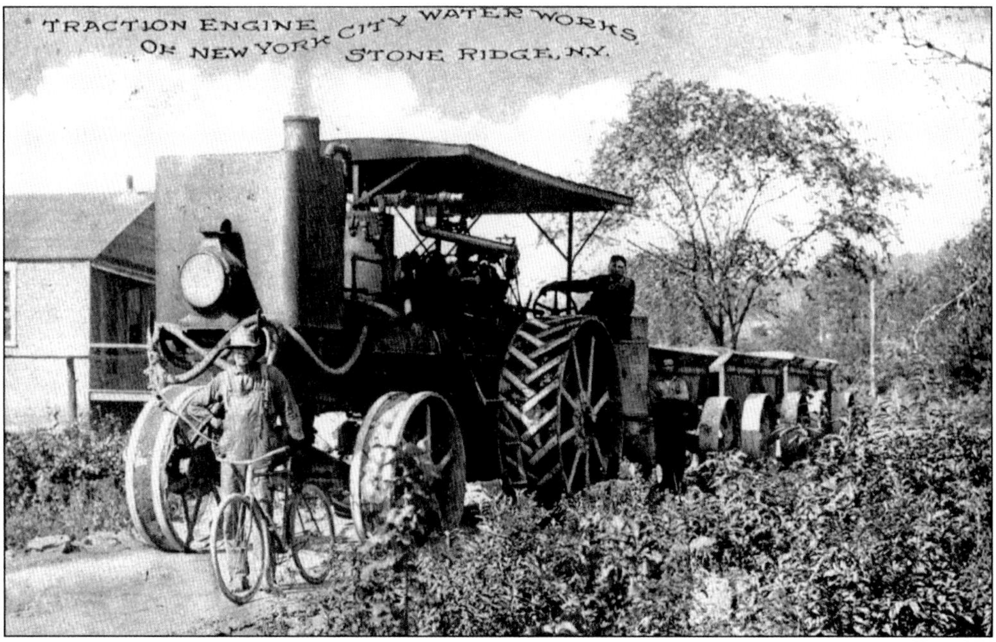

The newest technology was used in the construction of the nearby Ashokan Reservoir. This postcard shows a traction engine in Stone Ridge. (Courtesy Eric Fedde.)

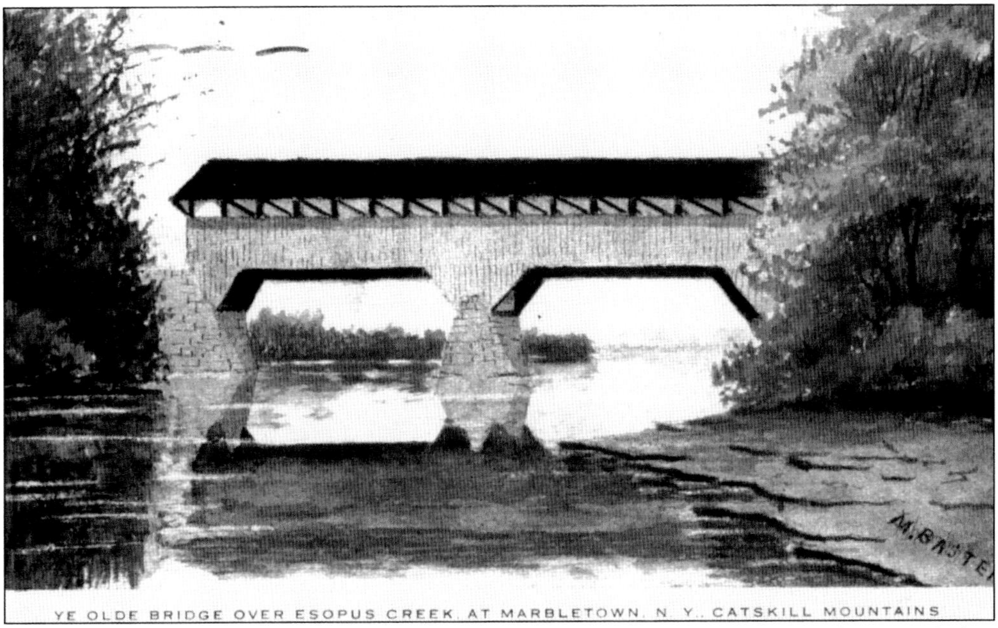

This bridge was located over the Esopus Creek near Lomontville. This postcard was mailed in 1910 by the artist who sketched the bridge, Minnie Basten Squires. The message reads, "I wish I could go back to the time I sketched this old bridge on my uncle's farm. I think it is the only picture of it." (Courtesy Eric Fedde.)

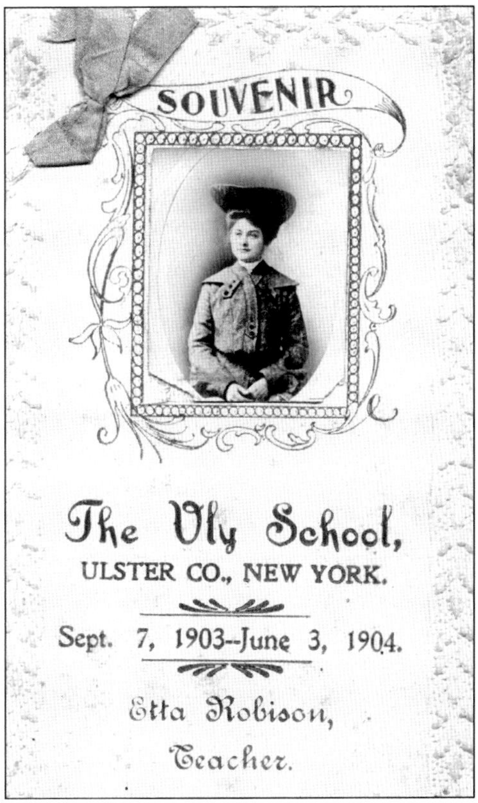

A souvenir from the Vly school shows 18 students attended in 1904. This one-room schoolhouse closed in 1943. As a private residence, the building still stands with several additions over the years. It is located at the intersection of Vly-Atwood and Scarawan Roads. (Courtesy Eric Fedde.)

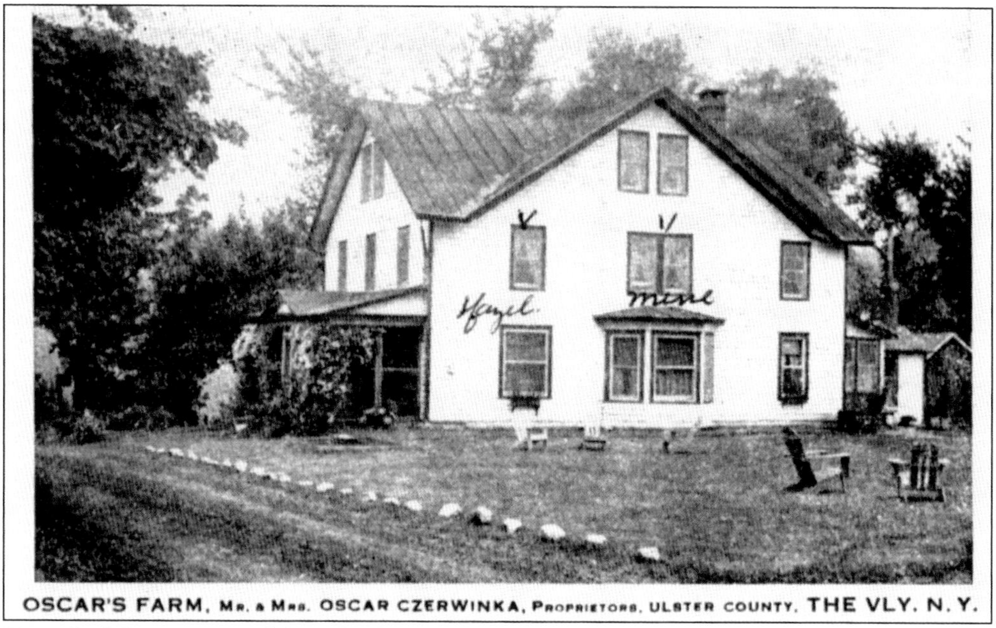

Typical of the many small boardinghouses operating in the Catskills in the 1940s and 1950s, Oscar's Farm offered home cooking, easy access to New York City, and the natural charm of the country. Today the main house looks much the same and is locally known as the Deerfield Inn. (Courtesy Eric Fedde.)

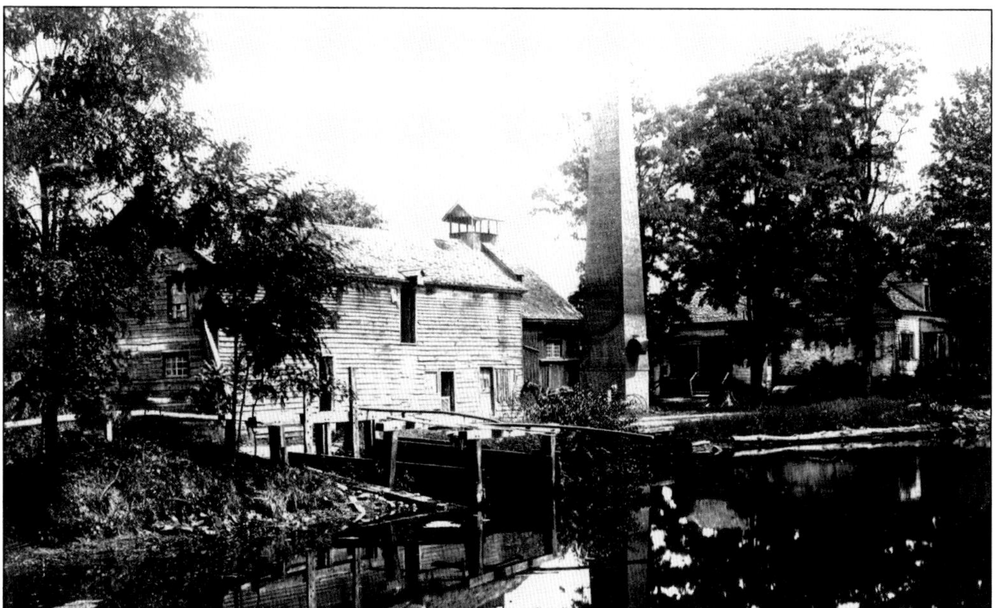

This c. 1910 postcard shows the gristmill that was located on Milldam Road in Stone Ridge. Today the mill is gone, but the house—known as the Hardenbergh house, built in 1762—still stands across from the pond. (Courtesy Eric Fedde.)

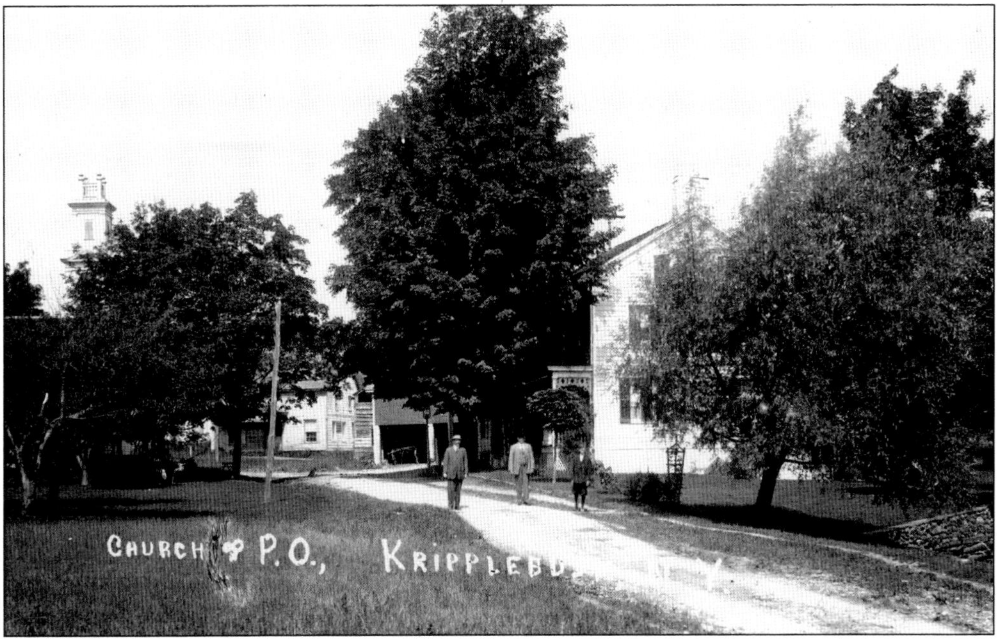

This view is looking west along what is now the county road in the village of Kripplebush. The building on the right was the Vandermark store and post office. This postcard was mailed in 1911. (Courtesy Eric Fedde.)

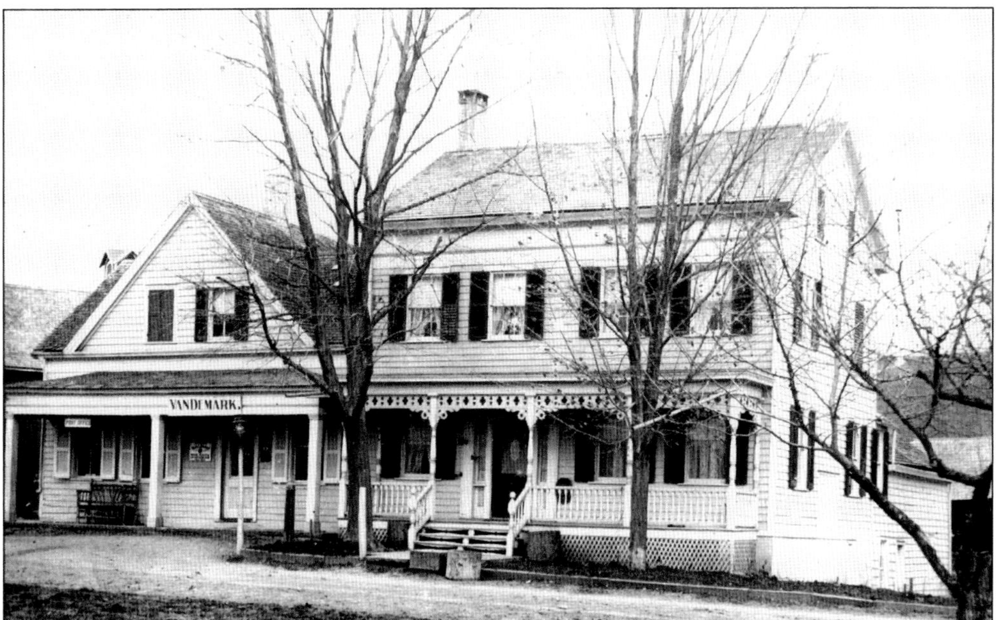

This view shows the Vandermark store and post office on the main street in Kripplebush. The message on this postcard sent in 1908 says, "I am staying at this place. Parties two to three times a week. Fine! Yaas! Yaas!" (Courtesy Eric Fedde.)

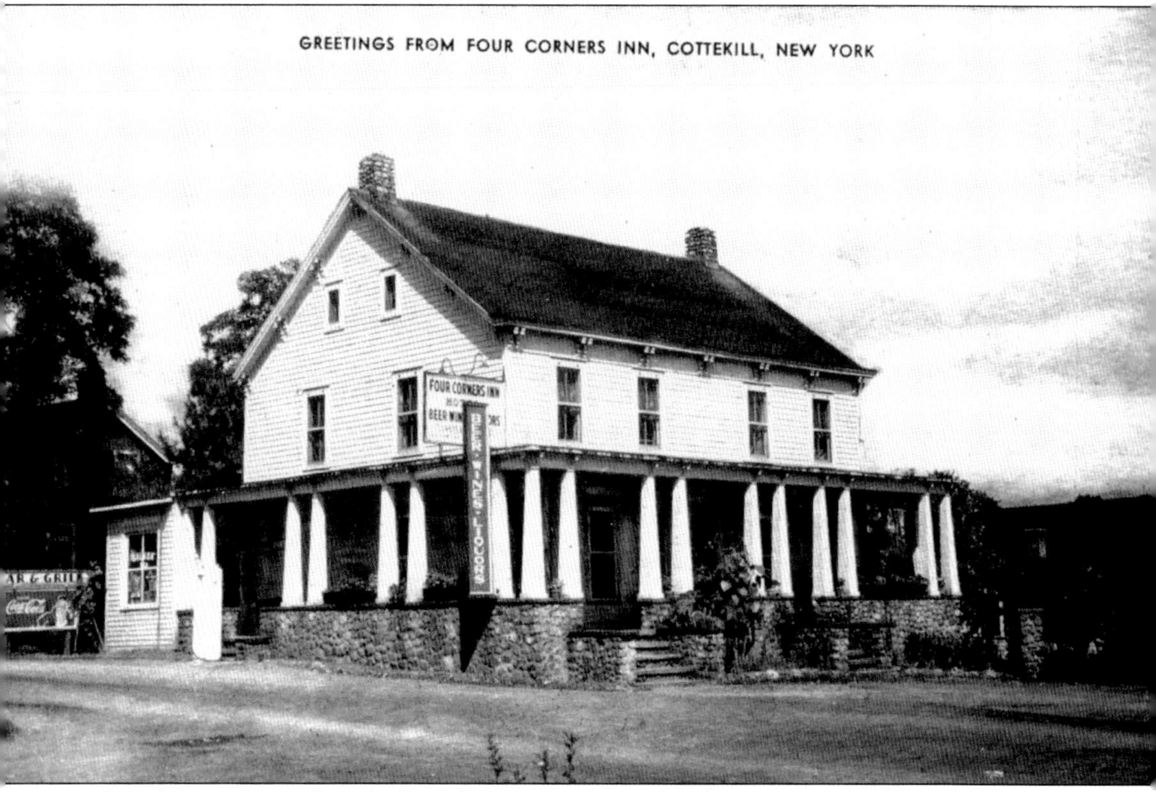

Seen here in the 1940s is the Four Corners Inn, located at the intersection of Cottekill Road and Lucas Turnpike. (Courtesy Eric Fedde.)

Four

LOMONTVILLE

Lomontville started as 17,000 acres of deeded land to Matthew Ten Eyck in 1712. The Ten Eyck family grew, and each child was given land in the area. Located on the flatland west of the Esopus Creek, it was to be named Lomont, but another community had that name, so *ville* was added to create Lomontville. Stone quarries in the Lapla area provided materials for bridge abutments. Residents connected Lomontville to the eastern side with a footbridge over the "fording place" at the creek. The largest influence, however, was the building of the Ashokan Reservoir in the early 1900s. The main overflow of the Ashokan flows directly through Lomontville, and the area lives in the shadow of the great reservoir.

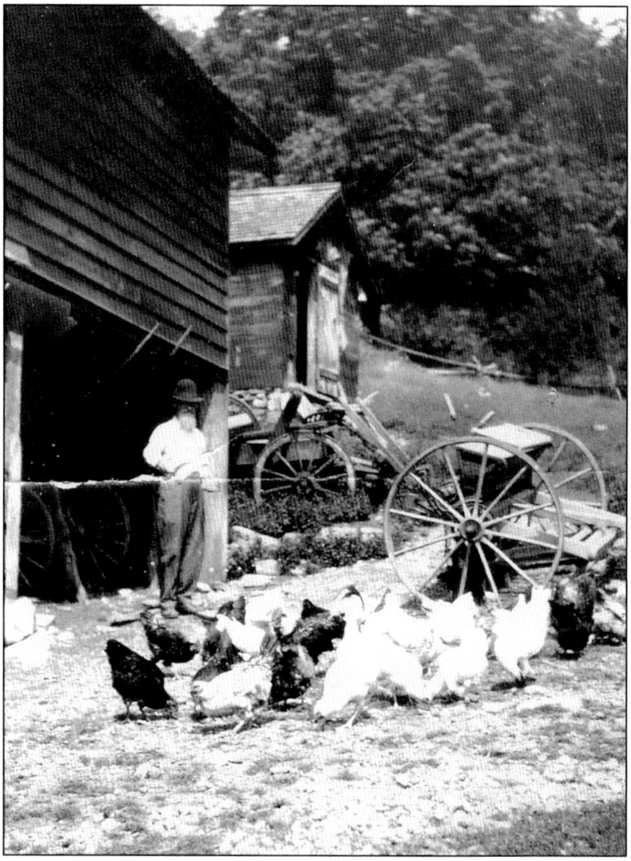

In the 1800s, farms had to be self-supporting. Here Simon Vandemark tends to a flock of chickens on his 99-acre Lomontville farm. This picture was taken on the old Ennist farm, one of the oldest farms in Marbletown. (Courtesy George K. Van Sickle.)

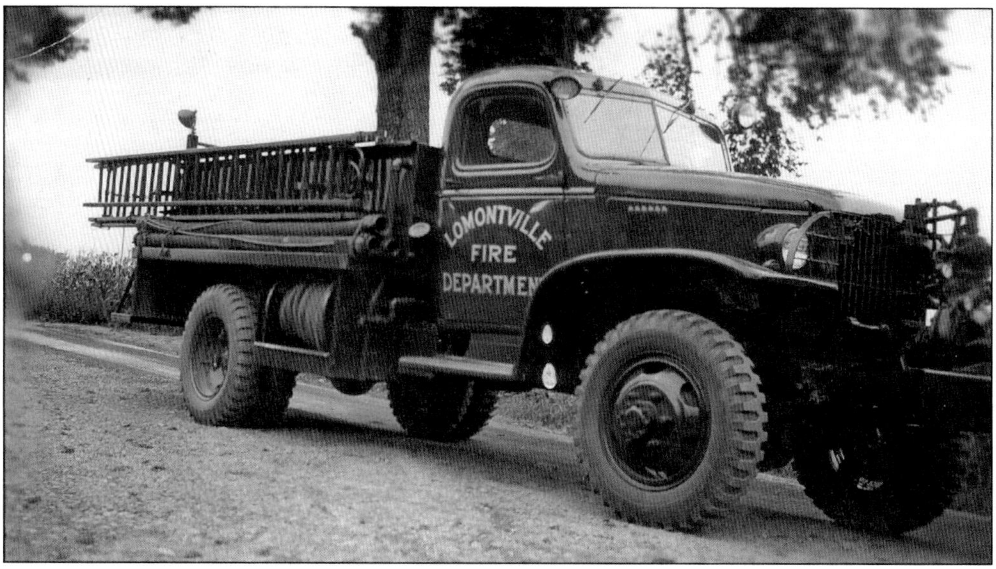

This 1942 General Detroit brush truck was purchased new from the army depot in Albany for $600 in 1947 and was put into service for the Lomontville Fire Company for over 50 years. Many surplus army vehicles were purchased by volunteer fire companies in the 1940s and converted to firefighting use. (Courtesy Chief Lou Cardinale.)

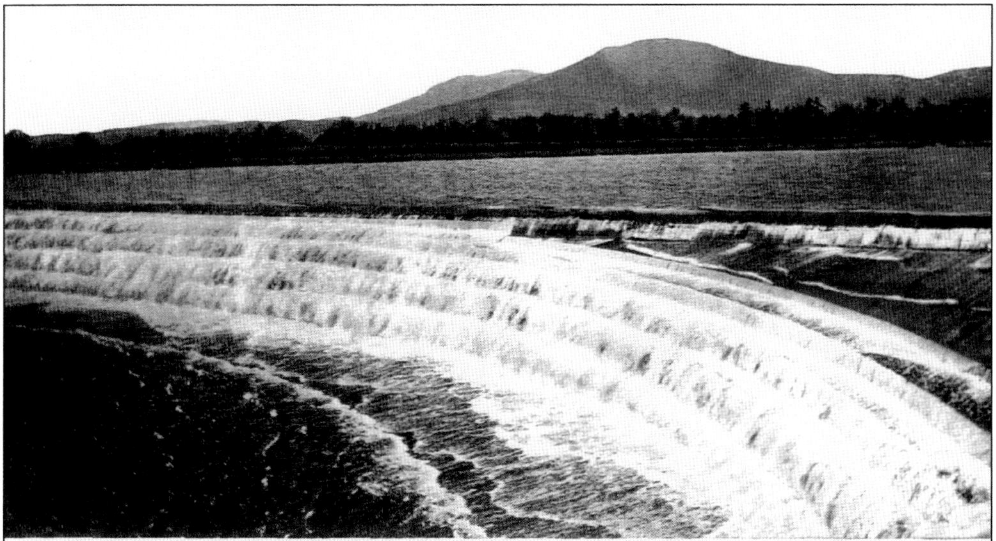

This *c.* 1915 color postcard beautifully shows the spillway overflow and waste weir in action. Located on the westernmost border of Marbletown, the overflow water travels down a long stone sluiceway to the Esopus Creek. High Point Mountain can be seen in the background. (Courtesy Betty Croswell.)

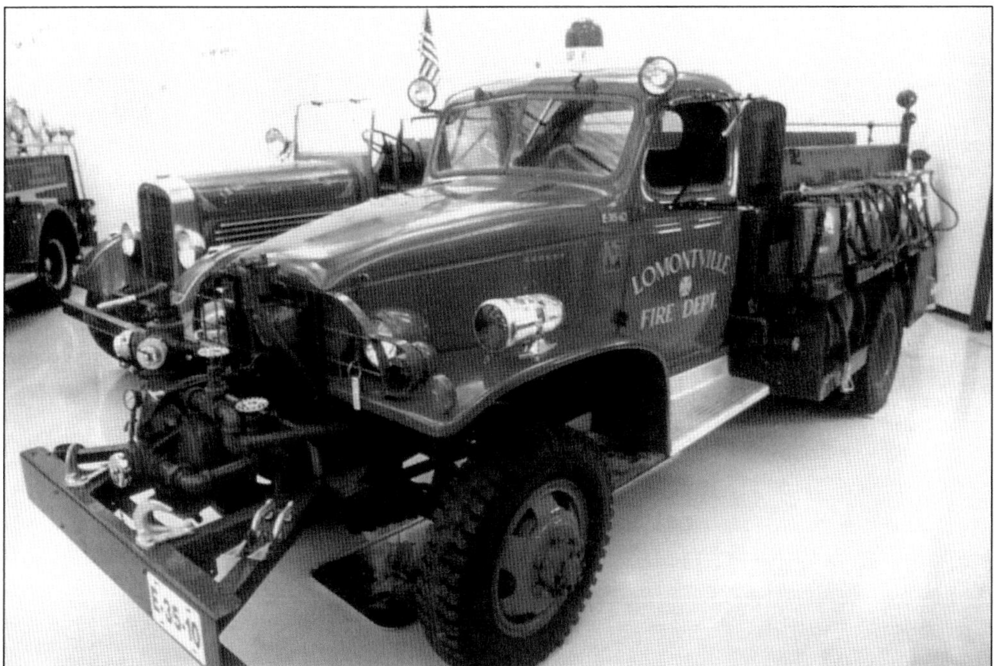

Donated to the Fireman's Association of the State of New York Museum of Firefighting, Lomontville's 1942 General Detroit brush truck is proudly on display at the Fireman's Home in Hudson, New York. (Courtesy Lou Cardinale.)

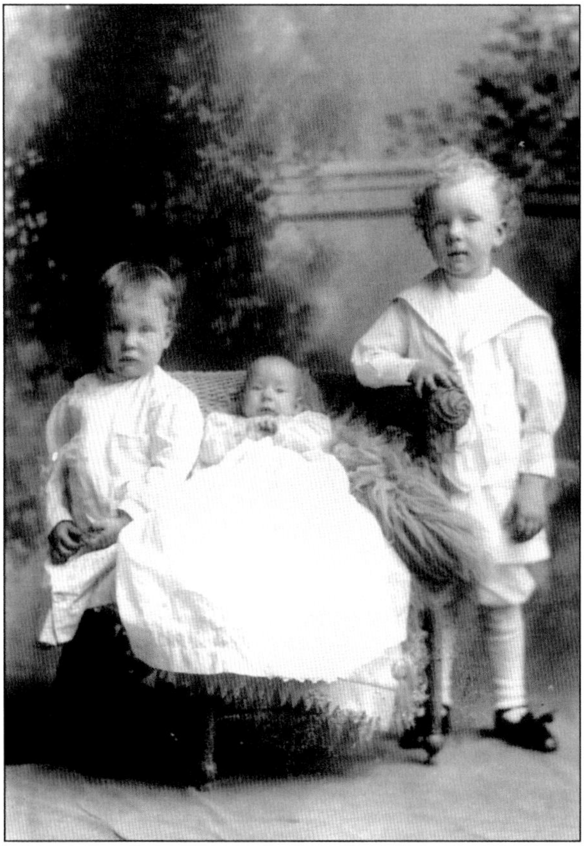

Pictured are the Forster family children. From left to right are Wilfred J., Hilda, and James. Wilfred eventually became owner of the Ennist family homestead in Lomontville until 1981. The photograph was taken on July 31, 1911. (Courtesy George K. Van Sickle.)

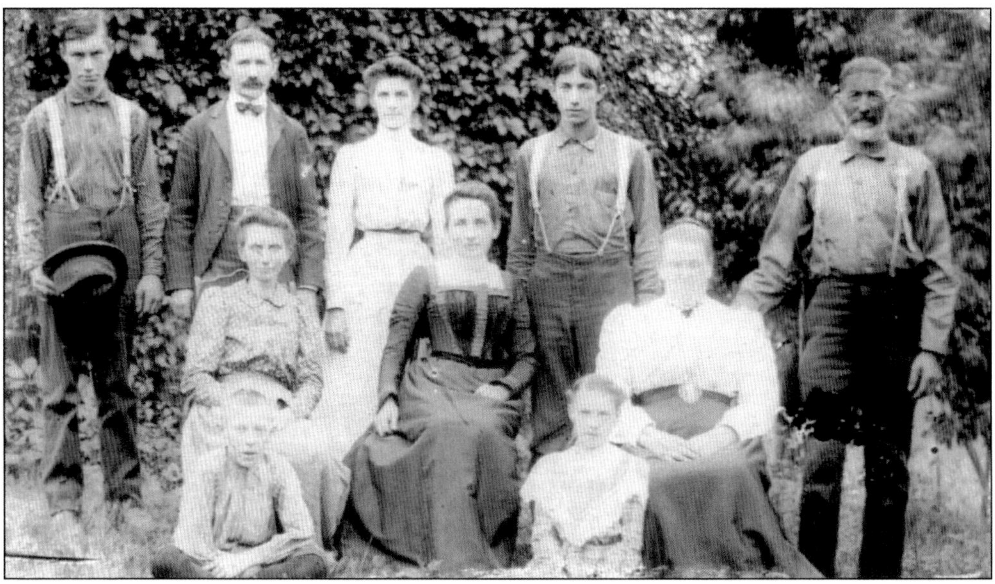

Friends and relatives of Aaron Krom pose during a family get-together in Lomontville around 1908. From left to right are (first row) two unidentified children; (second row) unidentified, Jenny Krom, Margaret Krom, and Aaron Krom; (third row) Russell Quick Krom, unidentified, Lida Krom, and unidentified. Aaron passed away in 1913. (Courtesy George K. Van Sickle.)

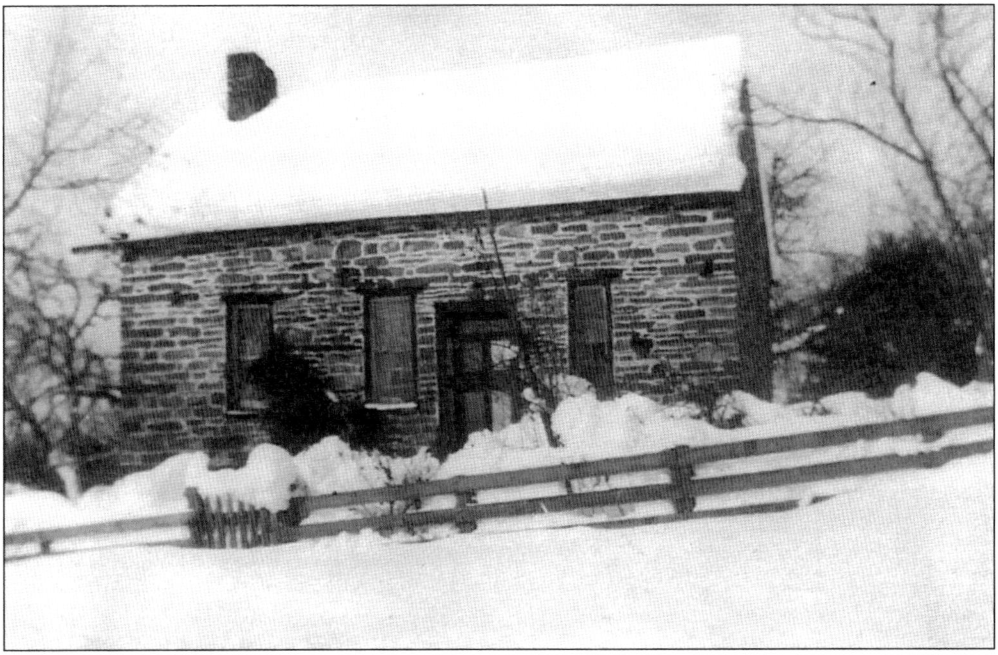

The original James Ennist homestead in Lomontville, built in 1825, is seen here as it looked in the early 1900s. This picture was taken prior to dormers that were added during modernization. The house sits on 99 acres that border the Esopus Creek. Also located on the farm is a private family cemetery. Taxes were based on many factors, including the size of windows. The small number of narrow windows in this house exemplifies this beautifully. (Courtesy George K. Van Sickle.)

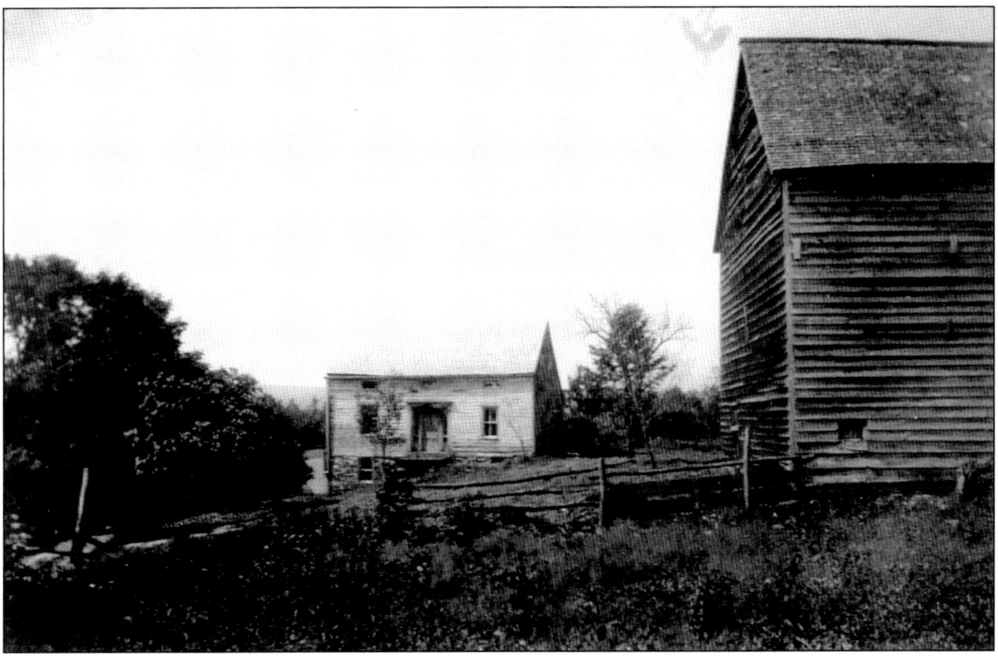

Pictured above is the Hunter family farm in Lomontville in the late 1800s. Located on Ashokan Road, the farm was on a barely passable dirt road. (Courtesy George K. Van Sickle.)

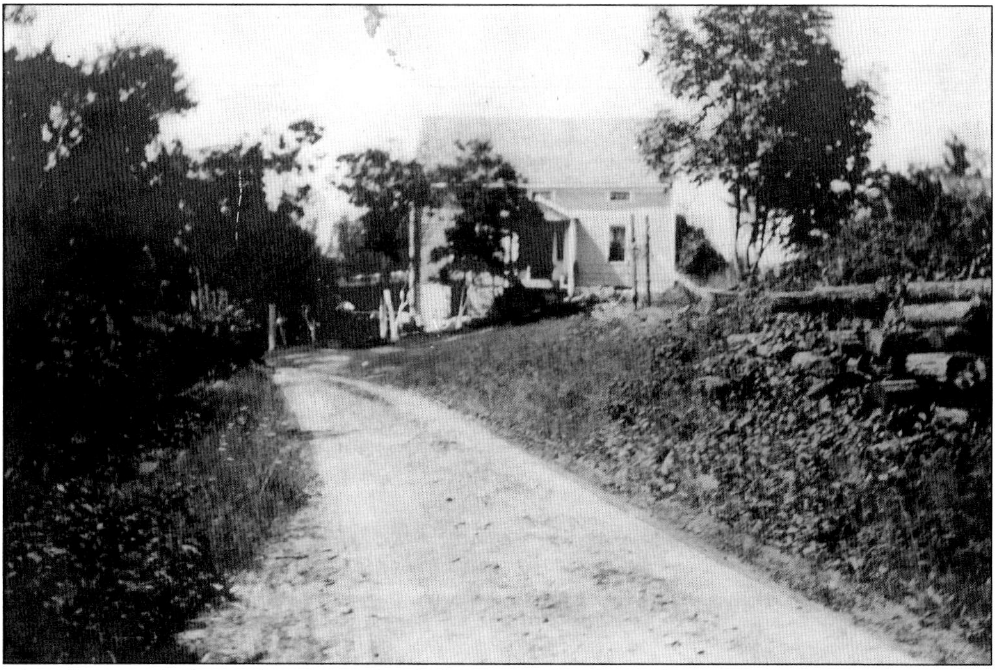

This photograph shows the Hunter family homestead in the early 1900s, after a front porch was added. Today Ashokan Road is one of the main roads connecting Hurley Mountain Road with the Ashokan Reservoir. (Courtesy George K. Van Sickle.)

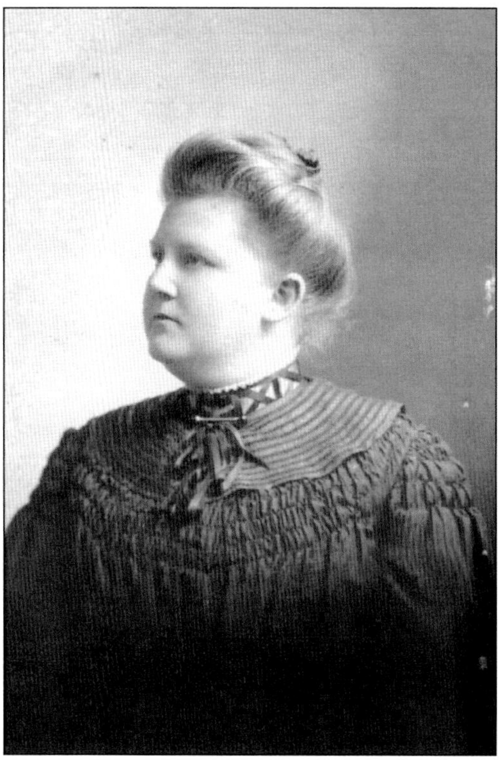

Caddie Hunter, a direct relative to the Ennist family, is shown in this late-1800s photograph in a characteristic pose of the era. It was not uncommon for family members to settle near one another, remaining in close contact with their parents and siblings. (Courtesy George K. Van Sickle.)

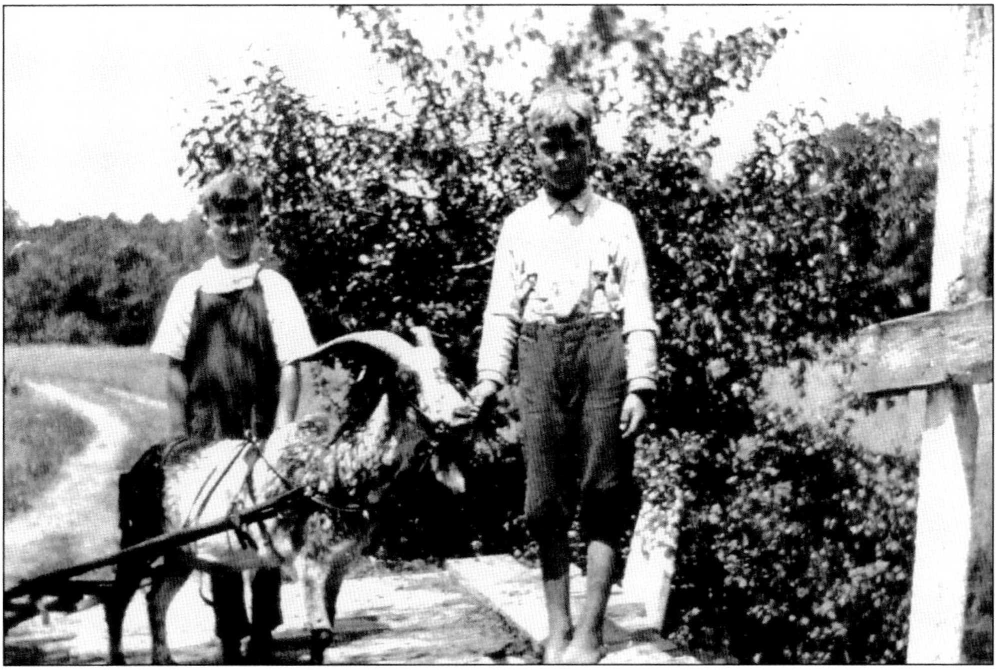

This early-1900s photograph shows two young boys with their goat hitched to a cart. Summertime was a busy time for youth, mostly tending to animals and crops and harvesting corn and hay. All animals had a specific purpose to earn their keep. (Courtesy George K. Van Sickle.)

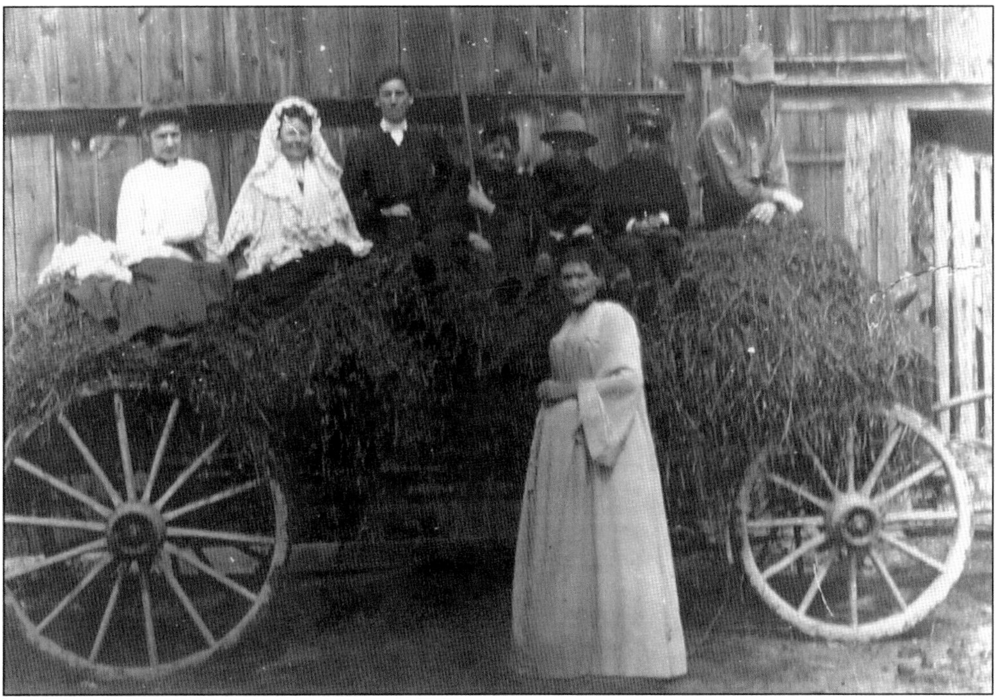

This happy wedding party celebrates and poses on the hay wagon at the Aaron Krom boardinghouse. This photograph was taken in the late 1800s. (Courtesy George K. Van Sickle.)

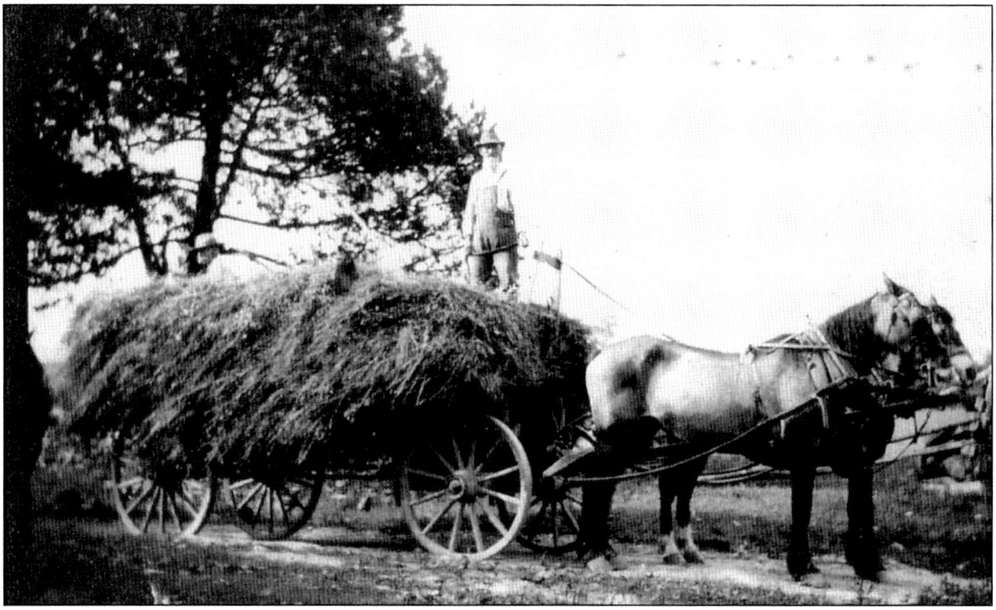

Russell Krom handles the team of horses while haying on the family farm in Lomontville. Haying was an important farm activity. Horsepower was essential in everyday farm life. Enough hay had to be stored away to last the winter. Spare crop was sold for profit. (Courtesy George K. Van Sickle.)

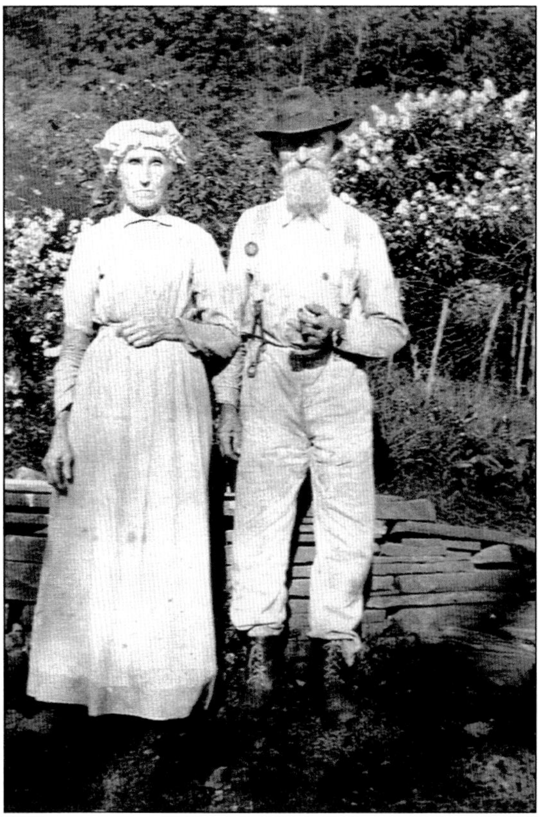

Life on the farm in the 1890s was difficult at best. Simon Van Demark and his wife Mary Susan (Ennist) of Lomontville are perfect examples of farmers in the Hudson Valley. Hard work started before the sun came up and lasted well until dark. (Courtesy George K. Van Sickle.)

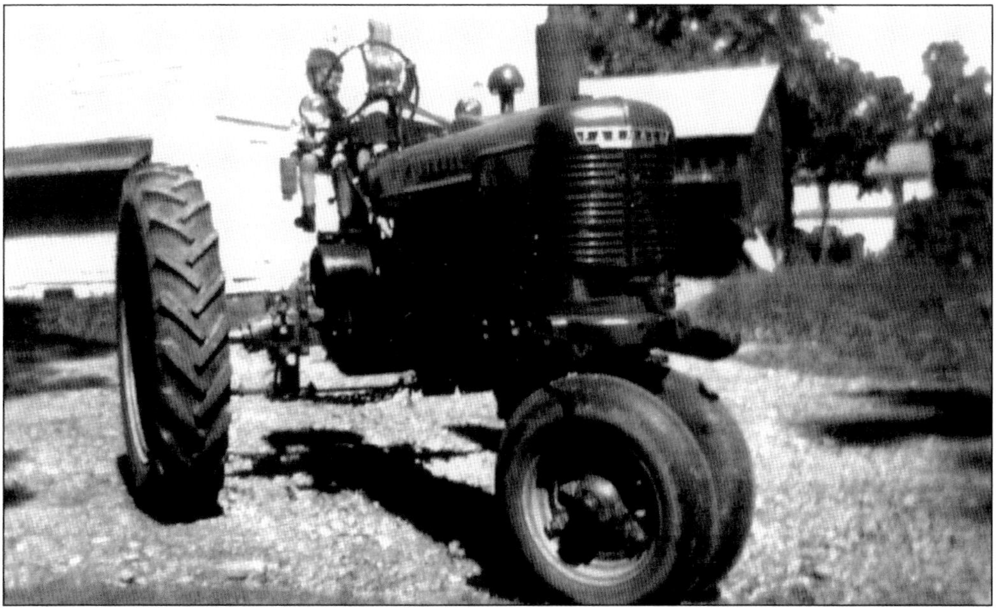

Robert (left) and Charles Van Wagenen pose with their father's new Farmall H tractor, dreaming of the day they can reach the pedals and take it for a spin. Family farms depended on offspring following in their parents' footsteps and continuing the tradition of working the land. (Courtesy Ed Croswell.)

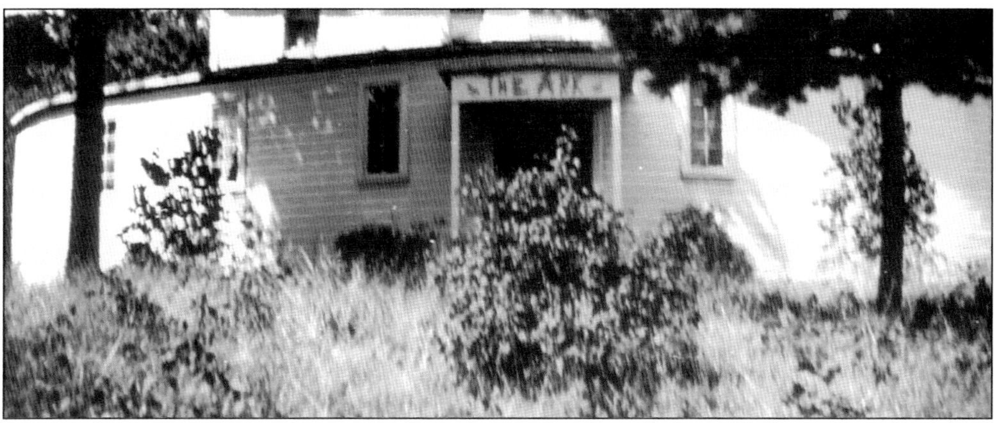

The Ark Church was built in the early 1930s in Lomontville. It obtained its name from the shape of the building, which resembled Noah's legendary ark in the Bible. Inside, the pulpit was set up to resemble the helm of a ship as well. Religious services contained much religious zeal and fervor. (Courtesy George K. Van Sickle.)

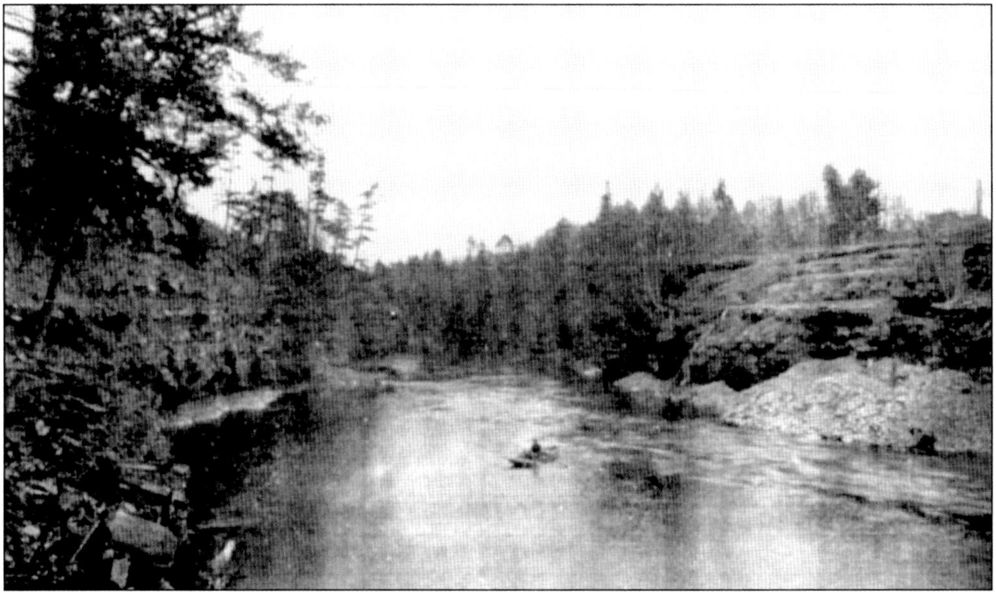

This vintage postcard shows the Esopus Creek before construction on the Ashokan Reservoir started near Brown Station. It was a wonderful area known for hunting and fishing. Work on the reservoir, which supplies water to New York City, would forever change the landscape in that area, flooding cities and forcing hundreds of families to relocate. (Courtesy Betty Croswell.)

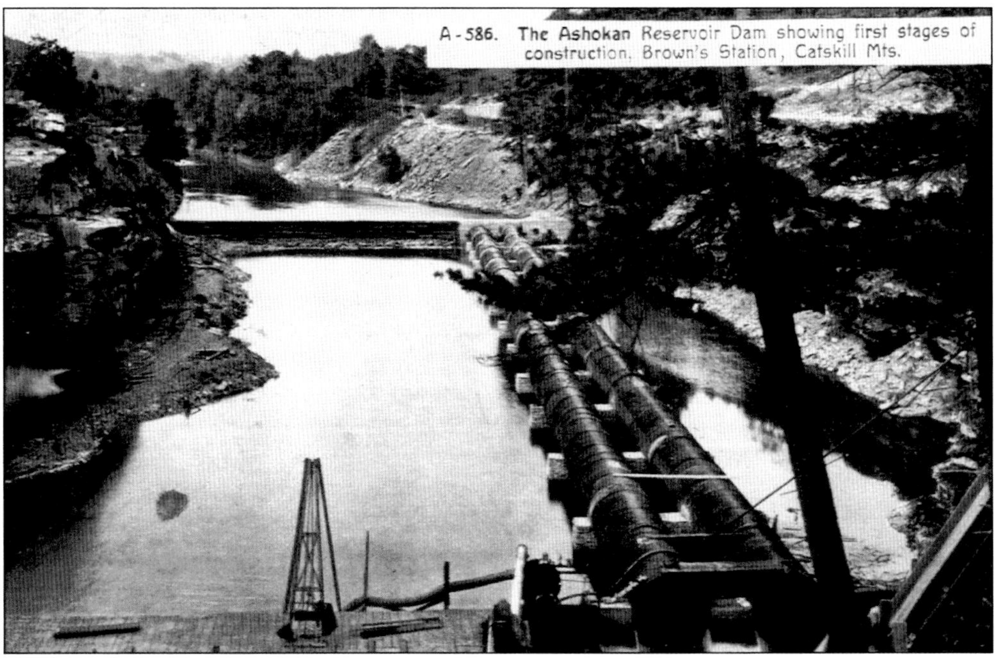

This was the first stage of many in the construction of the Ashokan Reservoir in Brown Station on the Marbletown line. It is the same area as pictured in the above photograph. (Courtesy Betty Croswell.)

Five

STONE RIDGE

Located in the center of the town is the village of Stone Ridge. It sits on stone ledges that act as watersheds for the Rondout and Esopus Creeks. The Old Mine Road formed the main street of the village. The first homes built were most likely log homes, and as settlers stayed, they built wonderful stone houses out of the abundant limestone that was available. The stage ran from the river port of Kingston to the ore mines of Pennsylvania. The large Hardenbergh mill—deeded to Johannes Hardenbergh in 1706 by Chief Kakawarium of the Esopus Indians—produced flour that was sold in exchange for salt. As one strolls through the hamlet of Stone Ridge, one will be struck by the Dutch influence in the architecture of the homes. One would almost expect to be transported back to a friendlier time. Today the government of Marbletown is striving to preserve the authenticity and uniqueness of this wonderful town for future generations.

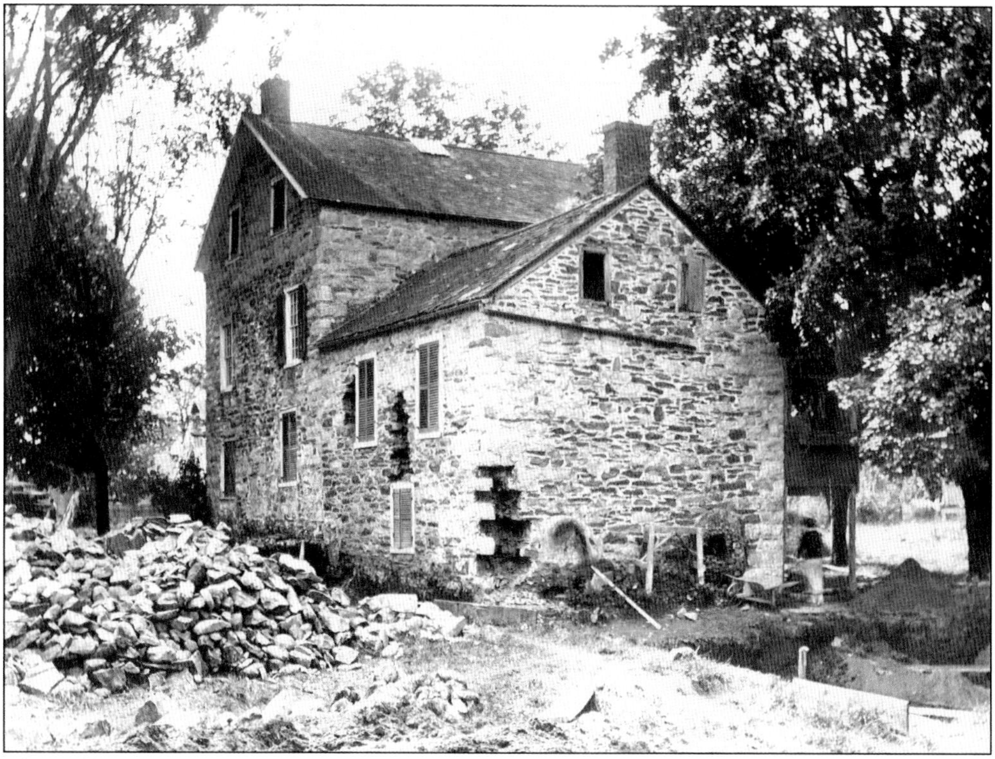

The Sally Tack Inn underwent extensive restorative work in 1919. This photograph shows repairs underway on the rear part of the structure. An addition was built onto the rear area for a Mrs. Chadburn, the home owner at the time. (Courtesy Jody Ford, Stone Ridge Library.)

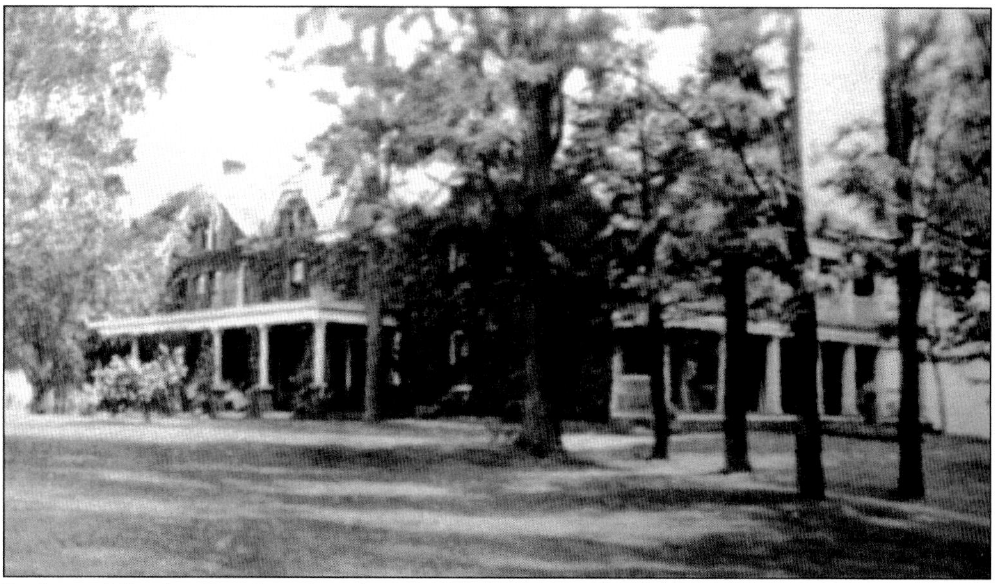

Built in 1757, this Dutch-Colonial mansion is known as the Hasbrouck house. Originally a private residence, it became a well-known pub/restaurant and bed-and-breakfast. It is owned by the Hauspung family and still offers travelers a chance to stay in its well-furnished rooms. (Courtesy Jody Ford, Stone Ridge Library.)

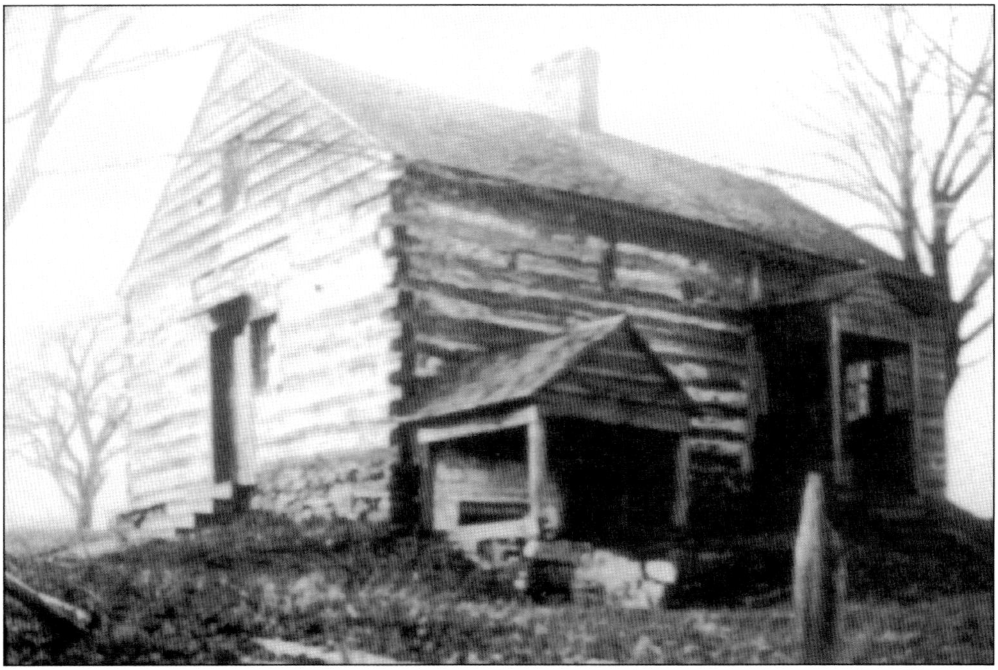

The exact location of this log cabin is unknown, but it was in the Stone Ridge area of Marbletown. It is an excellent example of the cabin-building methods used in the early 1800s. (Courtesy Jody Ford, Stone Ridge Library.)

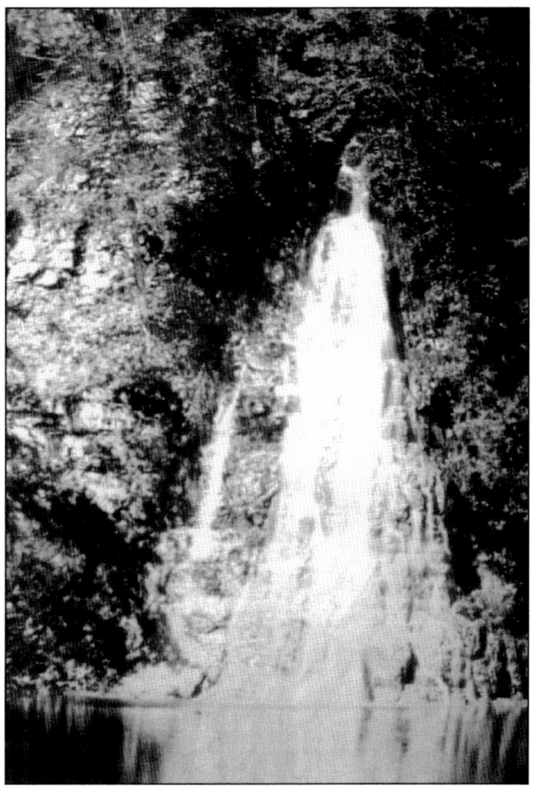

Bogerts Glen is an extremely picturesque waterfall located off Mill Dam Road behind the stone house of the Bogart family farm. One can see the limestone layering clearly in this photograph. (Courtesy Stone Ridge Library.)

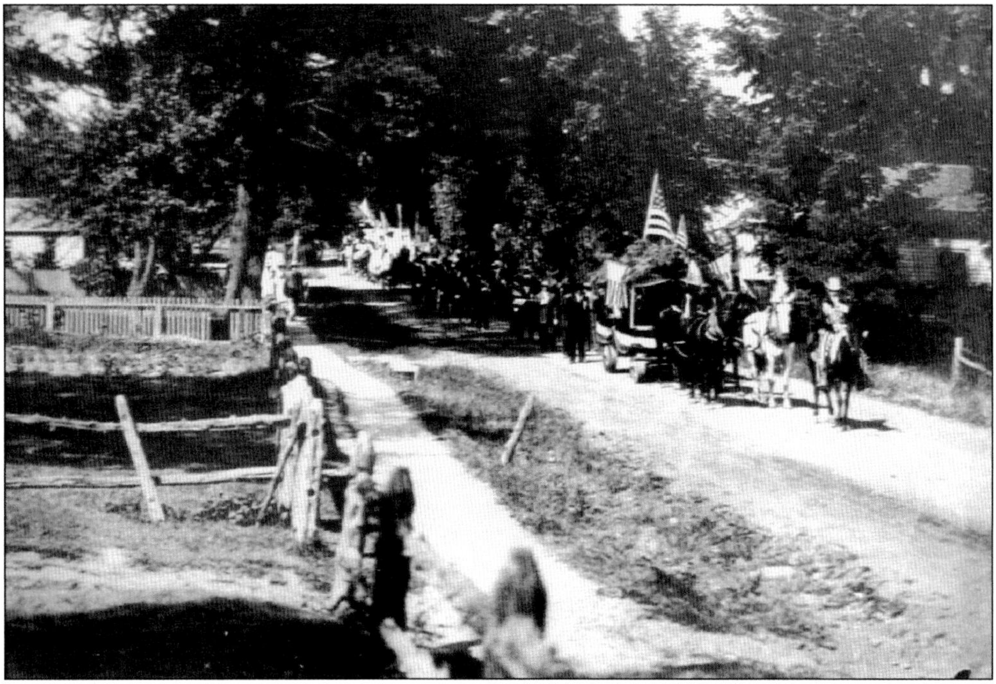

The exact dates of these photographs are unknown, but both are believed to be a Fourth of July parade down Main Street in the hamlet of Stone Ridge, taken sometime in the late 1880s to 1890s. The horse-drawn floats and patriotic flags waving, plus the finery the participants are wearing, suggest a large celebration. (Courtesy Jody Ford, Stone Ridge Library.)

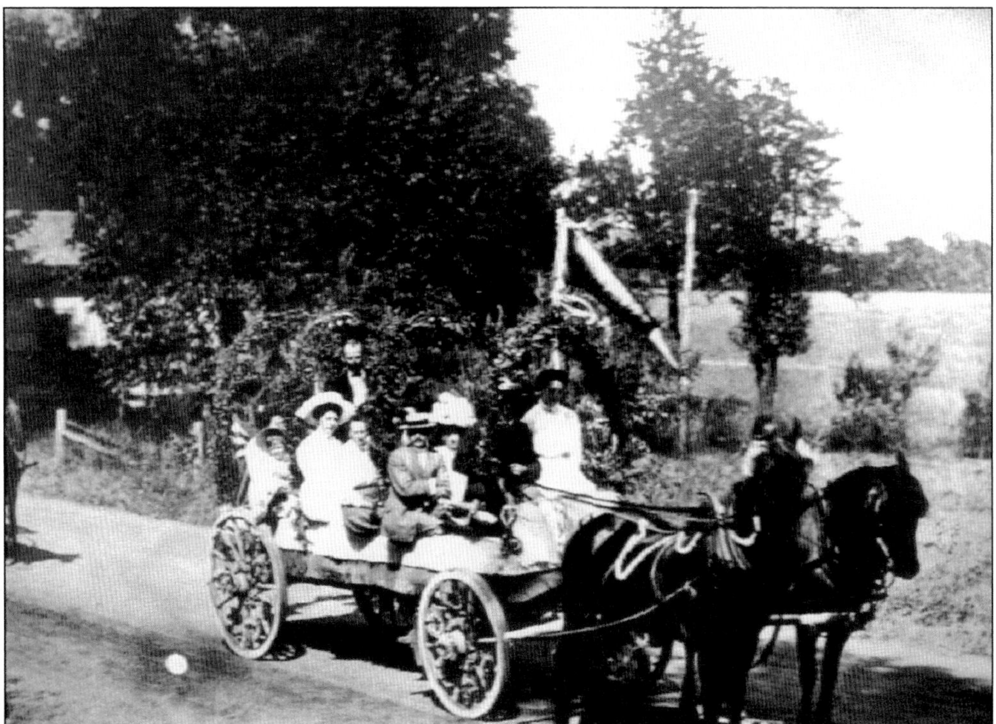

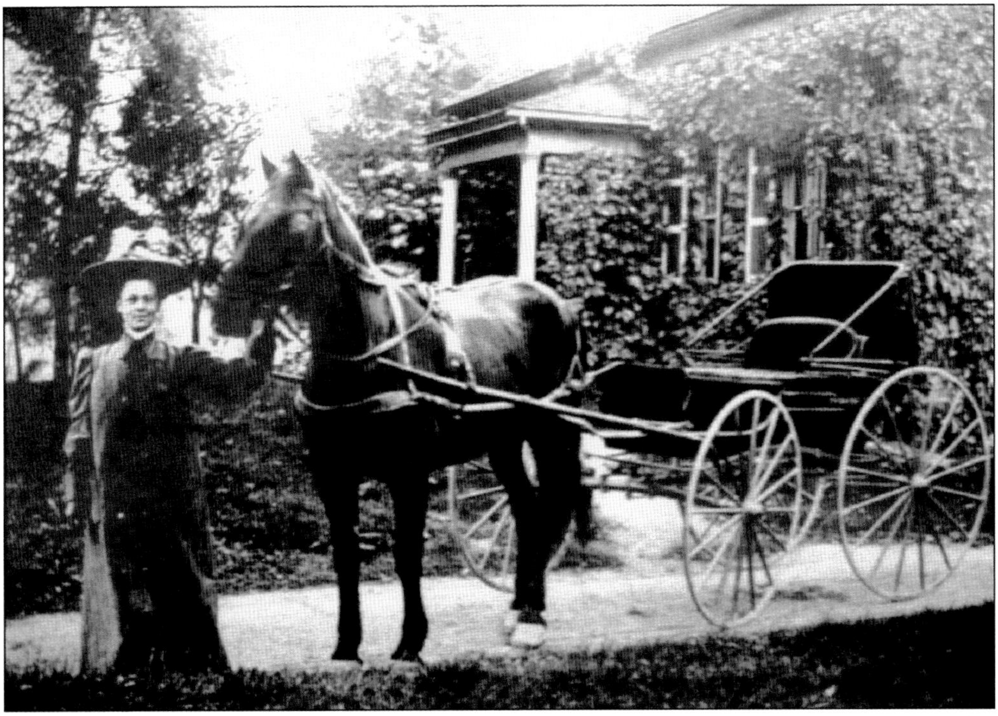

Sally Brink proudly poses with her horse and carriage in front of her Stone Ridge home in this late-1800s photograph. (Courtesy Jody Ford, Stone Ridge Library.)

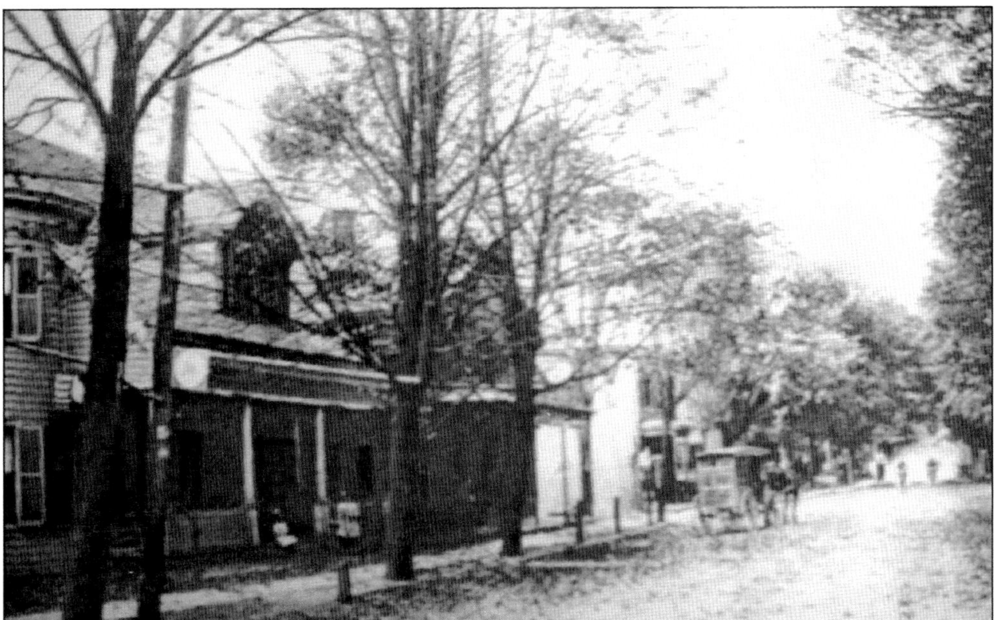

Looking south on Main Street in Stone Ridge, note the horse and covered carriage parked along the side of the street in this 1880s photograph. Hitching posts were conveniently located along the road. (Courtesy Jody Ford, Stone Ridge Library.)

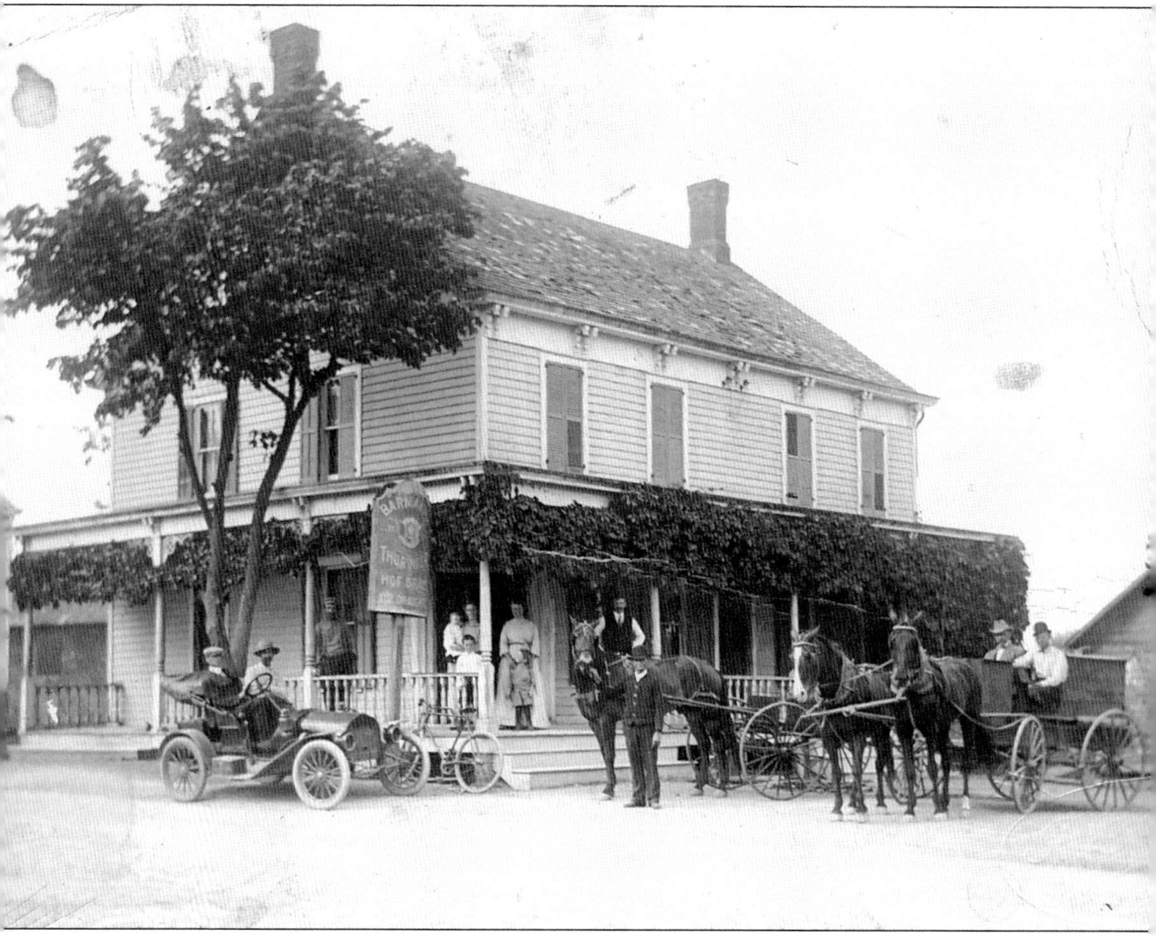

Man-made horsepower meets the real thing in front of the Burgess Hotel, Stone Ridge, around 1903. The earliest automobiles signaled the end to dependence on horse-drawn transportation. (Courtesy Jody Ford, Stone Ridge Library.)

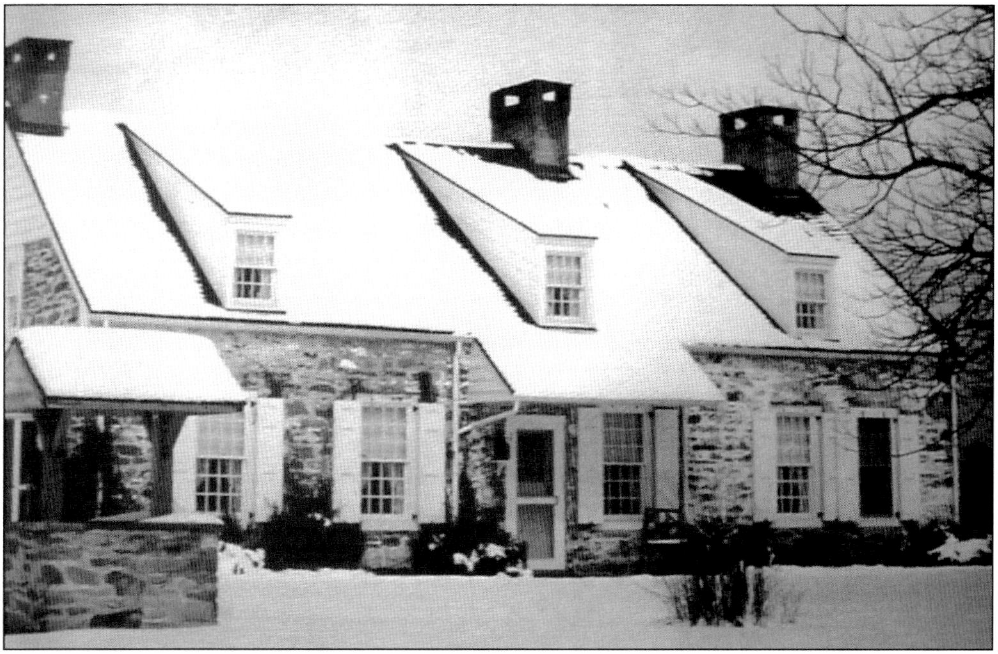

The McCorkle stone house is seen here in wintertime. Made of limestone, it featured large open hearths. Note the three large chimneys, typical of these houses. (Courtesy Jody Ford, Stone Ridge Library.)

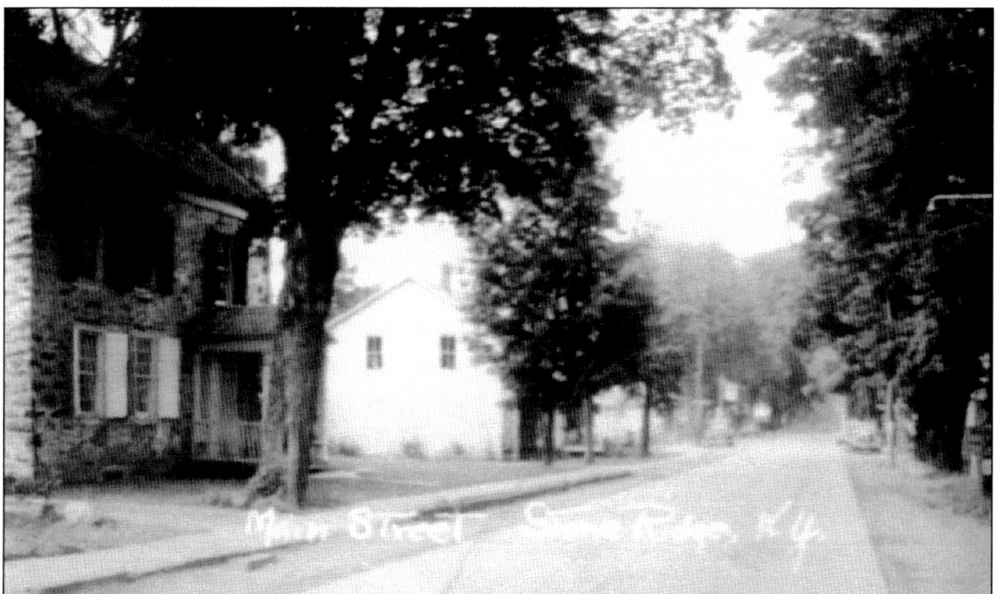

Looking north on Main Street in Stone Ridge, this photograph features the current Stone Ridge Library on the left. Originally owned by the Hasbrouck family, it hosts a wonderful library fair every June. (Courtesy Jody Ford, Stone Ridge Library.)

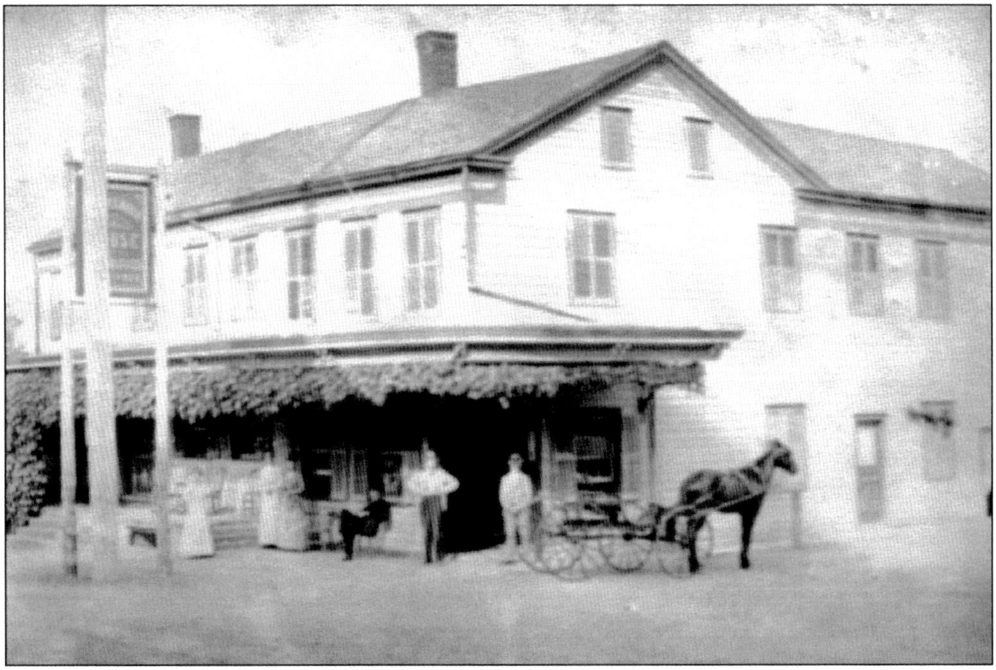

T. P. Ostrander owned and operated the Stone Ridge Hotel. This photograph was taken around 1886. It was a popular stopping point for travelers on the Old Mine Road. Horse and wagon was the mode of travel in those days. (Courtesy Jody Ford, Stone Ridge Library.)

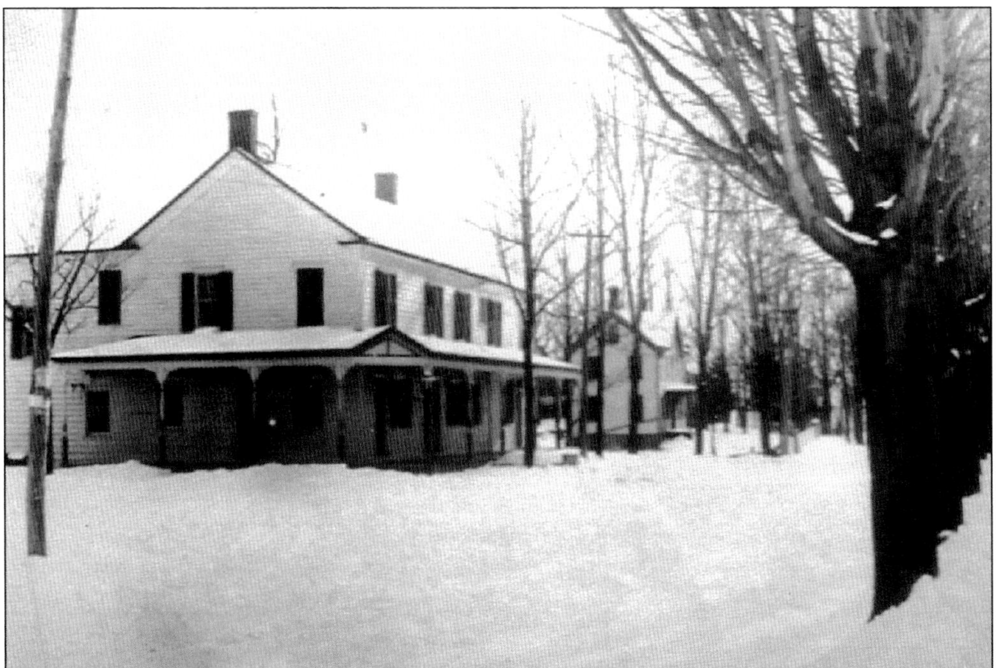

Pictured is the Stone Ridge Hotel, the former Summit Hotel, located on Main Street in Stone Ridge. The hotel was destroyed by a fire in 1925. The Marbletown Town Hall proudly sits on the site of the old hotel today. (Courtesy Stone Ridge Library.)

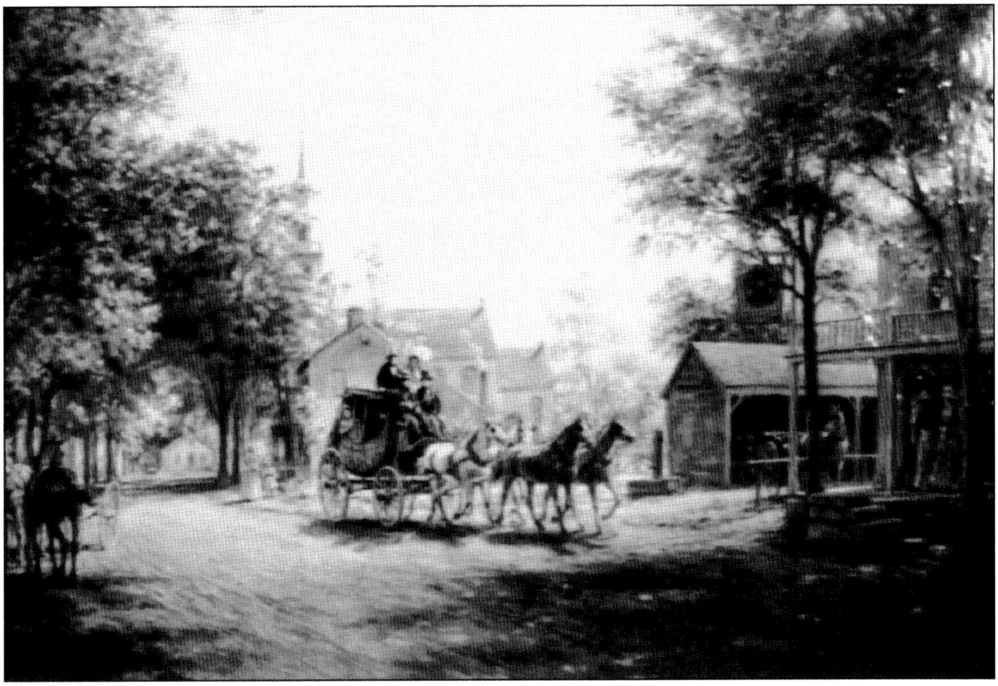

Arrival of Stage—Summit Hotel, Stone Ridge is a famous oil painting by E. L. Henry. Stagecoaches between Kingston and Pennsylvania regularly stopped at the Summit Hotel. (Courtesy Jody Ford, Stone Ridge Library.)

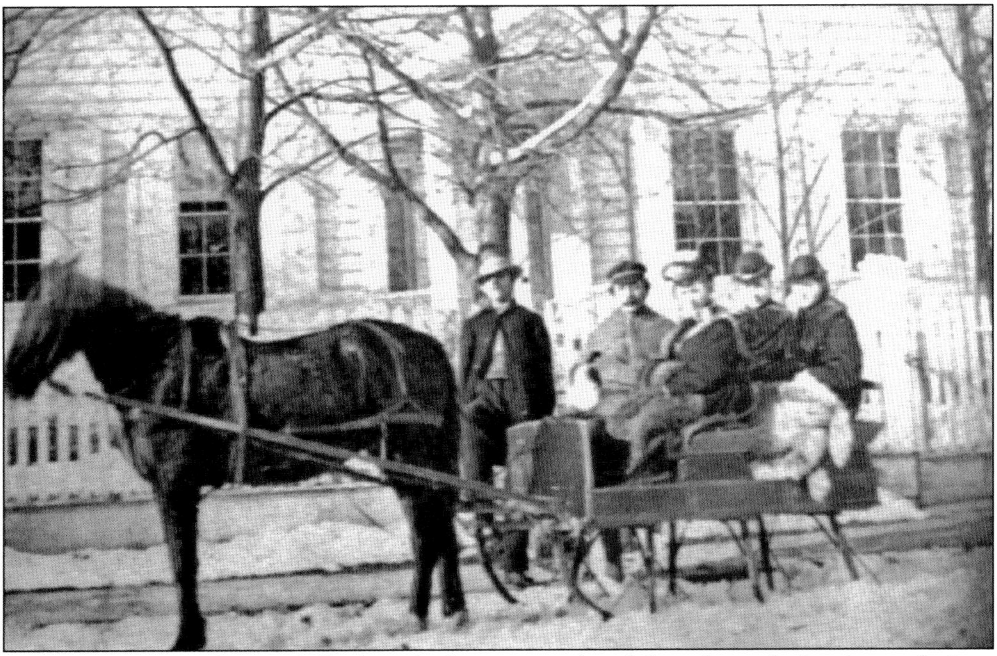

Winter travel proved more difficult under horsepower, but did not keep the hardy people from enjoying it. Sleighs with runners replaced wagons with wheels. These people are pictured in the 1880s on Main Street in Stone Ridge with their cutter sleigh. (Courtesy Jody Ford, Stone Ridge Library.)

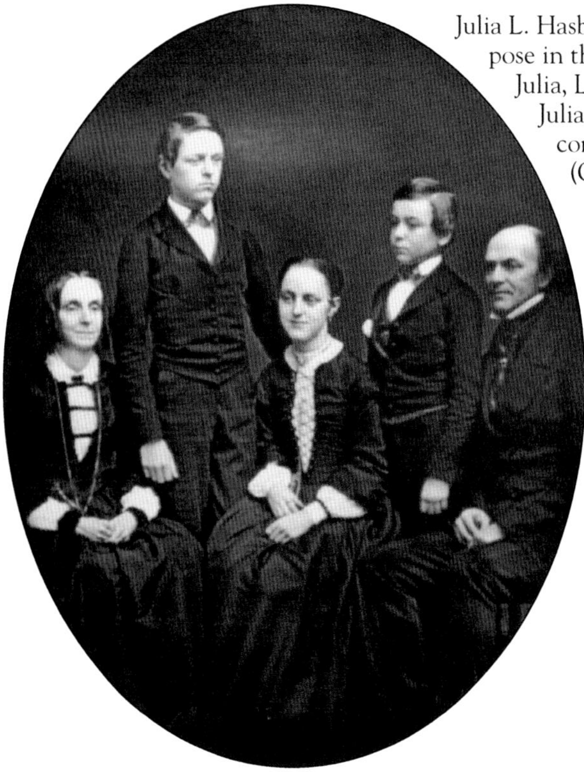

Julia L. Hasbrouck and Garret Decker Hasbrouck pose in the late 1880s with their children, Julia, Louis (second from left), and Remsen. Julia donated the family home to the community to be used as a library. (Courtesy Stone Ridge Library.)

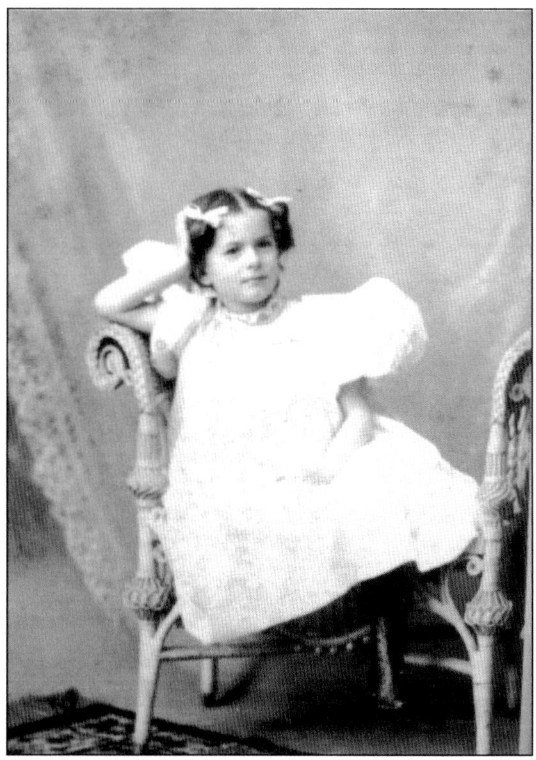

Sarah Lounsberry, pictured here as a child, lived in the Wynkoop-Lounsberry house. (Courtesy Stone Ridge Library.)

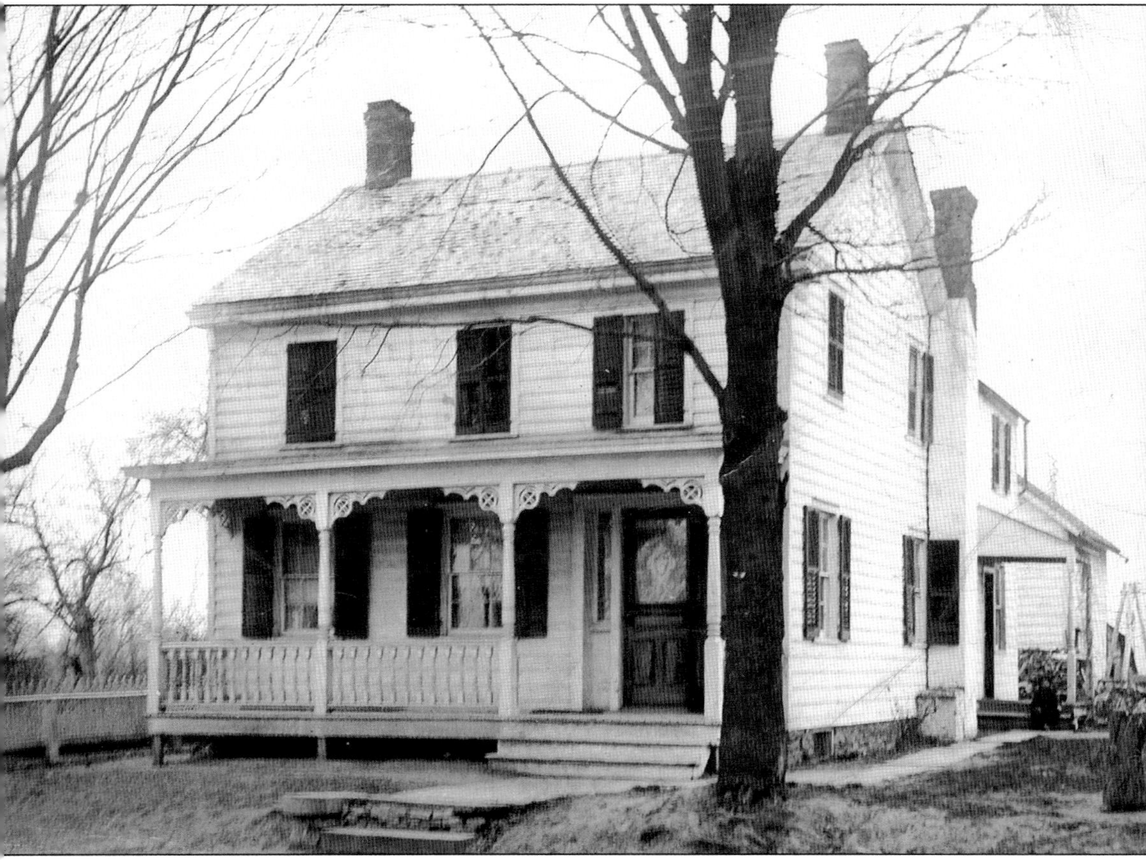

This wonderful old photograph shows the historic Roosa homestead on Main Street in Stone Ridge. (Courtesy Jody Ford, Stone Ridge Library.)

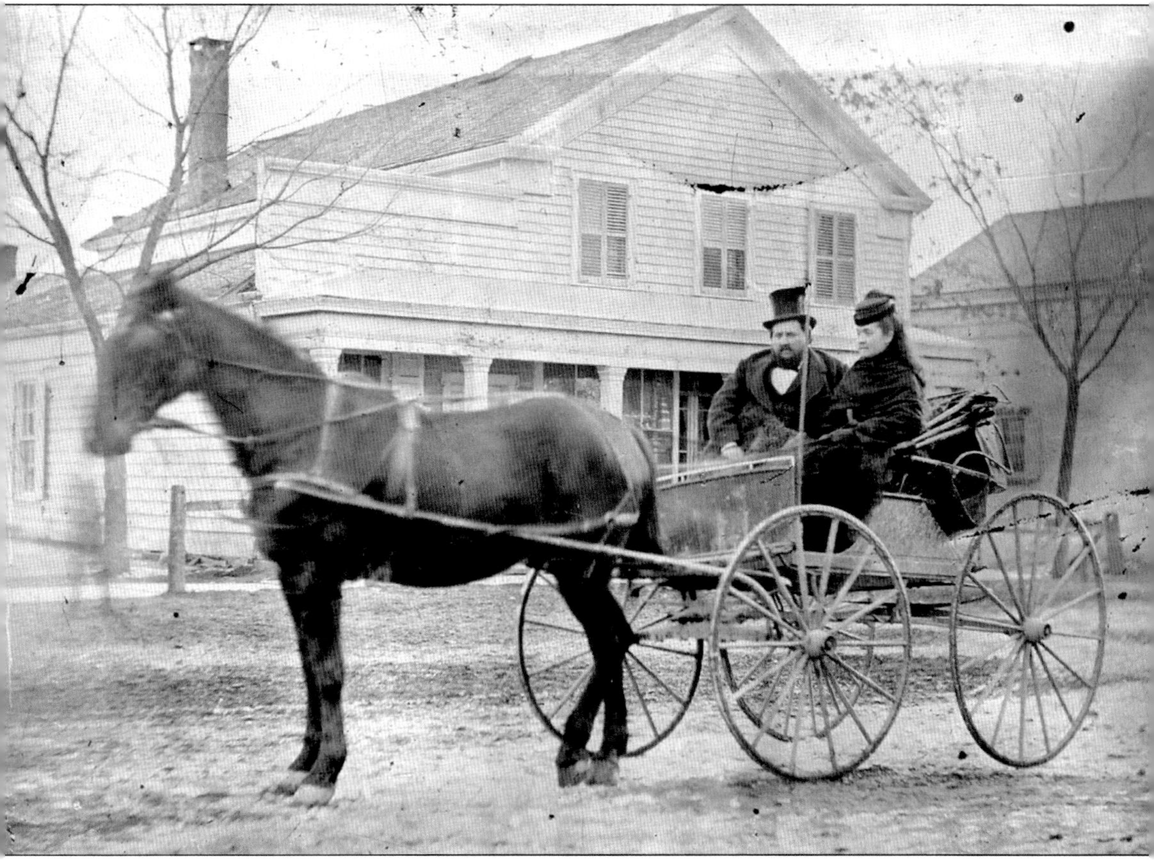

Taken from an original tintype, an unidentified couple and their handsome carriage and horse typify the customary transportation in the late 1800s. Travel was difficult. The Old Mine Road was a major thoroughfare of the day, connecting Kingston and the Hudson River with the mines of Pennsylvania. (Courtesy Jody Ford, Stone Ridge Library.)

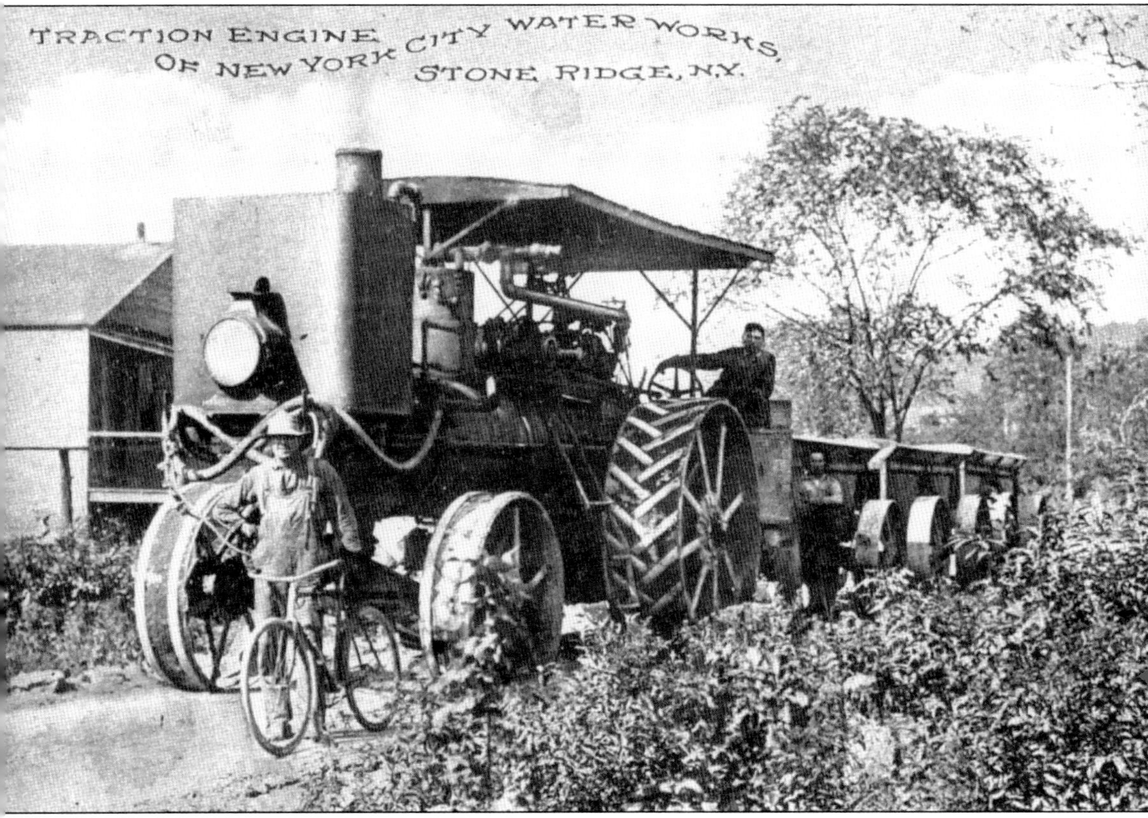

To provide water to the residents of New York City, the New York City Water Works built an underground aqueduct from the Ashokan Reservoir to reservoirs near Manhattan. The underground aqueduct ran through Lomontville, Stone Ridge, and High Falls and continued on past the Shawangunk Mountains. This postcard shows a large traction engine being driven down Main Street in Stone Ridge en route to the work site. (Courtesy George K. Van Sickle.)

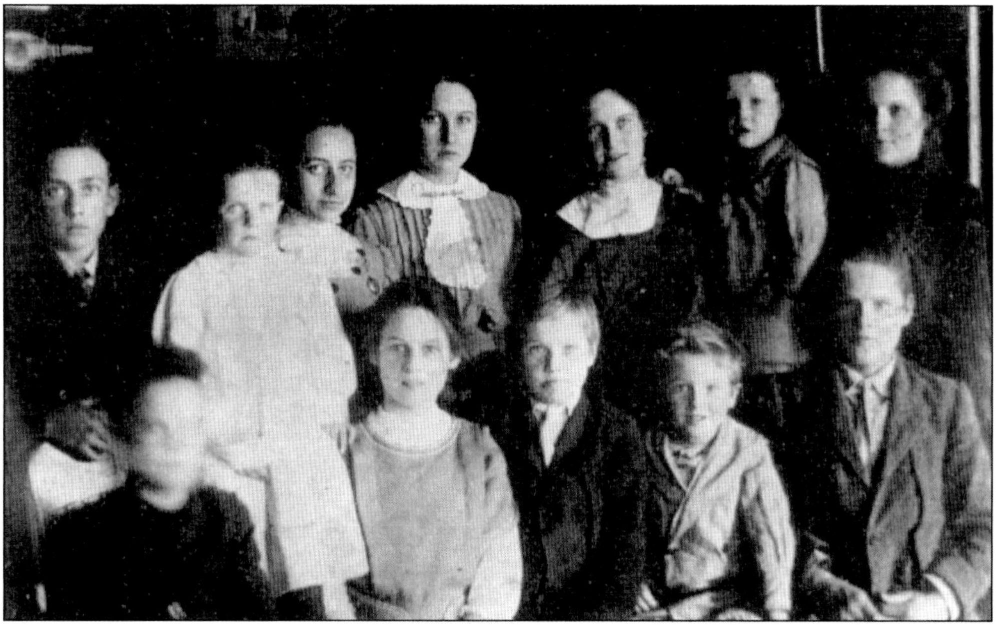

The Davenport family, well known in Marbletown, originally had its roots in Accord. This 1912 photograph was taken at a Christmas party held at the Dutch Reformed church in Accord. From left to right are (first row) Frances Davenport, Nellie Davenport, Maurice Davenport, Kenneth Davenport, and Edward Davenport; (second row) Ina Clearwater, Katherine, Ada Clearwater Osterhoudt, Helen Davenport Anderson, Edna Davenport LeFever, John Phillip Davenport, and Anna Davenport. (Courtesy Charles Greene.)

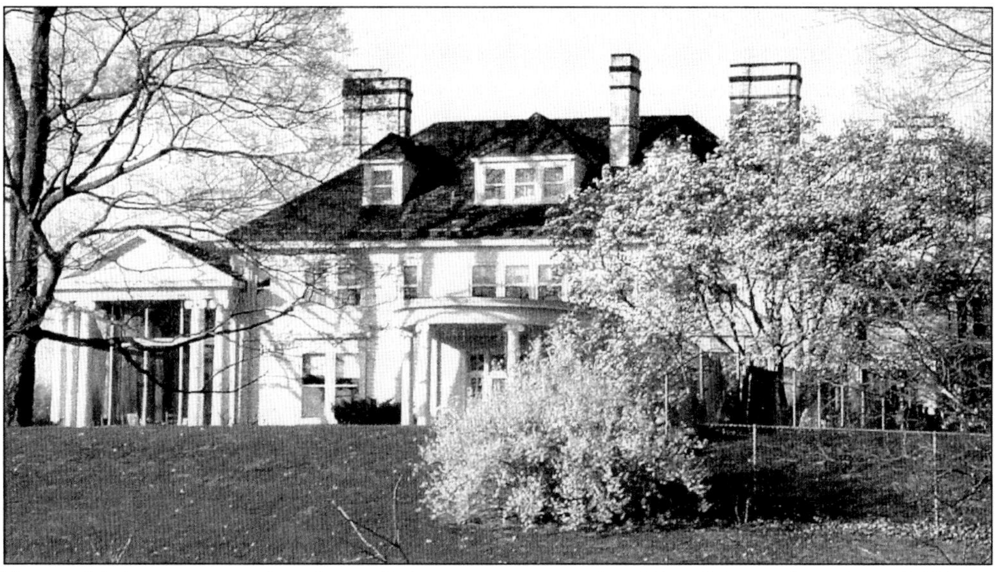

Francis H. Leggett moved to Stone Ridge sometime in the 1890s. He was friends with Henry Delafield, who managed the New York Cement Company in High Falls. He so enjoyed the area that he built Ridgely Manor on what is now Leggett Road. Several other houses on the property were rented to tenants by the season to bring in extra income. The grounds of the large estate were created by Frederick Olmsted, who also landscaped Central Park in New York City. (Author's collection.)

Six

Fire Companies and Rescue Personnel

This chapter is dedicated to the true unsung heroes of Marbletown, the firefighters and emergency medical service personnel of local fire companies and ambulances. Fire companies were formed due to the geography of the area, the need to respond quickly, and the desire of people to help one another. Many of these people are colleagues, neighbors, and friends. They all spend countless hours volunteering their time, training to respond to emergencies in town. Nothing is more difficult and at the same time more rewarding than responding to help one's fellow neighbors, friends, and even strangers when they are in need. The author salutes all the volunteers she has had the honor to meet and work with. Their dedication symbolizes the strength the original settlers of this area were so noted for.

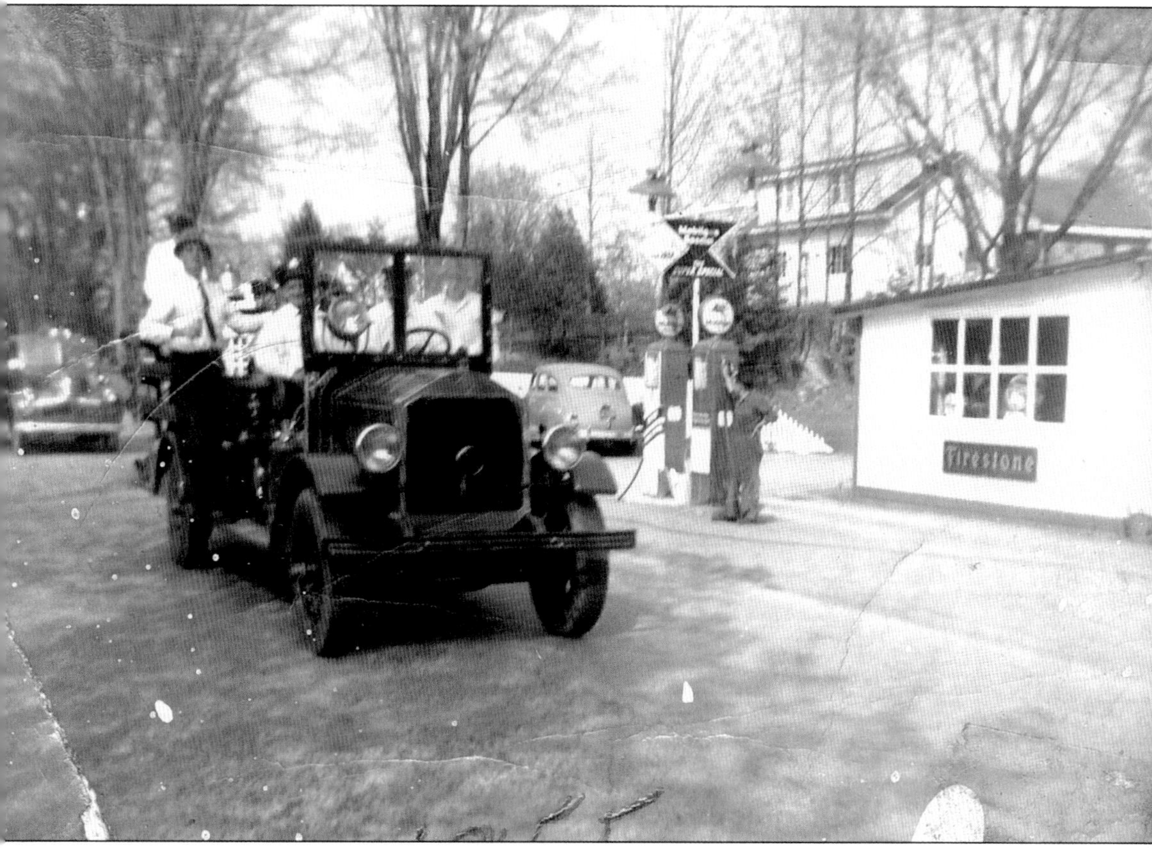

Steve Kowal drives the Marbletown Fire Company's 1928 Sanford Cub engine down Main Street in Stone Ridge, passing Tony Arra's gas station, during the 1955 Memorial Day parade. (Courtesy Marbletown Fire Company.)

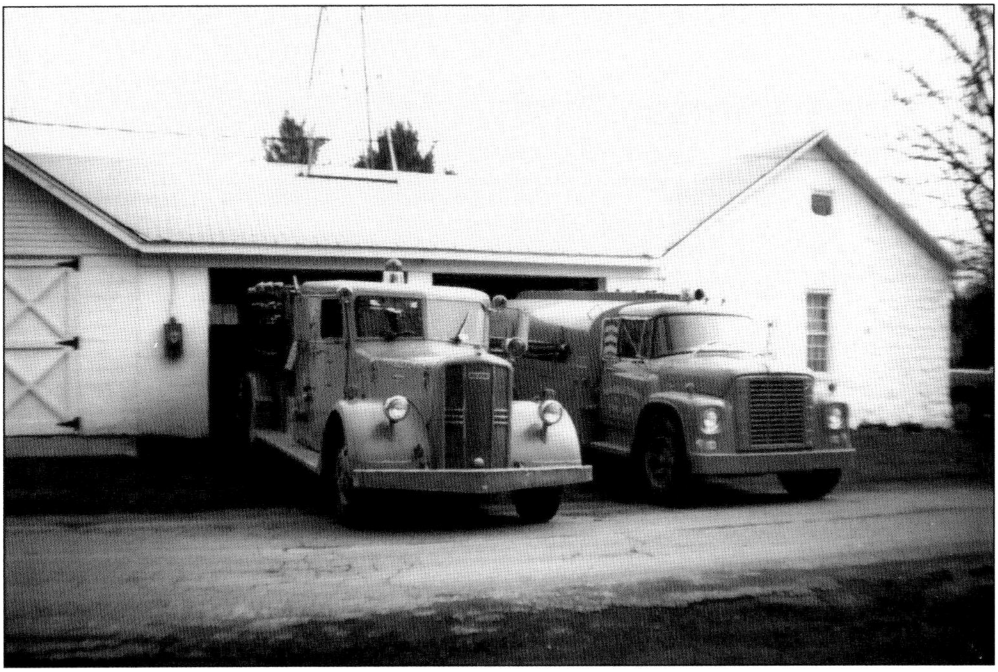

Pictured is the Marbletown Fire House around 1960, showing the 1947 LaFrance pumper and the 1963 International tanker. The right side of the firehouse was the Marbletown one-room stone schoolhouse. The schoolhouse and original firehouse on the left were joined by adding two truck bays between the buildings. (Courtesy Marbletown Fire Company.)

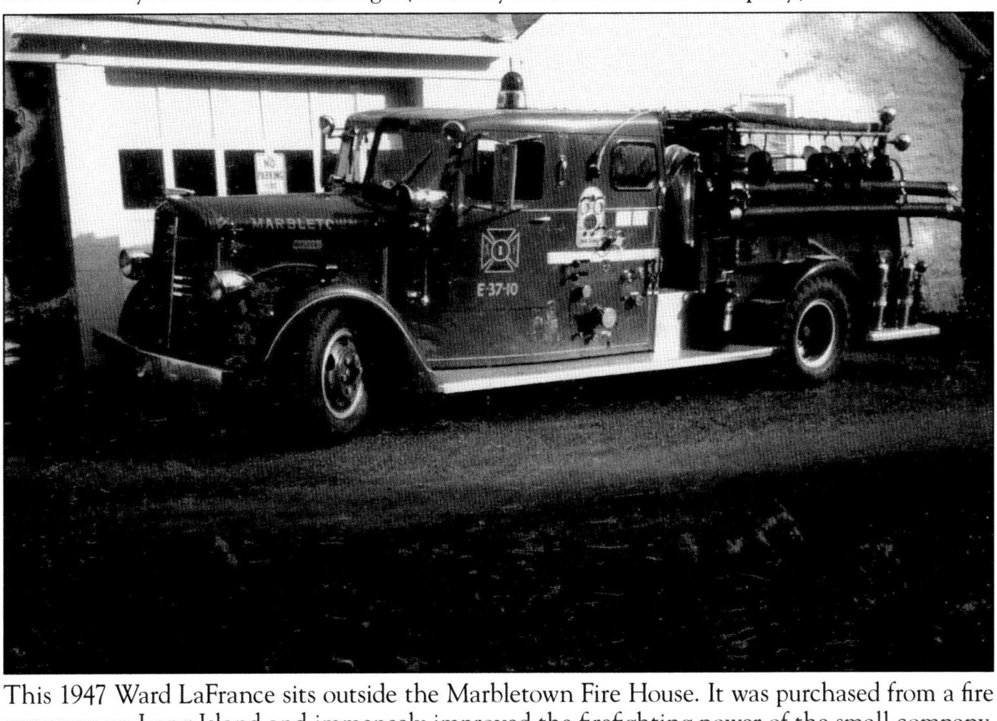

This 1947 Ward LaFrance sits outside the Marbletown Fire House. It was purchased from a fire company on Long Island and immensely improved the firefighting power of the small company. (Courtesy Marbletown Fire Company.)

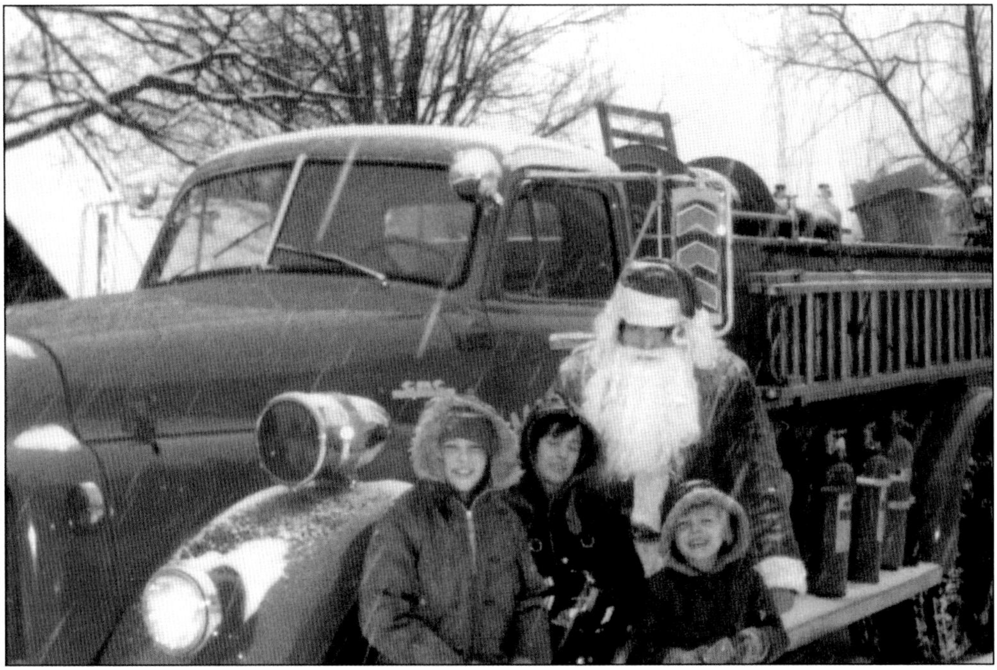

Santa, in the form of Vincent Guido Jr., visits district children during the 1975 Christmas season. Pictured from left to right with Santa are Brian, Timothy, and Stephanie Murphy. (Courtesy Marbletown Fire Company.)

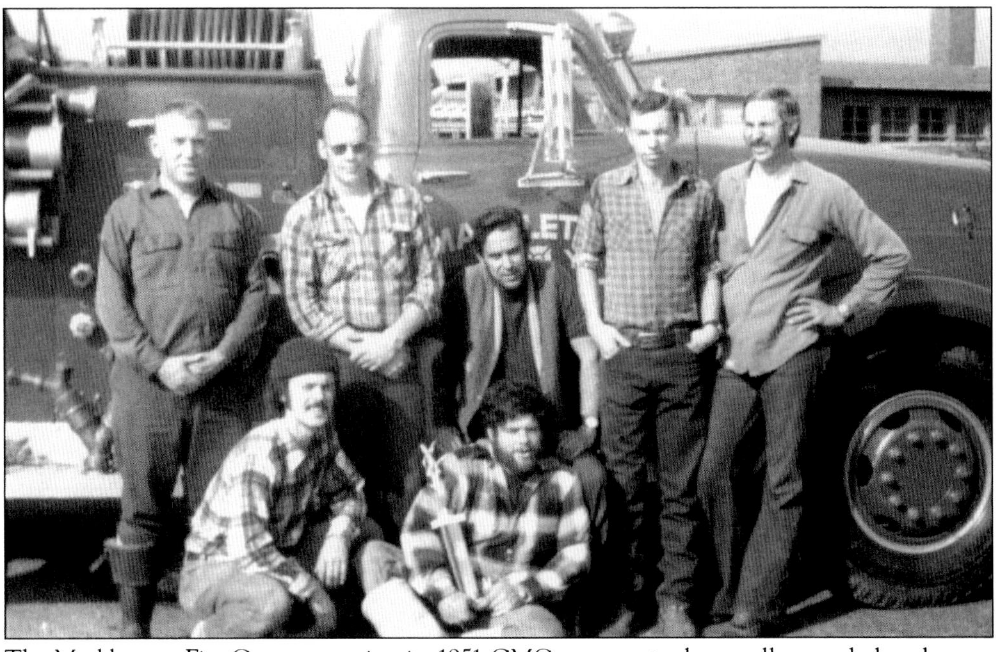

The Marbletown Fire Company, using its 1951 GMC pumper, took overall second-place honors at the Marbletown Volunteer Firemans Association competition in 1975. Pictured are, from left to right, (first row) Donald Hadden and Vincent Guido Jr.; (second row) George K. Van Sickle, Ed Croswell, Kenneth Cole Sr., Russ Van Sickle, and Dick Van Lear. (Courtesy Marbletown Fire Company.)

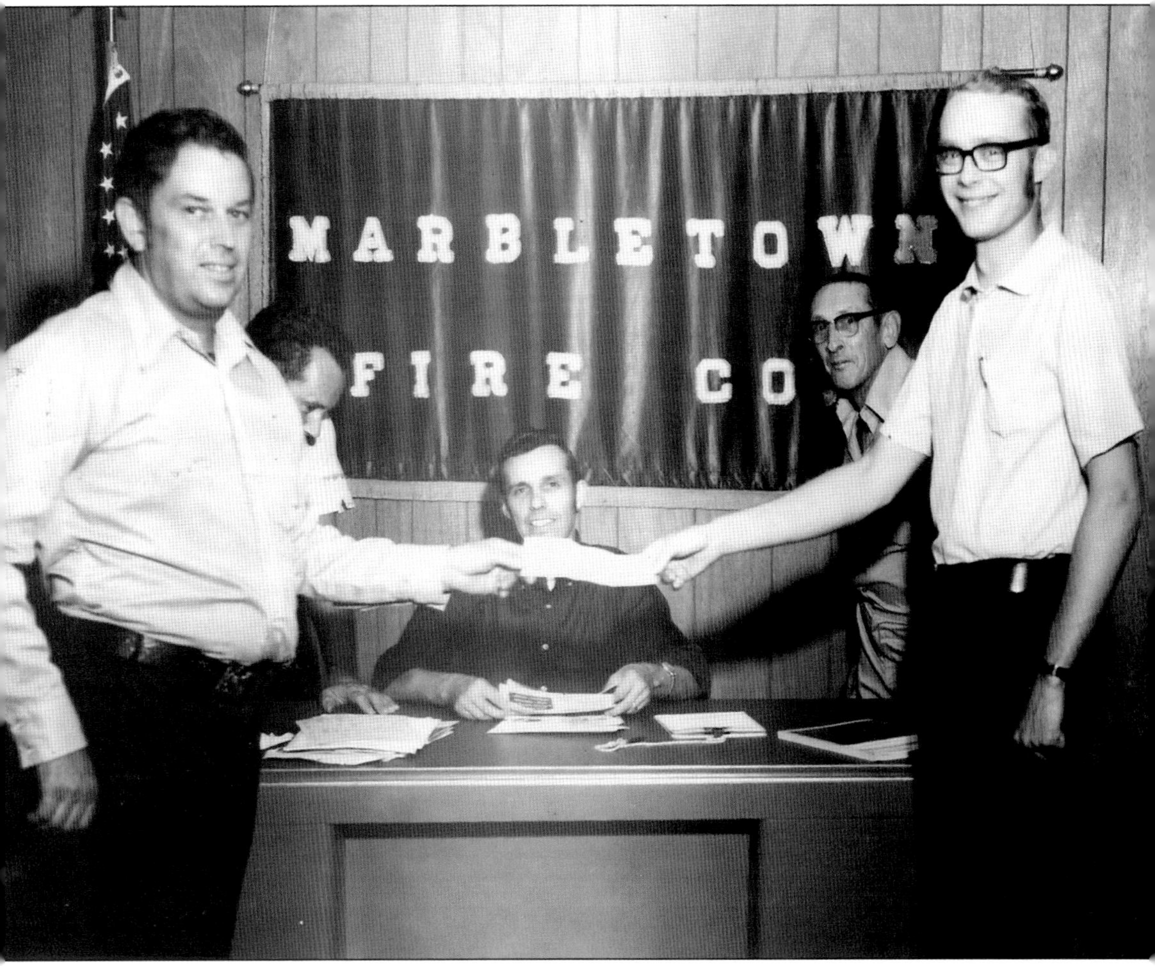

Kenneth Cole Sr. (left), then chief of the Marbletown Fire Company, accepts a check for first prize, presented by Alan Tyler. Tyler was in charge of a raffle sponsored by the Town of Rosendale in conjunction with the Ulster County Volunteer Fireman Convention. Looking on are, from left to right, secretary Dick Staubly, company president Bob Van Wagenen, and Assistant Chief Archie Robinson. (Courtesy Marbletown Fire Company.)

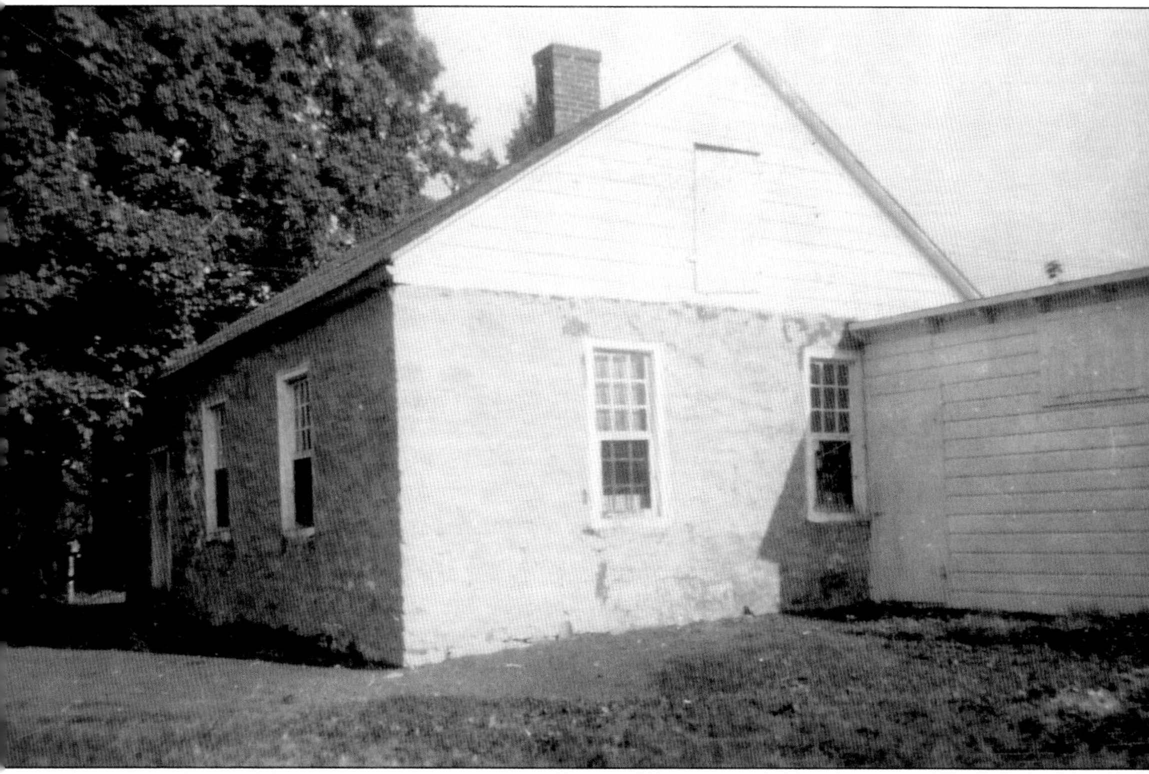

Here is the Marbletown stone schoolhouse around 1900. Of interest is the small wooden addition to the right. There was no indoor plumbing in the schoolhouse. The addition contained a small woodshed used to store wood for the woodstove and his and hers outhouses that the children used. (Courtesy Barbara Cole.)

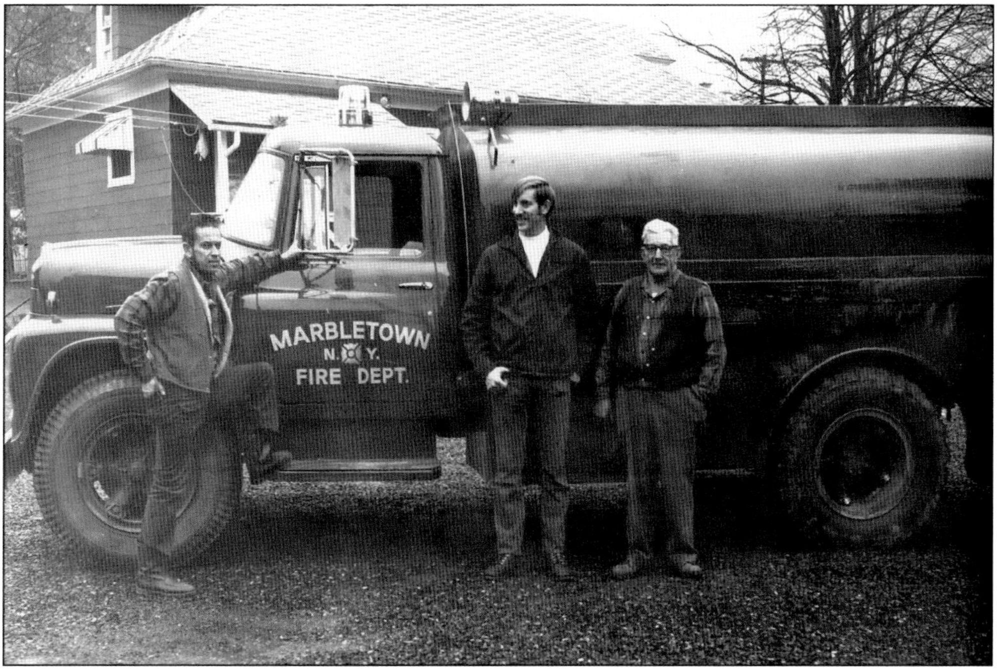

From left to right, Kenneth Cole Sr., Dick Van Lear, and Alfred Terwilliger pose with the Marbletown Fire Company's 1968 International tank truck. The company had purchased the used oil truck and converted it to a 1,850-gallon water tanker. (Courtesy Marbletown Fire Company.)

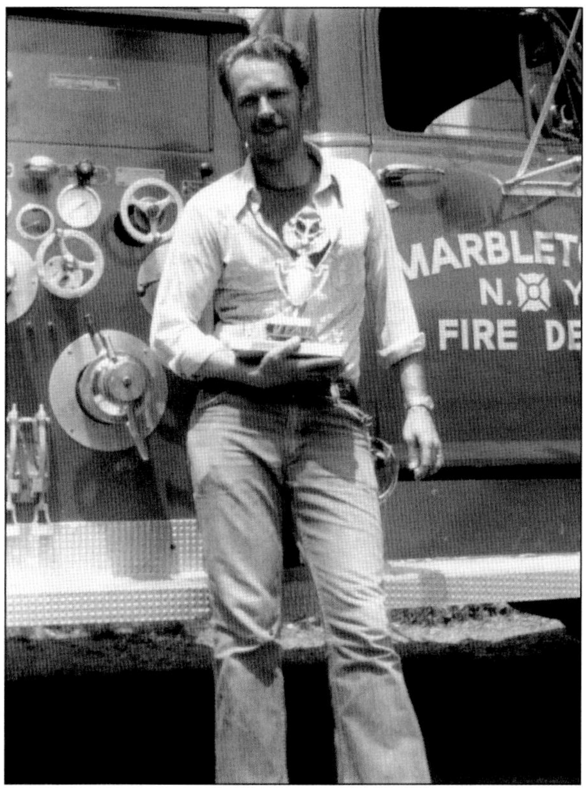

Willis Carney Jr. takes first place in the 1975 Marbletown volunteer firefighters' rodeo. He earned the honor by winning the driving competition. The rodeo was a yearly event held on the grounds of Marbletown Elementary School. (Courtesy Marbletown Fire Company.)

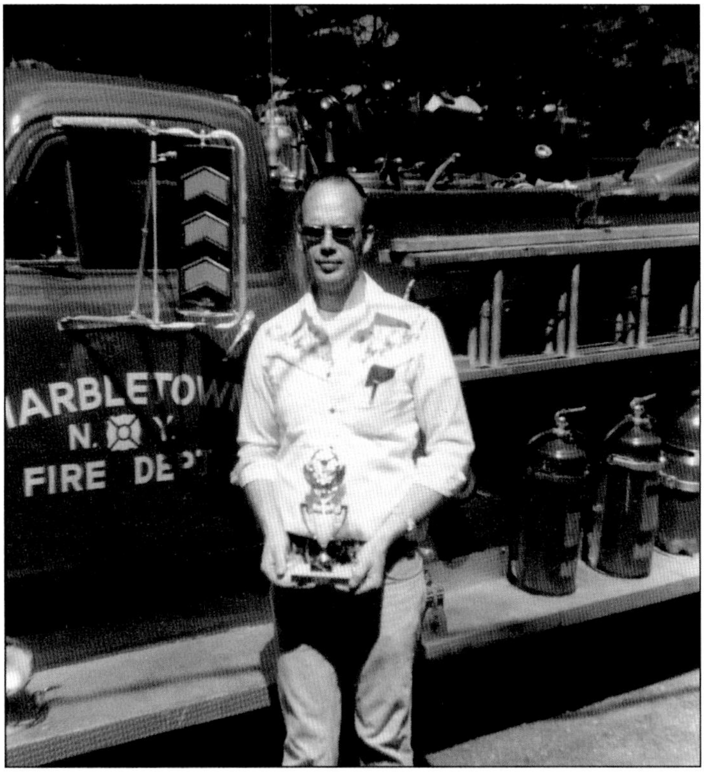

Ed Croswell proudly displays his driving trophy for the firemen's "road-eo" sponsored by the High Falls Fire Company in 1976. Drivers maneuvered trucks through obstacle courses, showcasing their expertise in handling the large fire trucks. (Courtesy Marbletown Fire Company.)

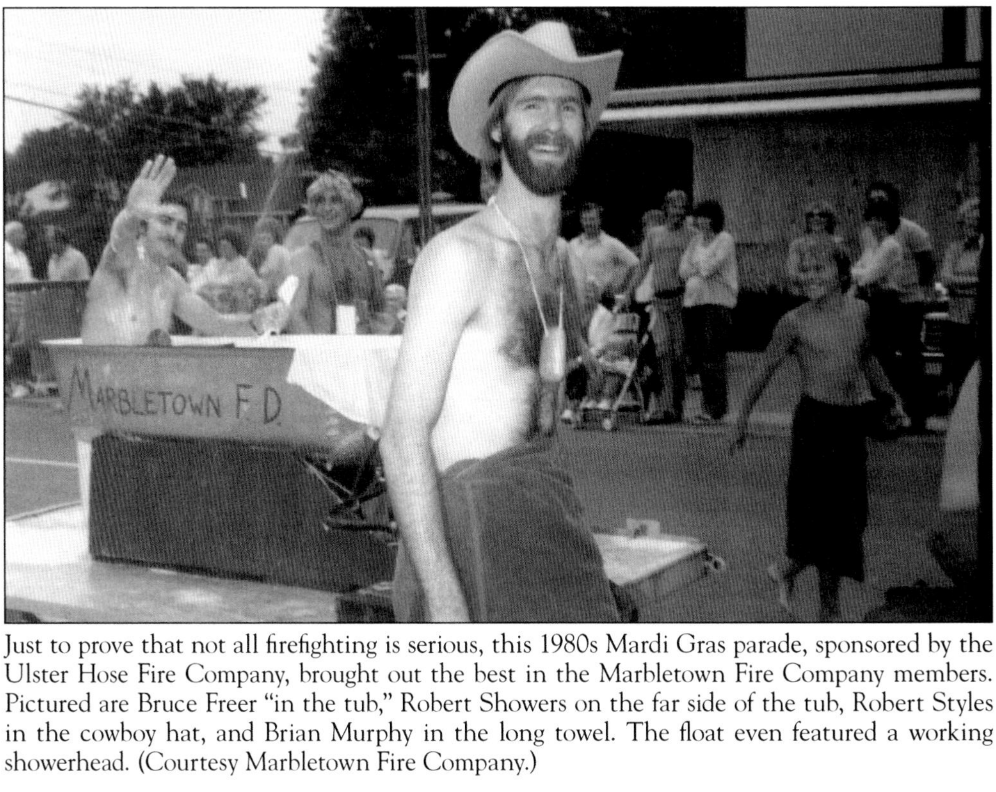

Just to prove that not all firefighting is serious, this 1980s Mardi Gras parade, sponsored by the Ulster Hose Fire Company, brought out the best in the Marbletown Fire Company members. Pictured are Bruce Freer "in the tub," Robert Showers on the far side of the tub, Robert Styles in the cowboy hat, and Brian Murphy in the long towel. The float even featured a working showerhead. (Courtesy Marbletown Fire Company.)

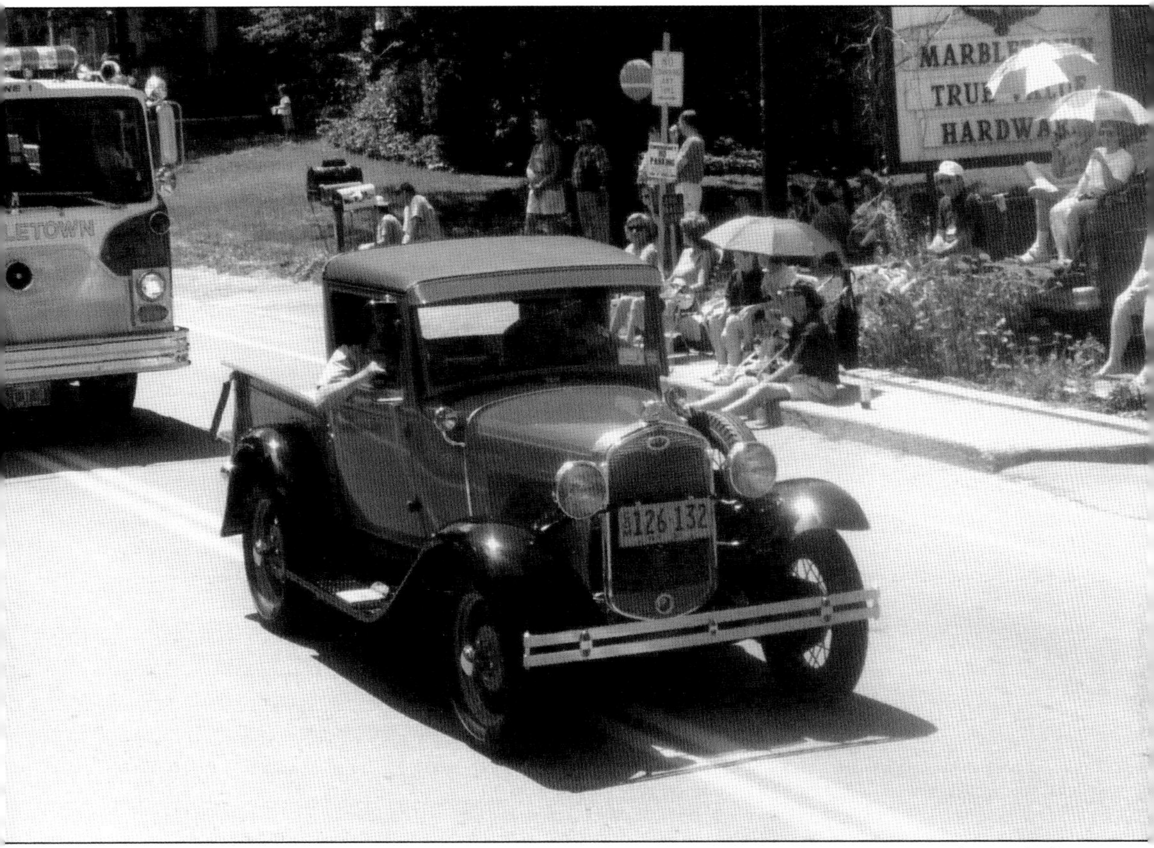

Ed Croswell, past chief of the Marbletown Fire Company, carries honorary grand marshal Kenneth Cole Sr. in his restored 1931 Ford Model A pickup truck in the 1997 Ulster County Volunteer Fireman's Association parade held in Marbletown. (Author's collection.)

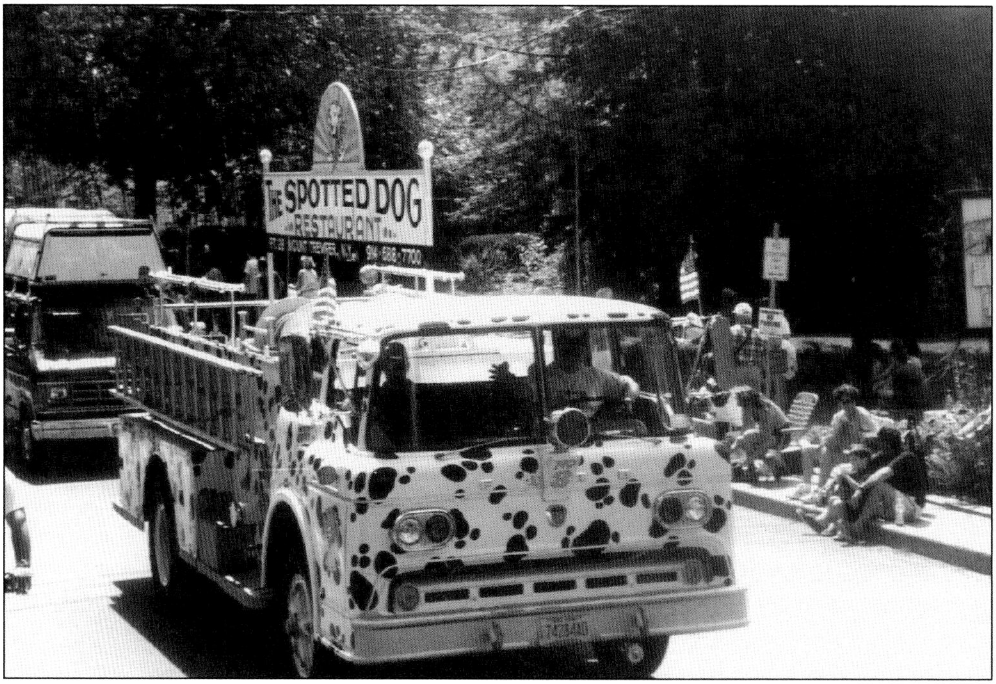

During the 1997 Ulster County Volunteer Fireman's Association parade in Marbletown, the grand finale of the parade was the Spotted Dog Restaurant's dalmatian fire truck. The Spotted Dog was a popular eatery in Mount Tremper, New York, that sported a firefighter theme. (Author's collection.)

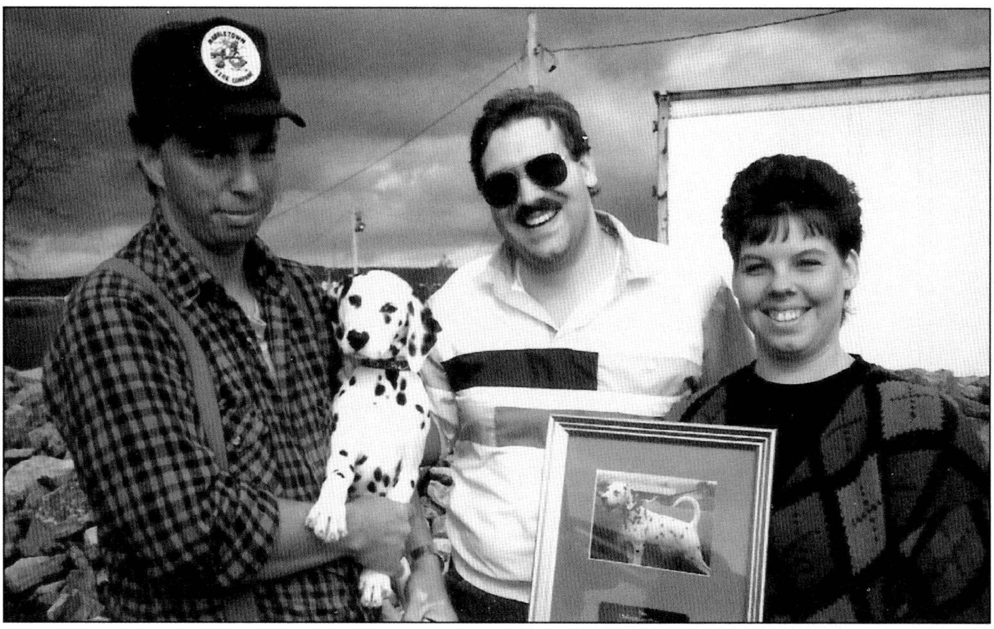

Chief Russ Van Sickle of the Marbletown Fire Company presents a dalmatian puppy to Chief Gary Verstraete and his wife Michelle, of the Marbletown Fire Department in Wayne County. The puppy, bred by a member of Van Sickle's fire company, was given in friendship to be used as a mascot for the Wayne County department. (Author's collection.)

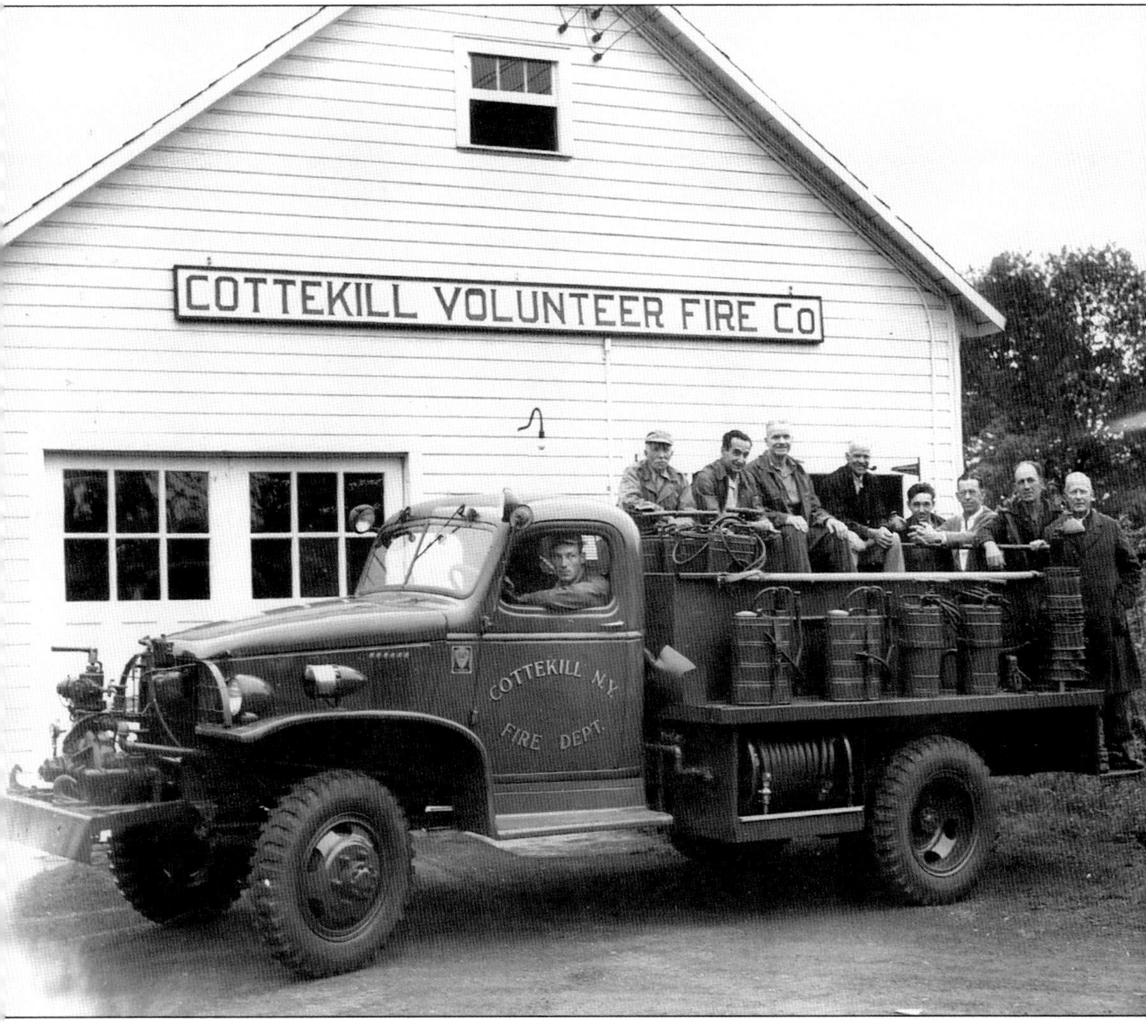

Cottekill Fire Company members pose with their new 1944 Chevrolet four-wheel-drive fire truck. This truck served as the department's second truck, the first being a chemical truck. Ben Hayes, Grant Addis, and Harry Van Wagenen repainted the truck prior to its going into service. Richard Barringer is shown in the cab of the truck, and from left to right are Henry Meyer, Jack Curci, Arthur DePuy, Grant Addis, Harry Bush, William Conner, Vernon Davis, and L. R. Conner. (Courtesy Chief Brad Fiore, Cottekill Fire Company.)

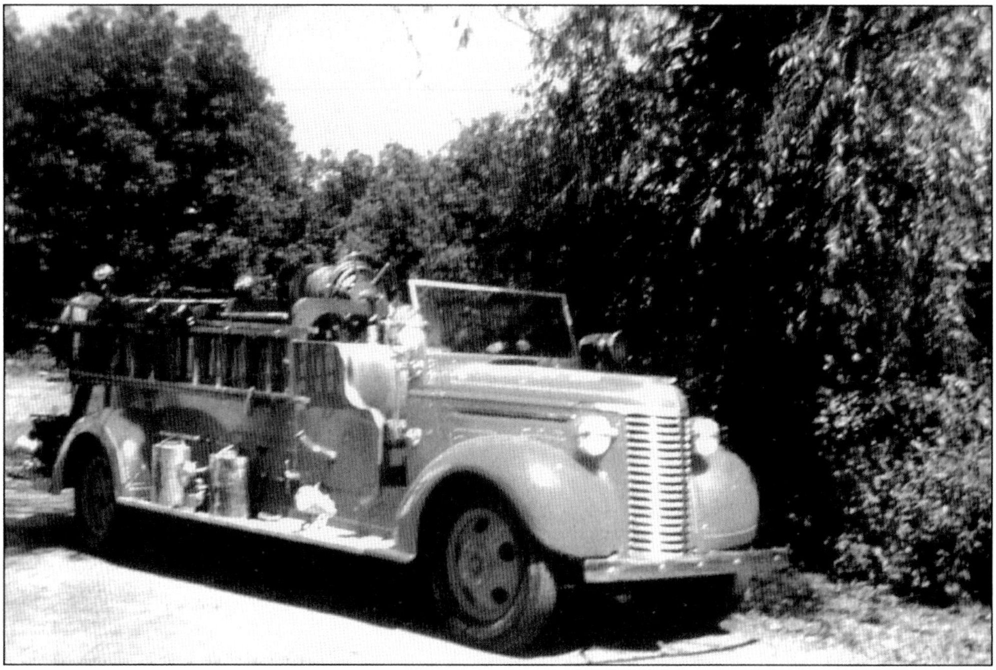

This 1935 Chevy fire truck was purchased by the Cottekill Fire Company from the Stone Ridge Fire Company in 1959. Indian tanks, used to fight brushfires, are mounted on the running boards. The large reel on top of the truck provided larger amounts of water to fight larger fires. It was very common for old fire trucks to have open cabs. This was quite unhandy when fighting fires in the winter months. (Courtesy Cottekill Fire Company; photograph by Joe Raymond.)

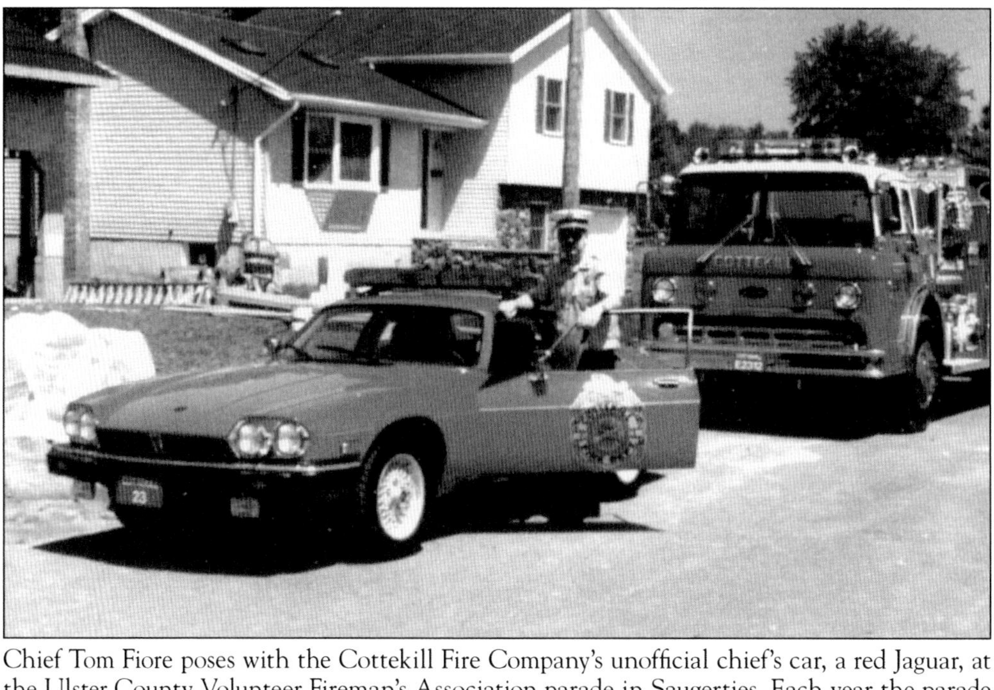

Chief Tom Fiore poses with the Cottekill Fire Company's unofficial chief's car, a red Jaguar, at the Ulster County Volunteer Fireman's Association parade in Saugerties. Each year the parade is hosted by a different zone company. (Courtesy Cottekill Fire Company.)

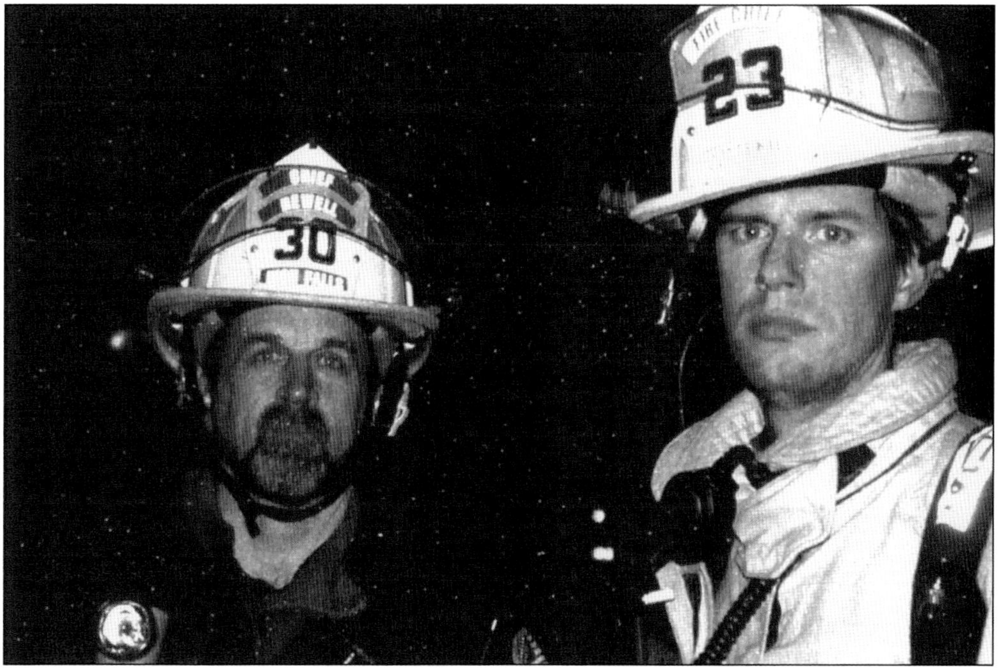

Fire Chief Donald Newell Jr. (left) of High Falls and Fire Chief Brad Fiore of Cottekill pose in full turnout gear while at a mutual aid fire call on Mohonk Road. Most fire companies have mutual aid agreements with neighboring companies to assure manpower at calls. (Courtesy Cottekill Fire Company.)

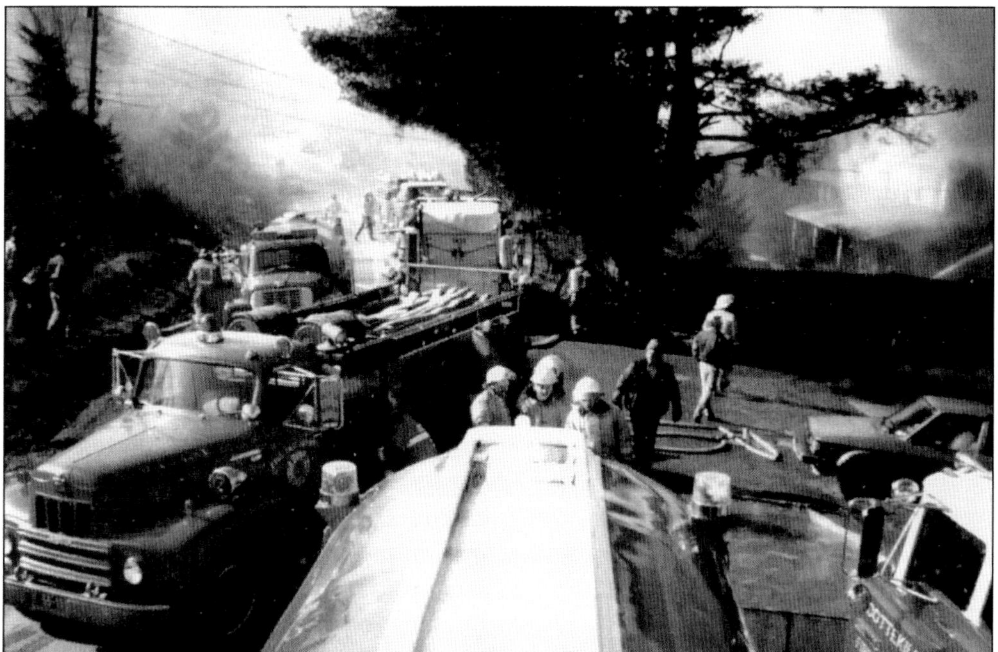

This fire scene was a large garage fire at Elliott's Speed and Custom Shop in Cottekill on February 6, 1993. Mutual aid responded by most companies in Marbletown. It took several hours for the fire to be extinguished. The building was a total loss. (Courtesy Cottekill Fire Company.)

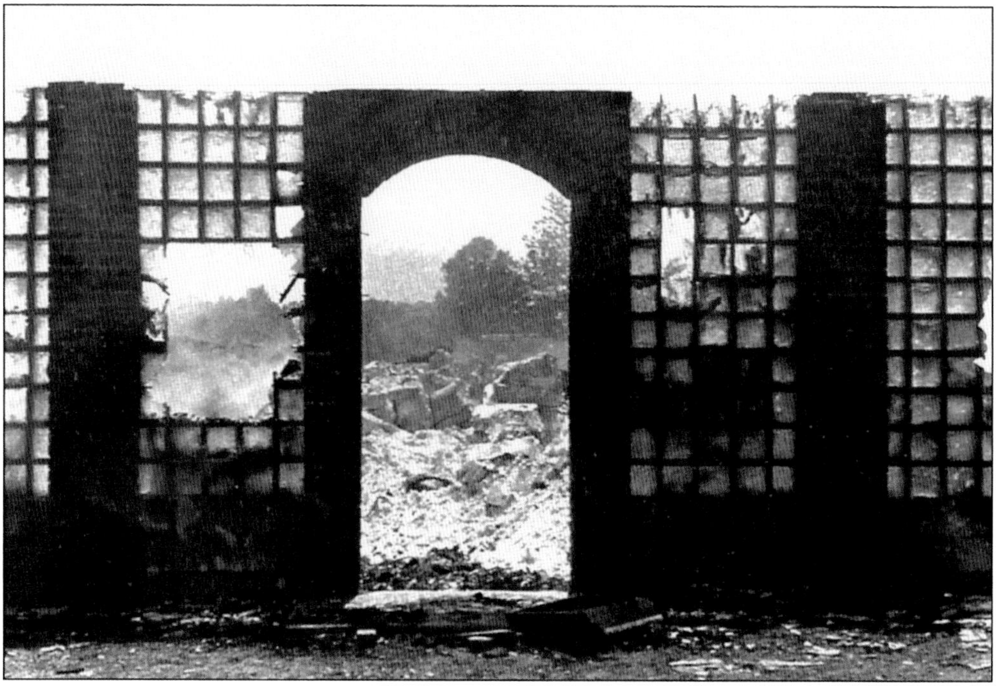

This glass block wall acts as a stark frame with the feed mill remains showing behind it. The intense heat from the fire destroyed most of the solid glass blocks. (Courtesy Cottekill Fire Company.)

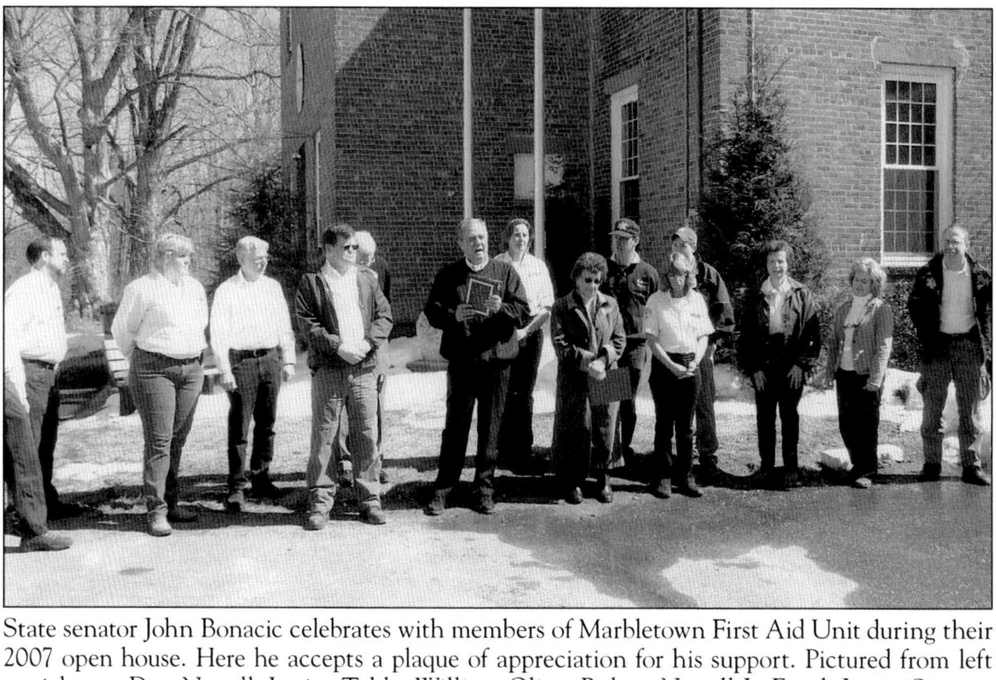

State senator John Bonacic celebrates with members of Marbletown First Aid Unit during their 2007 open house. Here he accepts a plaque of appreciation for his support. Pictured from left to right are Don Newell, Jessica Tokle, William Oliva, Robert Newell Jr, Frank Joynt, Senator Bonacic, Di Countryman, Sue Sarr, Peter Sarr, Captain Annabelle Sarr, Nate Johnson, Jeri Weber, Lois Frazzetta, and Paul Medici. (Courtesy Marbletown First Aid Unit.)

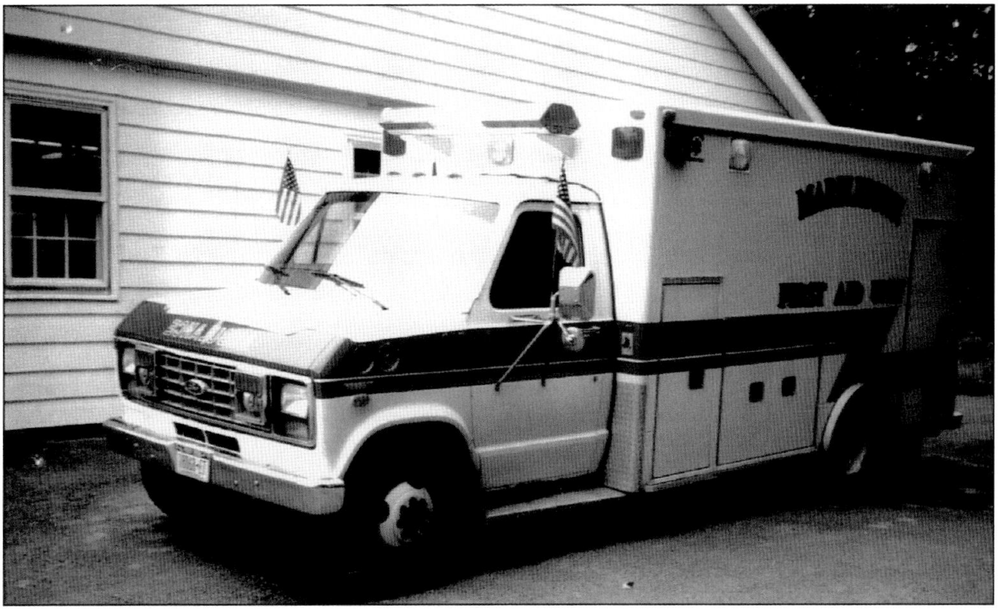

The Marbletown First Aid Unit's brand-new ambulance, unit No. 612, was purchased in 2002 from Road Rescue. The large box patient care compartment offered ample room to treat a patient from both sides. Marbletown First Aid Unit is staffed 100 percent by dedicated volunteer community members. (Courtesy Annabelle Sarr.)

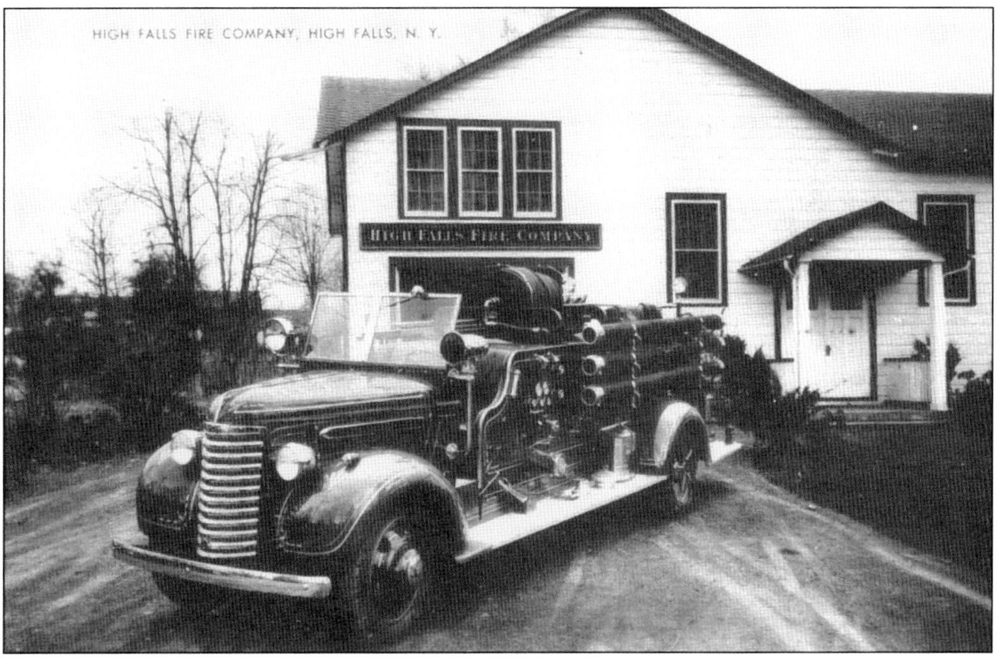

This c. 1930 GMC fire truck sits outside the High Falls Firehouse on this lovely postcard. The open cab and large running boards were common for that era. Firefighters would stand on the running boards so more members could go to the fire. The firehouse had a single-truck bay at that time. (Courtesy Paul Wikane.)

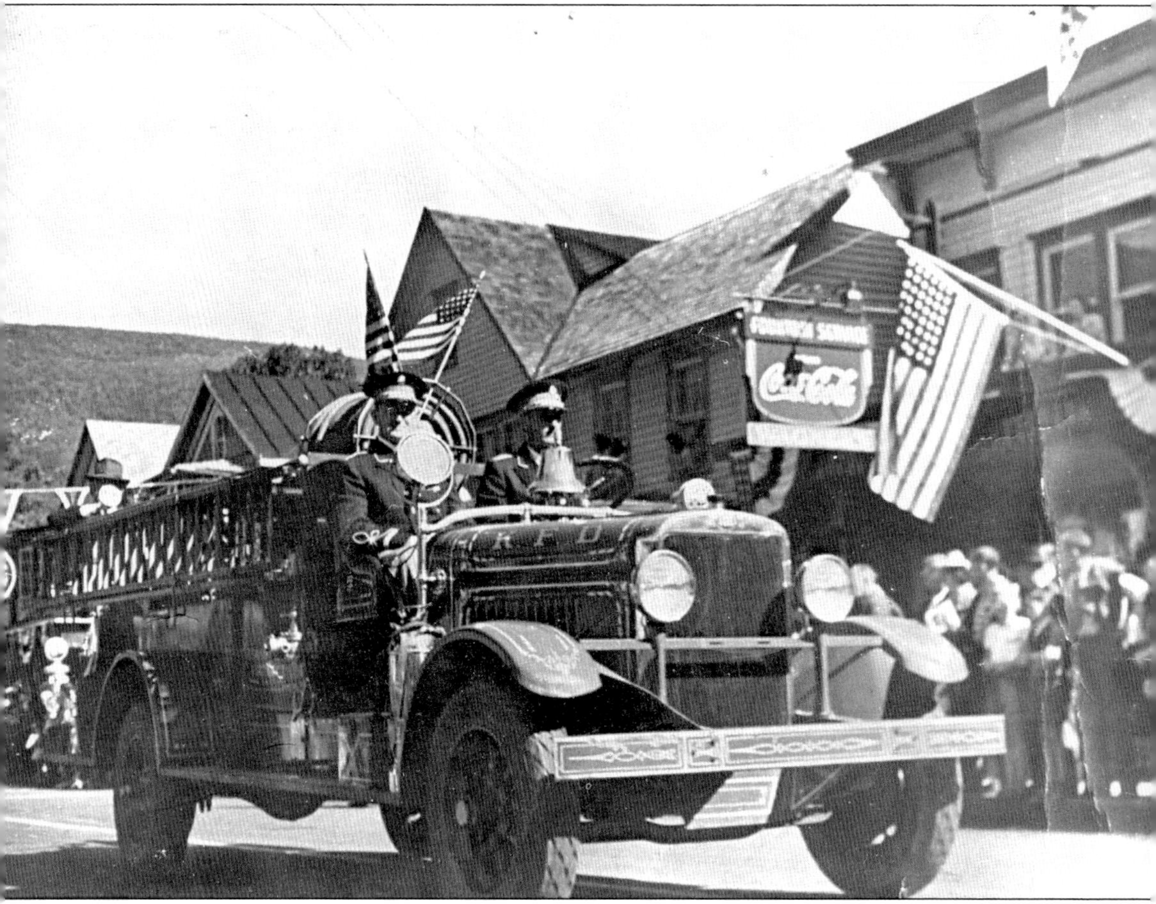

This Sanford fire truck is shown during one of the yearly fire company parades. The truck was originally owned by Kerhonkson Fire Company and later sold to the Kripplebush Lyonsville Fire Company and then resold to the Marbletown Fire Company. It carried approximately 200–300 gallons of water and had a hose reel on the top. (Courtesy John Snykus.)

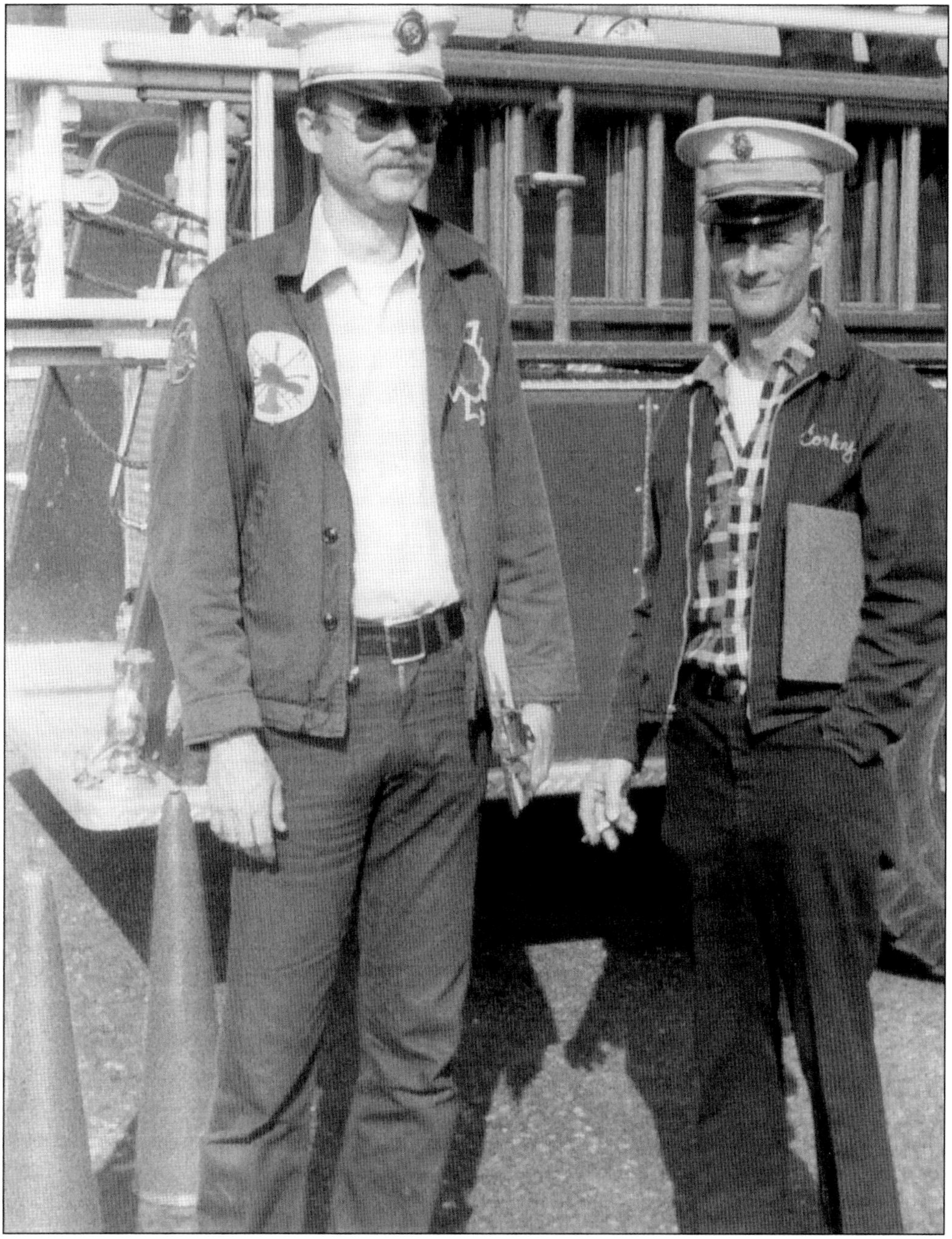

Alan Tyler (left) of the Bloomington Fire Company and Corky Sommer of the Kerhonkson Fire Company were frequent judges at fire company competitions. They were both well-respected firemen. These drill competitions were a good way to showcase the firefighting skills that every town fire company tried to perfect. This photograph was taken at the 1975 rodeo held at the High Falls Fire Company. (Courtesy Russ Van Sickle.)

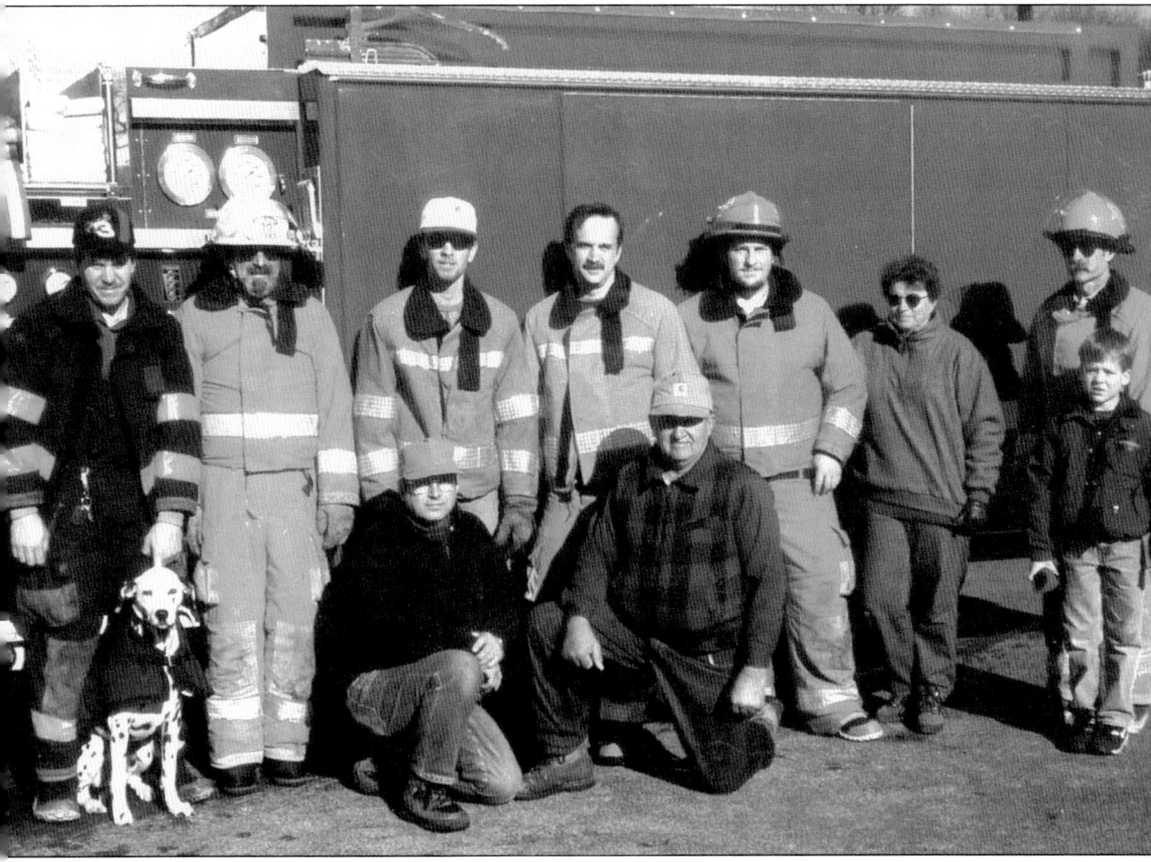

Members of the High Falls Fire Company pose in front of their new 1997 Ferrara fire engine. This engine was purchased to house the company's Jaws of Life. Pictured are, from left to right, (first row) Timothy Shea and Art Lapp Sr.; (second row) Art Lapp Jr. with dalmatian Missy, Assistant Chief Otto Scherrieble, Jerome Lendvay, Chief Donald Newell Jr., Shawn Marks, Elisa Scherrieble, Robert Hamm Sr., and son Robert Hamm Jr. (Courtesy High Falls Fire Company.)

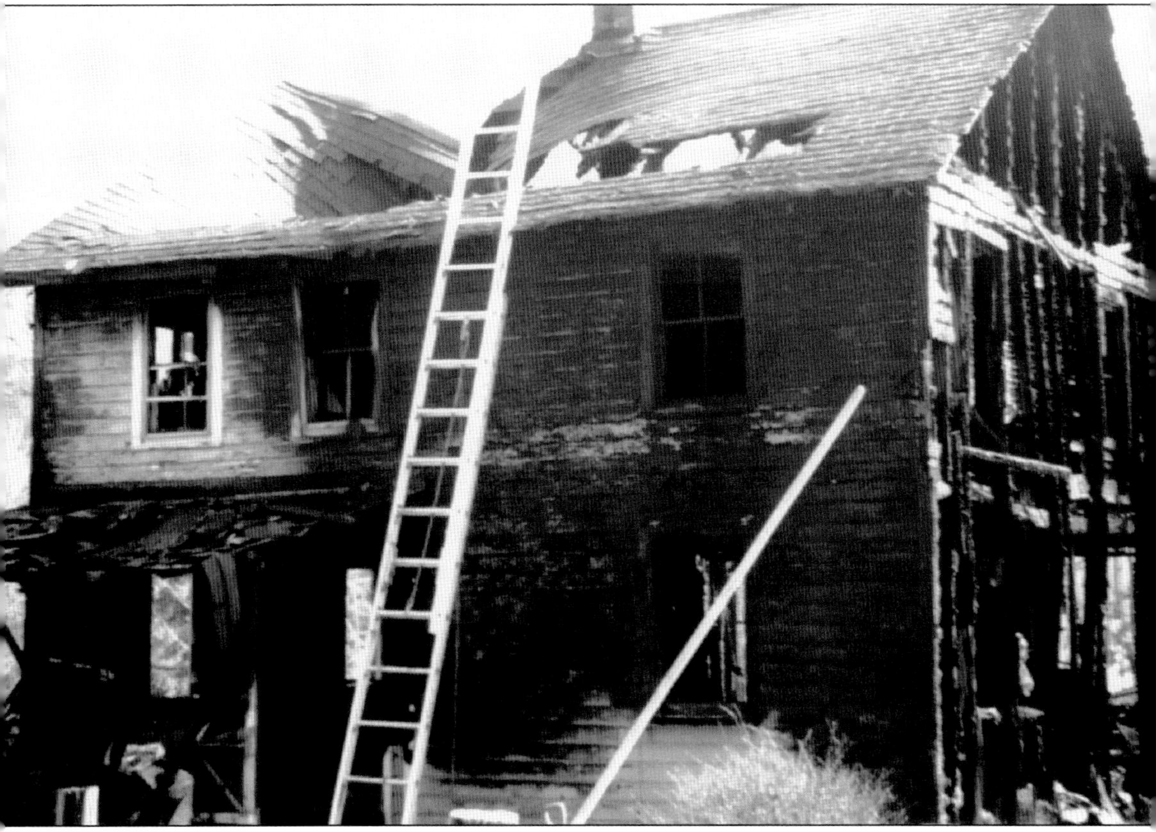

On March 1, 2003, the High Falls Fire Company responded to a fully involved structure fire at the home of longtime Marbletown residents Richard and Emily Stokes. Emily is the town historian. Tragically, Richard perished in the fire that consumed their home. (Courtesy High Falls Fire Company.)

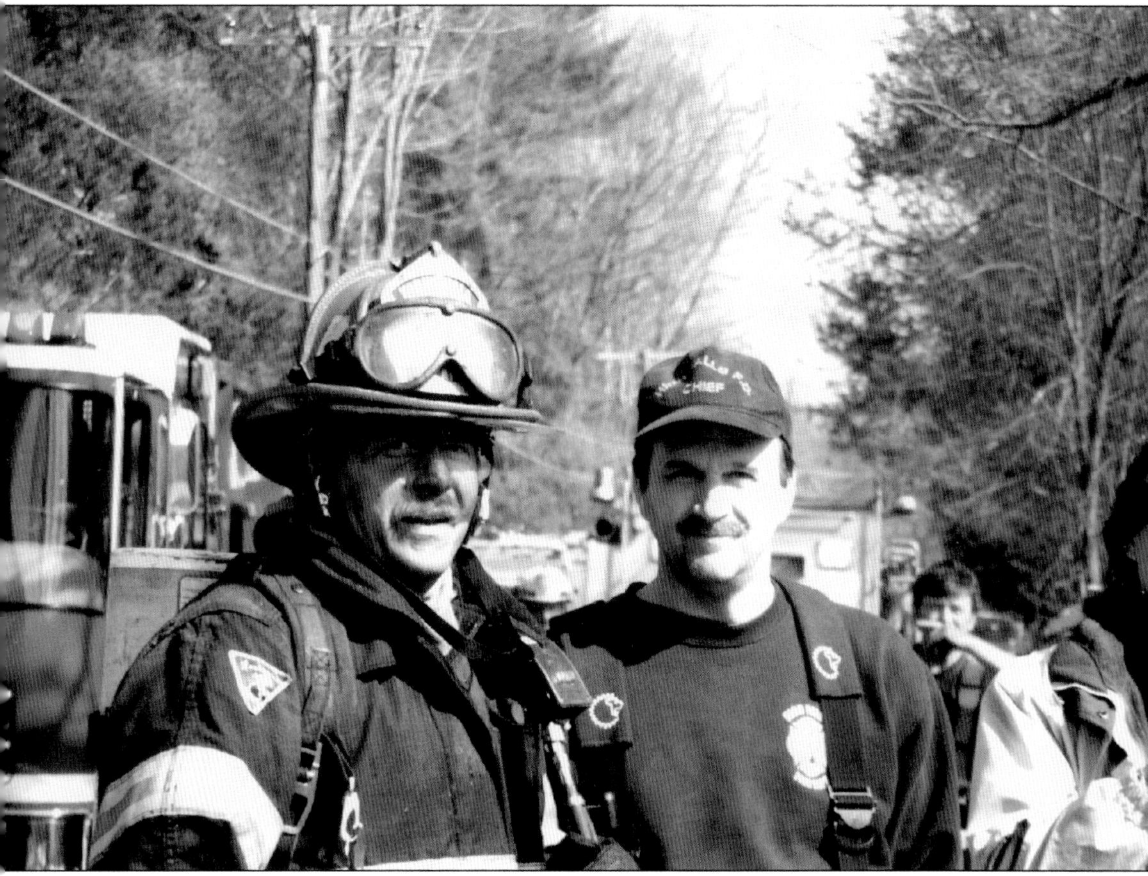

The stress of fighting the large fire at a neighbor's house shows on the faces of Lt. Art Lapp Jr. (left) and Chief Donald Newell Jr. while taking a breather during the Stokes fire on Mohonk Road. (Courtesy High Falls Fire Company.)

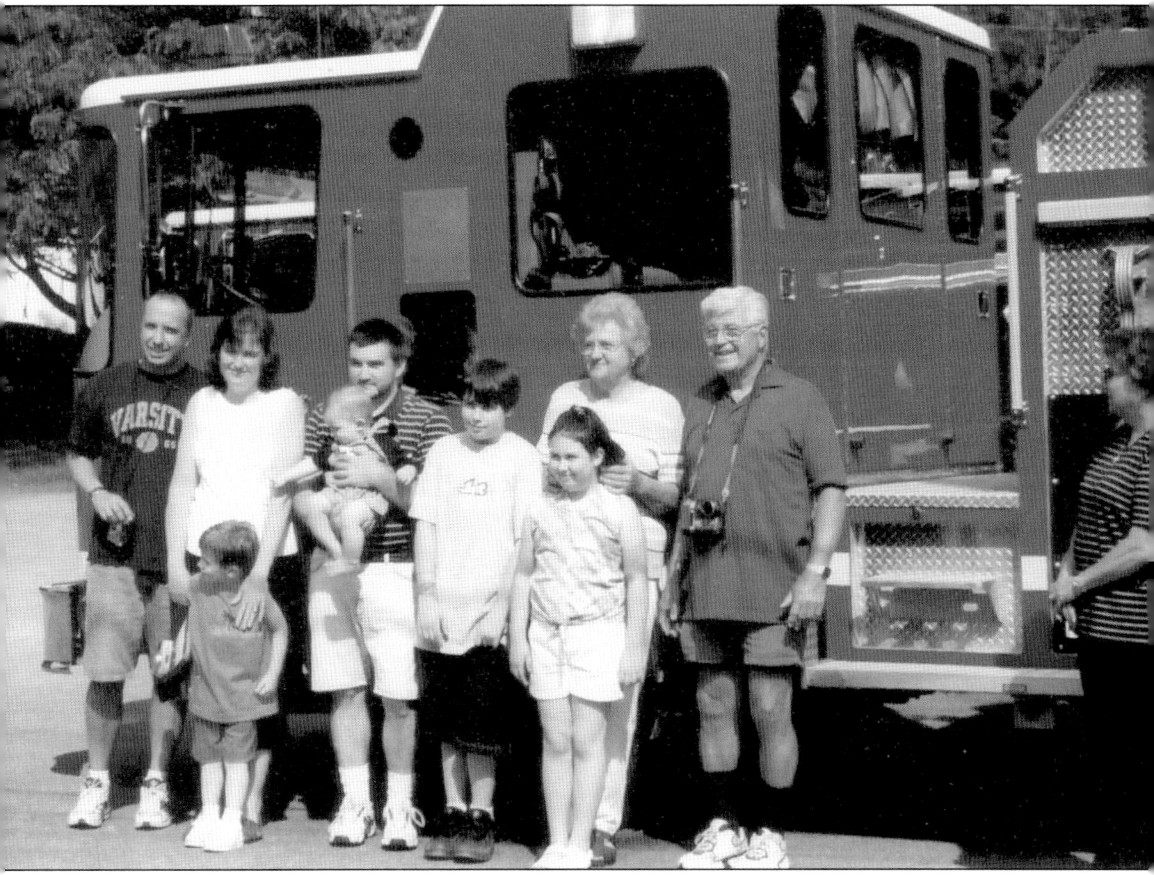

On June 14, 2003, the High Falls Fire Company dedicated engine No. 30-12 to the memory of fallen firefighter Charles Haas. "Charlie," as he was affectionately known, died in the line of duty performing routine roof ventilation work at a structure fire. He was only 17 years old. Pictured are, from left to right, family members Ed Wainwright, Denise Turner with son Brandon, Keith Turner holding son Bradley, Kyle Wainwright, Emily Wainwright, and Charles's parents, Jean and George Haas. Looking on from the right is chairman of the board of commissioners Elisa Scherrieble. (Courtesy Chief Donald Newell Jr.)

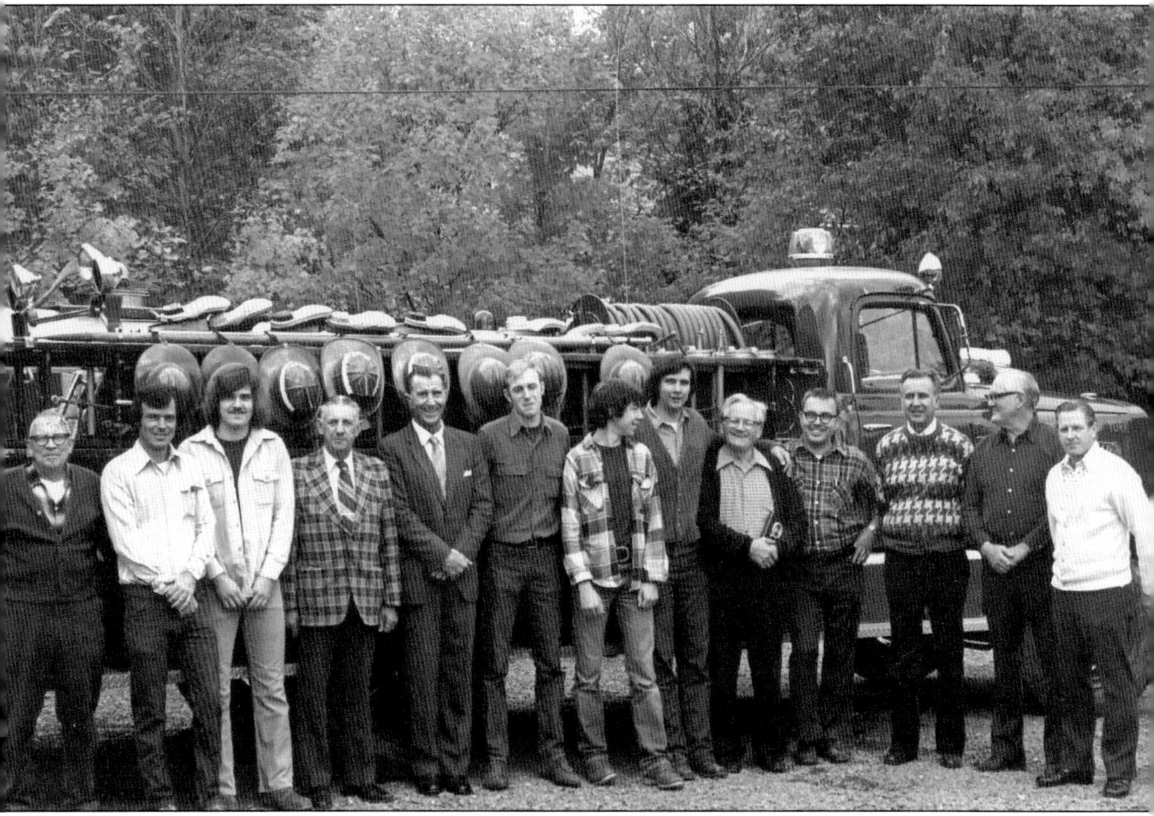

Kripplebush/Lyonsville firemen held an open house for their 25th anniversary in October 1977. They honored the founders of the company, which was incorporated in 1952. Charter members include Elmer Wager, Robert Kelder, Milford "Red" Van Demark, George Zellner, and Robert Hough. Pictured are, from left to right, Elmer Wager, James Del Pizzo, Robert Beatty, S. Robert Kelder, Oscar S. Christensen, Richard Henry, William Eggers, Gary Johnson, George Zellner (holding the 25-year plaque), John Snykus, Robert Hough, Milford "Red" Vandemark, and John Walker. (Courtesy Kripplebush/Lyonsville Fire Company.)

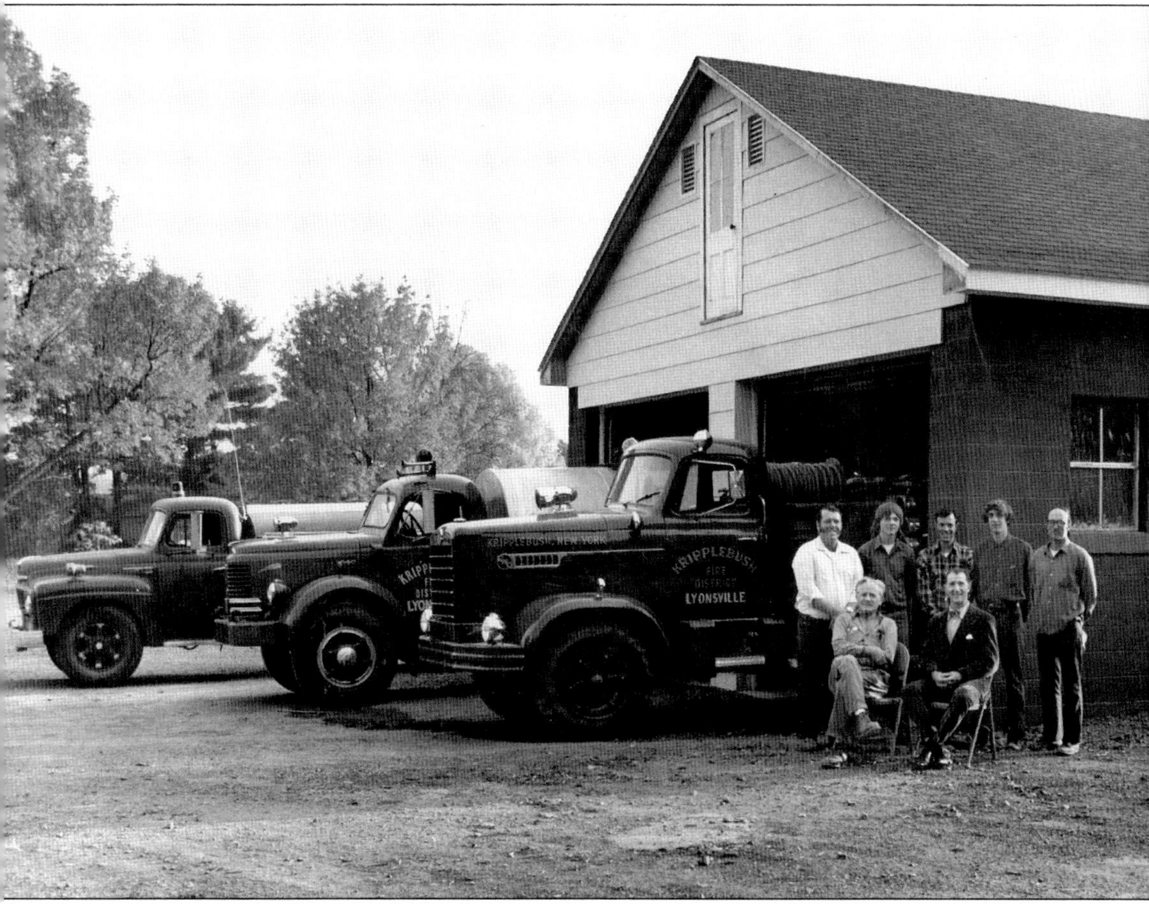

Several Kripplebush/Lyonsville Fire Company members take a moment to celebrate the opening of their new firehouse addition. The building was completed through the volunteer efforts of members of the company. Shown in front of the building are, from left to right, (first row) building committee chairman George Zellner and assistant building committee chairman Oscar S. Christensen; (second row) then fire chief Ronald Roosa, Marion Davis, Capt. James Del Pizzo Jr., Gary Johnson, and Lawrence Skalla. (Courtesy Kripplebush/Lyonsville Fire Company.)

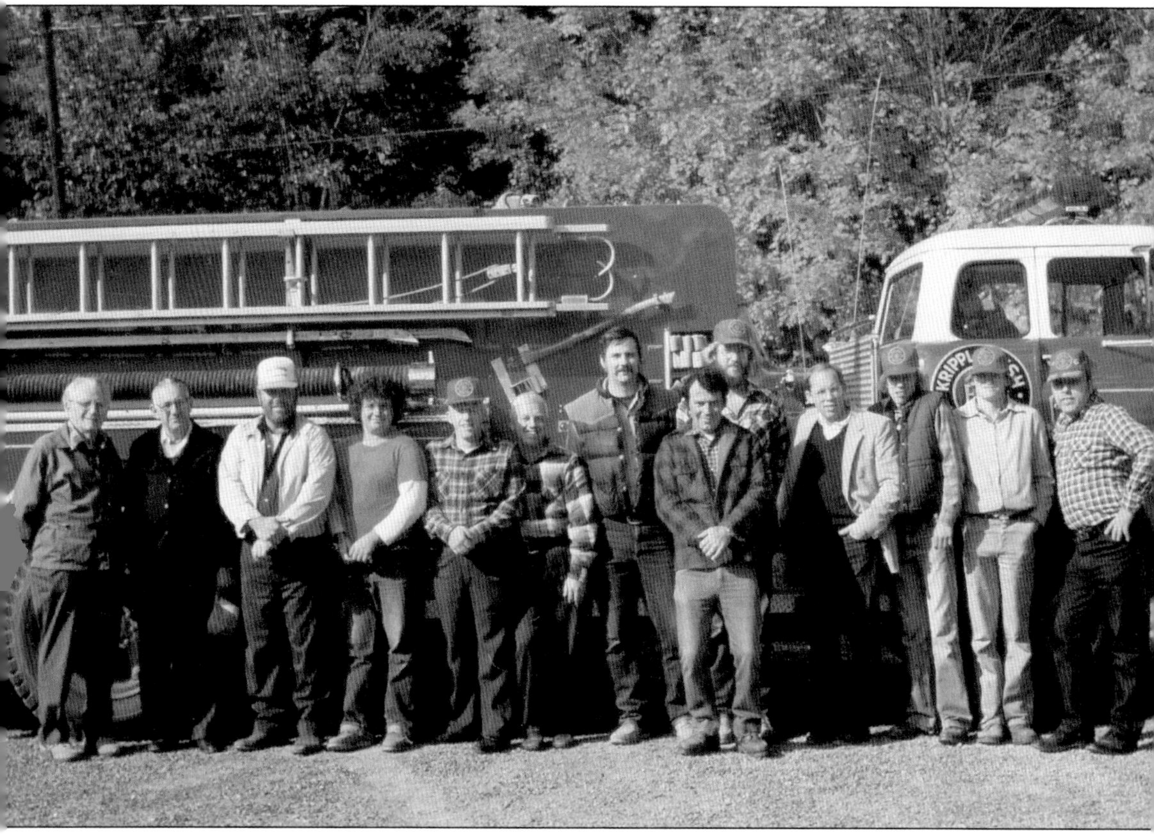

From left to right, George Zellner, S. Robert Kelder, Bill Lahl, Jesse Myer, Arthur Waterfall, Skip Waterfall, Gary Johnson, James Del Pizzo, Bruce Grupe, Steve Hilsenbeck, Norman Hough, Robert Newell Jr., and John Snykus proudly stand by their new class-A pumper. (Courtesy John Snykus.)

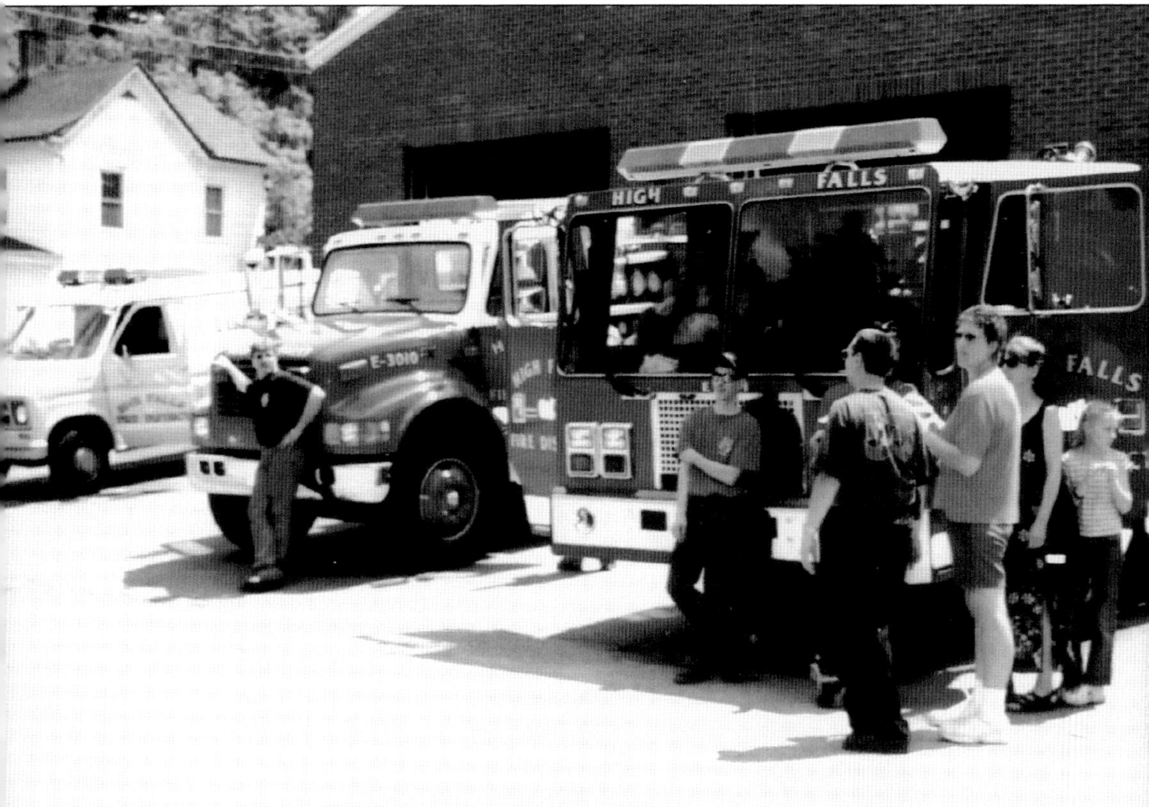

Members of the High Falls Fire Company stand proudly in front of their firehouse on June 14, 2003, during dedication ceremonies for engine No. 30-12. Art Lapp Jr. stands by engine No. 30-10, while Joe Creegan is in front of No. 30-12. Local residents look on. (Courtesy High Falls Fire Company.)

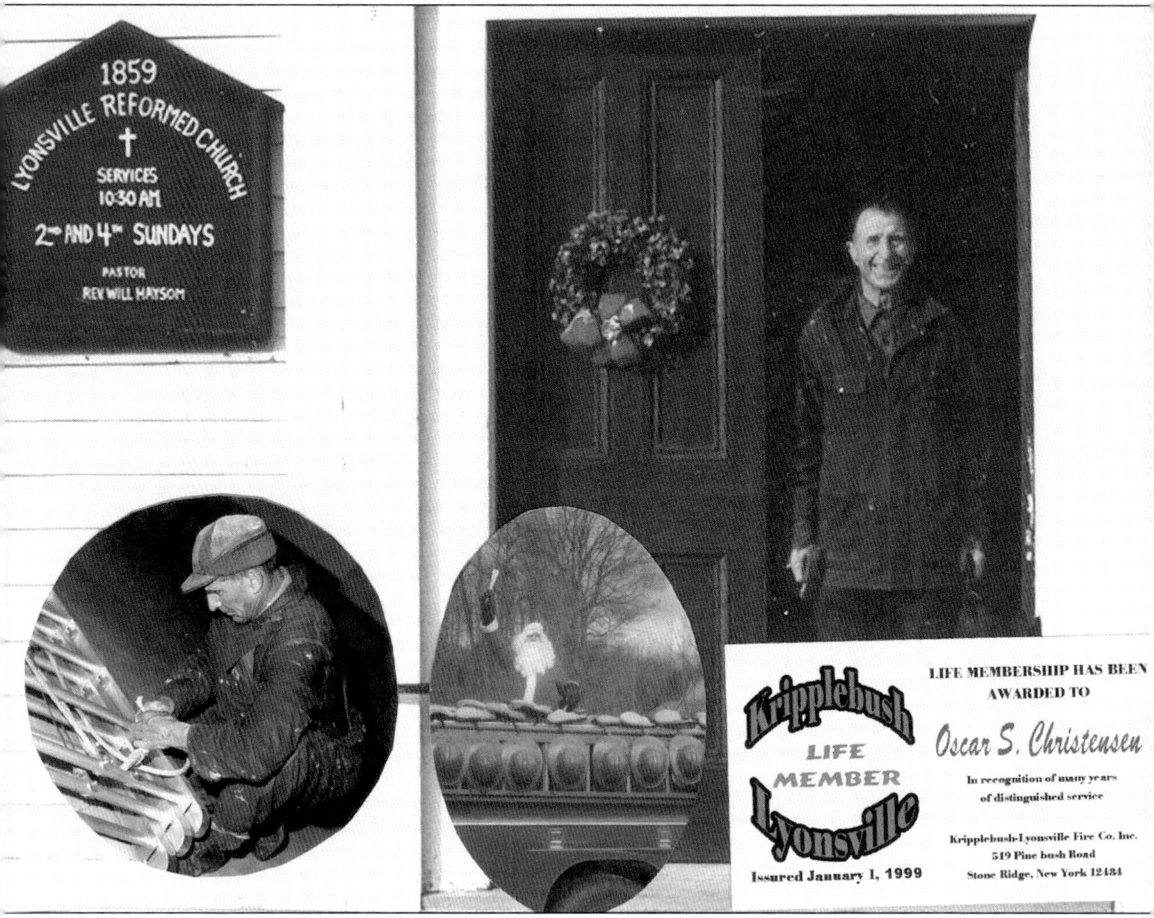

Lifetime member Assistant Chief Oscar S. Christensen was honored by members of his company as a dedicated member. He was an integral part of the expansion the Kripplebush/Lyonsville Fire Company experienced. He also enjoyed playing the role of Santa on the fire trucks. He was an avid member of the Lyonsville Church. This collage was put together by the fire company and hangs proudly in its hall. (Courtesy John Snykus.)

BIBLIOGRAPHY

Evers, Alf. *The Catskills: From Wilderness to Woodstock*. Woodstock, NY: Overlook Press, 1982.

Fried, Marc B. *The Early History of Kingston and Ulster County, N.Y.* Marbletown, NY: Ulster County Historical Society, 1975.

Hine, C. G. *The Old Mine Road*. New Brunswick, NJ: Rutgers University Press, 1963.

History of Ulster County: With Emphasis in the Last Hundred Years 1883–1983. Compiled by the Ulster County Historians. Kingston, NY: Self-published, 1984.

Consistent with our mission to preserve history on a local level, this book was printed in South Carolina on American-made paper and manufactured entirely in the United States. Products carrying the accredited Forest Stewardship Council (FSC) label are printed on 100 percent FSC-certified paper.

MADE IN THE USA